The Art of Healing Childhood Grief

A School-Based Expressive Arts Program

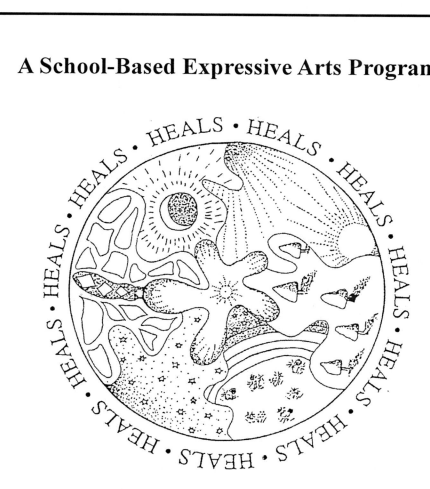

Promoting Social and Emotional Literacy

Anne Black, Ph.D.   Penelope Simpson, LCMHC

authorHOUSE

1663 LIBERTY DRIVE, SUITE 200
BLOOMINGTON, INDIANA 47403
(800) 839-8640
www.authorhouse.com

The Art of Healing Childhood Grief: A School-based Expressive Arts Program Promoting Social and Emotional Literacy

First published by AuthorHouse 08/24/04

ISBN: 1-4184-6903-3(e)
ISBN: 1-4184-2219-3(sc)

Library of Congress Control Number: 2003096597

Printed in the United States of America
Bloomington, Indiana

This book is printed on acid-free paper.

Illustrated by Bronwen Sommer

Published by Black & Simpson
114 Westminster Road, Putney, Vermont 05346

www.artofhealingchildhoodgrief.com   ahcg@sover.net

1. Bereavement & grief in children
2. Primary Prevention
3. Death, Loss
4. Psychology, Expressive arts
5. Social & emotional literacy
6. Education, grief support curriculum

The Art of Healing Childhood Grief

TABLE OF CONTENTS

Section II: The Heartbeat Program Delivery System........55

We fondly dedicate this manual to our students,
all of whom have been our teachers
whether young in years or young in heart,
especially Jamin and J.T., who guide us from above.

Jamin Ernes
1984-1988

James T. Cribben
1963-1972

Acknowledgments

From the beginning we have likened the development of The HEALS Program to that of a child. As parents we went through the pondering stage and ultimately decided to commit to a creative endeavor that seemingly wanted to come through us. Once HEALS was birthed, we made a conscious choice to trust the spark of creation to light the way. Many gifted human beings entered our path at significant points to assist us in our early parenting of HEALS. We have been influenced by many mentors and wish to thank the spiritual essences of Carl Jung, Abraham Maslow, Joseph Campbell, and Carl Rogers for their pioneering contributions to the human potential movement which created the space for this work to develop.

We wish to thank Sandra Fox and The Good Grief Program for contributing to the foundation of The HEALS Framework which guides our sessions. Thank you, Elizabeth Kübler-Ross, for lighting the candle and beginning to address the bereavement needs of children.

Harriet Tepfer, known as "Hattie" within The HEALS Program, unleashed her creative juices time and time again as she facilitated bereavement groups and then generously shared her successes with us. Hattie's imprint on this body of work is present in ways more numerous to recount.

And special thank-yous to Natalie Rogers for bringing the expressive arts to the Person-Centered work of her father, Carl Rogers, and to Cornelia Brunner of Zurich, Switzerland, friend and pupil of Carl Jung's, for gently opening the veils to the unconscious—and to both of these women for agreeing to be the honorary godmothers for The HEALS Program.

We wish also to extend deep gratitude to:

> • Don Hayes at Brattleboro Area Hospice who, in 1990, believed in the initial concept of bereavement support in the schools and helped open the door to Martha Ward, the school psychologist at Brattleboro Union High School, who receptively responded to the use of art in griefwork with the students in Brattleboro Middle School;

> • Dr. Donna Harlan, principal at Guilford School, who recognized the creative healing potential of the expressive arts and availed it to a segment of her students;

> • Virginia Fry who trained us in the use of art and ritual when working with children in grief;

> • Shellee Davis' facilitation skills and creative spark at the Person-Centered Expressive Institute which has inspired us and served as a model for safety, flexibility, and approach;

> • The powerful work of Lucia Capacchione, Gabrielle Roth, and Tria Reed which has been into The HEALS Program as we continue to observe the empowerment and healing effects of their contributions;

• Sandy Hartley, ATR., whose inspiration it was to name our program HEALS (HEALS Expressive Arts Loss Support Program) which beautifully incorporates the various aspects of this work;

• Dale Schwarz and Guillermo Cuellar at the New England Art Therapy Institute for their support in the early vision of bringing the healing world of art to children in traditional school settings;

• Our original HEALS School Counselors: Laurie Gorham, Lucille Messina, Diana Sprague, Tom Hudac, Marion Abell, and Kathy McEvily who welcomed us into their schools and recognized the need to help grieving children face their pain in order to go on with their lives;

• Our early HEALS Facilitators: Carol Grobe, Wren Gore, Harriet Tepfer, Molly Hyde, Patti Rivinus, Susan Palmer, Emily Bullock, Elizabeth Pitman, Mary Ann Abney, and Teta Hilsdon, who responded to the call, gave generously of their inner resources, and taught us so much; and our later facilitators who continued to add their creativity to this body of work with new ideas and activities: Lori Greenberg, Jen Bailes, Marian Rose, Nan Mann, Heather Booth, Jeff Speigler, Sue Aldridge, Eileen McFerran, Gretchen Webber, Noree Ennis, Patrick Skater, Collin Leech, Marki Webber, Mary Ellen McDurfee, Elizabeth Christie, Katherine Barrett, Kerri Moriarty, Nancy Wohl, Stephen Coronella, and Sydney Crystal.

• Bronwen Sommer, our graphic artist, who came into our lives during the spring of 1992 (on the anniversary of her mother's death) and allowed her own images of healing to inspire the written word; and David Ritchey for his patience and photographic wizardry;

• Our text editors, Elizabeth Christie, Patti Rivinus, David Ritchey, John Adams, and JoEllen Tarallo Falk, and Nancy A. Olson who graciously extended themselves to assist us in synthesizing, clarifying, and fine-tuning our writings;

• Ed DeRosha at Lotus Graphics in Brattleboro, Vermont who patiently worked with us in the execution of the printing and lay-out of this material; all our trained HEALS facilitators and other community members who gave of their time and support in many practical and helpful ways;

• The Vermont Teddy Bear Company and Mary Meyers, Inc. for their frequent donations of cuddly bears for our program; all the students in our HEALS support groups who have been our teachers along the journey into healing through the expressive arts;

• To anyone whom we may have forgotten and whose contribution to the field of childhood bereavement has inspired us, or our facilitators, we extend our heartfelt gratitude.

• And most importantly our families who believed in this work and loved and supported us in a way that made it possible for "something bigger than all of us" to be born into our needy world. Thank you: John, David, Jennifer, Andrew and Vada. We love you.

～✿～

∼ Foreword: The HEALS Story ∼

When one follows the course of the hospice movement in the past few decades, it is not difficult to imagine that something like The HEALS Program was inevitable.

People began to realize that the way people were dying (mostly in institutions) was not only a cold and lonely process away from their familiar environments and families, but also it was becoming an increasingly expensive process. The hospice movement grew out of a need to help people die with dignity and to provide trained, understanding people to assist in the personal business of terminal illness.

In the same time interval, behaviorists understood more and more about the process of grieving, and seeing its dynamic in both short-term and long-term emotional distress. Making use of the large body of work, both written and used therapeutically, hospice began very effective work in the area of bereavement counseling. However, an area that was less addressed was: How do children grieve? And what is being done for them? Children seem to be grieving so many losses in these times that the school services and social agencies are hard pressed to keep up with their needs and, in some cases, even fail to see the needs as valid.

It was upon this stage that a series of synchronistic events brought together Penelope Simpson and Anne Black, two extraordinary women who, over many years of their lives, had been gathering knowledge, tools, and skills which, when put together, met a need that was almost critical in its timeliness.

It's a magical trail when one follows these two back to their own paths and pursuits, and watches them converge and give birth to the unique gift for grieving children that today is called The HEALS (Hospice Expressive Arts Loss Support) Program.

Penelope Simpson was a Montessori-trained teacher who owned and administered a school in California. During a sabbatical she attended a LDT (Loss, Death & Transition) workshop with Elisabeth Kübler-Ross, then went on to Switzerland where she studied with Cornelia Brunner, a Jungian analyst, and several art therapists.

Following her return from Switzerland in 1987, Penelope experienced the loss of one of her students. This profoundly moving experience illuminated for her how much of a taboo the subject of death still is among teachers and parents. She also witnessed how children can, and do, create their own paths for healing and caring for one another if allowed to do so.

Shortly after her move to Vermont in 1990, she had the opportunity to combine her interests in education for children, Jungian psychology, and the arts, and meld them together with her volunteer hospice work for Brattleboro Area Hospice. She presented her idea to the local middle school where, with the assistance of school psychologist, Martha Ward, she was able to offer a unique support group for students within the school who had experienced the loss of someone special in their lives.

Through the Brattleboro Area Hospice, Penelope was introduced to Virginia Fry, an artist/educator, who had worked with children in bereavement for ten years in northern Vermont. As Penelope related her experiences to Virginia and expressed a need for more trained help to facilitate support groups in the Windham County area, she learned that Virginia was just completing a grant to develop two "Children in Grief" pilot training projects. One of the two designated Hospices had withdrawn from the pilot project, and Virginia immediately invited Penelope's fledgling program to take its place.

Meanwhile at Guilford School in the Brattleboro area, Anne Black was using the expressive arts of movement, art, sounding, and writing coupled with guided visualization to invite students to open the doors of their inner worlds in order to explore their emotional landscapes. Many of these children had experienced various traumas which were crippling them emotionally and interfering with their classroom performance. The safe, aesthetic, verbal and non-verbal environment had a calming effect on many of these children, and Anne knew that a deeper hunger was being reached.

As an educator, Anne's dream was to develop a creative healing approach to provide children with support, give them practical tools to express their feelings, and to address these needs within the school system where many children would not otherwise have such an opportunity. With this intent in place the magic began to unfold, and a string of enlightened individuals, training programs, music, workshops, and books began entering the scene—each one contributing a new, fresh piece for what would eventually synthesize and ultimately manifest. Seeds were planted during the course of studying with Lucia Capacchione, Gabrielle Roth, Robbie Gass, and Tria Reed. Each was grounded in one of the expressive arts, and when Anne was exposed to The New England Art Therapy Institute and then studied with Natalie Rogers at the Person-Centered Expressive Therapy Institute and experienced her "Creative Connection®" process, and it all began falling into place.

One day while Penelope was ordering books on art therapy at The Green Mountain Bookstore in Brattleboro, the owner suggested that she get in touch with Anne, who was also using the arts to help children heal. On April 10, 1990, at the Whetstone Cafe, over tea and scones, Penelope and Anne brought together their love of working with children, their varied educational experiences and trainings, and a commitment to "following their bliss." The chemistry was immediate, and the creative energy began to flow. As if to confirm that the two women were to pursue their converging paths, Anne, who lived several towns away from Penelope, inexplicably received in the mail a letter addressed to "Penelope Simpson." It was from the phone company and its message was "Reach out, America."

The uniting of Penelope and Anne's dreams, loves, ideas, and skills was an effortless endeavor, and they agreed to become co-facilitators to implement the grant project under Virginia Fry during the fall of 1990. Following Virginia's training sessions, Penelope and Anne offered five more sessions to help prepare the first fourteen volunteers to go into the schools. That same autumn, an advisory committee was formed to guide the direction of the fledgling bereavement program. The name HEALS, (Hospice Expressive Arts Loss Support) was the inspiration of Sandy Hartley, an art therapist on the committee. The program was now birthed, named, and ready to be in the world.

Following a HEALS presentation to area principals and guidance counselors, the schools began requesting Anne and Penelope to come in and facilitate support groups. Several counselors welcomed the opportunity to learn how to use the expressive arts and ritual to create paths for healing in a group setting. Being with grieving students naturally brings up unresolved grief within the adult, and the counselors agreed to work through one of their losses in the support group with their students in order to experience the program directly.

Penelope and Anne were soon to discover that HEALS had no intention of having a slow and steady development. The next nine months were to be a most creatively stimulating and busy time for them as they and three volunteers facilitated nine support groups in the schools. The HEALS Program was also asked to assist the schools following four separate death crises: a teenager with a congenital heart defect died at a school dance; a three-year-old day-care child was accidentally run over and killed by his father's car; a teenager who learned her cancer had returned committed suicide; and a beloved music teacher who had taught in six local schools was brutally murdered. In each of these instances, HEALS went into the schools with death crisis protocols, teddy bears, and art materials. These experiences became Penelope's and Anne's teachers, and each experience became part of their ongoing training. The two women had been literally catapulted from their theoretical perspectives into the experiential mode.

In 1991 it became obvious that more trained volunteers would be needed to handle all the requests for assistance. Consequently, Penelope and Anne developed the HEALS Training Program and this HEALS Training Manual, which are both based on their experiences, backgrounds, trainings, their work with Virginia Fry, and their actual field work. Although a lot of the work is experiential and not tangible due to its nature, you who are reading this manual are holding the synthesis of their inspiration in your hands.

The facilitators who train in this work must go through what Elisabeth Kübler-Ross terms "the tumbler." They must search out their own unresolved grief issues, bring them into their awareness, and then learn how to set them temporarily aside while working with the children they serve. Only then will a facilitator be clear and open enough to give helpful support to those in grief. This challenging work is best served by those who are personally dedicated to their own self-growth and are willing to utilize the expressive arts to communicate their life experiences in order to operate with integrity.

Anne Black and Penelope Simpson have provided our communities with the magic of the HEALS experience where children and adults are permitted—in a safe, non-judgmental environment—to express their life experiences from their hearts. Many nurturing adults have been magnetically drawn to HEALS, not only because they are committed to providing a safe, nourishing place for children to grow, but also because each of them has an inner child who also yearns to heal and grow.

—Patti Rivinus
Writer, editor & HEALS Facilitator
Brattleboro, Vermont

~ Preface ~

This manual has been conceptualized and developed so school counselors, educators, mental health professionals, lay volunteers and other adults can learn how to use the expressive arts to help grieving children feel their varied responses to loss. Walking in the shadow of death with these children takes a special person, a person who sincerely wants to give them a context in which to embrace the joy and suffering of living and offer child-centered ways to release the feelings of grief, both the uncomfortable feelings—and the love.

Yes, even love must be released to keep the heart of a child open. Otherwise, all emotions become stuck inside, engulfing the child (or adult) in a sea of confusing energy. Experiencing this phenomenon, it is common for those who are grieving to use their vital life force to hold down, and frequently dam, the flow of what longs to be innocently freed. The expressive arts is a potent tool, a gentle approach that, when responsibly used, creates a pathway for the energy of grief to be liberated from the body.

For those eager to use this expressive arts program, we want to make two important statements. First, we highly recommend that you continue to do your own work to deepen yourself, because the deeper you are able to access yourself, to that depth you are able to be present with children—and everyone else—including yourself! And second, this program begs for a huge investment of love and care, coupled with a commitment to attend to the many details it takes to create each session with impeccability.

Yes, it takes work to create each expressive arts session. As such, every session is a unique labor of love as it is composed. Every session longs to be presented from a place of being mindful and respectful of each child's specific situation and what will be most helpful for the children to express who they truly are beneath the pain. Every session holds the opportunity for the facilitator to plan and then let go of their agenda, so something fresh and "in the moment" can manifest. Rest assured that as you witness the opening of childrens' hearts, you will be so grateful you extended yourself and pushed the boundaries of what you thought were your limitations in time and ability. There is a force that is available to all of us when we surrender to it.

When healing energy flows through facilitators who have gone the extra mile to prepare themselves, as well as each expressive arts session in the curriculum, children experience the power of this unconditional love. These two essential ingredients mix together and hold the potential to help children heal. Whether this love and care is experienced consciously or unconsciously, children are keenly aware of being valued, validated and loved—which is what every human being seeks.

Saying "yes" to life and service creates an opening in our minds and our hearts, an opening that frees us to let something new and unexpected happen. For it is from this opening that guidance and inspiration can flow into us—so that out of this open state can flow our own unique expression.

We welcome you to the world of childhood grief. May this manual inspire you to explore the expressive arts and give you a set of golden keys to unlock a place in grieving children (and yourself) so that the precious gem held within every human being can be revealed—and each person's natural energy can be invested in living life more fully.

HOW TO USE THIS MANUAL

If you are taking The HEALS Training

This manual, The Art of Healing Childhood Grief, is designed to accompany The HEALS Training Program. As you progress through the process of understanding childhood grief, in light of your own grief experiences, you can most thoroughly understand the content of this manual and the HEALS approach to emotional literacy using the expressive arts. This training has been designed for school counselors, therapists, educators and paraprofessionals seeking to meet the needs of grieving children. This Creative Healing Approach can be adapted to be used in a variety of other settings and age groups.

If you are using the manual
independently from The HEALS Training

We have attempted to explain The HEALS Program as carefully as possible. Given that the training is largely experiential, it is impossible to obtain the pure substance of this work through this manual alone. It is our hope that the spirit of this work will filter through the words on these pages and inspire you to use some of these ideas and sessions when working with children in grief, even if you have not taken the training.

~ **Caution:** The Expressive Arts have the potential of taking both children and adults to very deep places. Allow ample time for participants to fully return to present-time before ending each session. Please refer to "HEALS Centering Exercises" for more information.

A Brief Synopsis of the Sections of this Manual

Section I: This is the **Backbone** of the program where The HEALS story and the philosophy of The HEALS Program is outlined. How children grieve based on their social and emotional development is explained as well as the signs of grief and how to listen to grieving children. Since the expressive arts are a significant part of our work, each of the arts is explored in a modicum of depth to provide some insight and awareness into the Creative Healing Approach of The HEALS Program.

Section II: The **Heartbeat** is where the threads of the program are carefully knit together. The HEALS framework begins the section; the roles of the counselor and facilitators are defined, and the forms are explained and gathered here. Creating the physical environment and establishing the psychological climate are discussed as well as The HEALS Rights for the program and how to handle behavioral problems.

Section III: The **Creative Mind** begins with The HEALS Program Framework followed by the learning objectives, sample HEALS plans for a variety of age levels for each session, and the core curriculum. This section also includes a segment on attunements, centering exercises, circle closures, imaginary journeys, and puppet shows. A resource list of our favorite books and films can be found in the Bibliography.

Section IV: Helpful information on **Death Crisis Intervention** can be found in this section as well as how to develop a HEALS Death Crisis Intervention Team to support schools in the event of a sudden and traumatic loss. Valuable troubleshooting tips, guidelines for dealing with students in grief, sample letters to send to parents, and information on secondary losses are also included. Specific information to help support children, staff and parents pertaining to suicide, homicide, disaster, and terrorism can also be found here.

Section V: Anyone who is in the position of facilitating and supporting groups of children or adults in grief can be most effective when they take care of themselves physically, mentally, emotionally, and spiritually. **Facilitator Sustenance** is a special section full of nourishment for the body and soul and offers gentle ways for facilitators to take time every day to nurture themselves.

Section VI: In the **Bibliography and Resource** section you can locate bibliographies for both children and adult referencing, resources, networking organizations, websites, related articles and references used for this publication.

Section I: The Backbone

History & Foundation

The HEALS Program for Children in Grief

What HEALS Is ～

The HEALS Program, an expressive arts bereavement and SEL (Social Emotional Learning) program, was founded in 1990 by Anne Black and Penelope Simpson to offer educational support for grieving children. This primary prevention project of Windham County, Vermont, has expanded to other communities where adults have been trained in this work.

HEALS Goals & Objectives ～

The HEALS curriculum and educational support groups are carefully designed to:

- ～ give grieving children an opportunity to meet in an accepting and caring environment;
- ～ decrease the isolation and loneliness children often feel following a loss;
- ～ help children experience safe and creative ways to express their feelings of grief;
- ～ increase a child's sense of self-worth and belonging;
- ～ provide activities and experiences to enhance social and emotional literacy;
- ～ strengthen resiliency skills needed to navigate future losses and life transitions;
- ～ reduce the need for substance abuse to deaden feelings of grief.

The eight HEALS sessions provide a framework to guide a group through the stages of grief while introducing each participant to techniques that can become lifelong tools for self-expression.

The HEALS Model: Using The Expressive Arts ～

Self-expression through the arts can be a doorway to deep communication, insight, and healing, especially in those who have difficulty with expression, or who are just learning to do so. Using art, movement, sound, imaginary journeys, writing, ritual, and relaxation in a special sequence, participants are encouraged to express their thoughts, feelings, and dreams to access healing energy and inner wisdom.

The HEALS Intensive Trainings ～

HEALS training programs are available for professionals and volunteers interested in using the expressive arts to assist grieving children and adults. This experiential training gives each participant a direct opportunity to experience the power, the process, and the procedures of the HEALS curriculum as they explore a significant childhood loss. Facilitators can most effectively guide others where they have been themselves.

The HEALS Connections ～

Monthly or quarterly support groups and in-services provide ongoing support and continuing education for HEALS facilitators.

The HEALS Curriculum Manual ～

The Art of Healing Childhood Grief: A School-based Expressive Arts Program Promoting Social and Emotional Literacy is a comprehensive manual designed to accompany The HEALS training. This how-to resource contains everything needed to implement a bereavement program for children as it weaves theory with practice in grounded, practical ways. As educators, therapists, and humanitarians, Black and Simpson draw on their diverse backgrounds to create this careful blending of techniques and disciplines that takes the mystery out of how to create safe, effective programs for grieving children.

The HEALS Program Framework & Objectives

Based on the work of Sandra Fox, founder of the Good Grief Program, and expanded by Anne Black and Penelope Simpson for The HEALS Program.

SESSION I: WE ARE NOT ALONE WITH OUR LOSS

To acknowledge that each member in the group has experienced a loss. To allow for the opportunity to share the death of the significant person in a child's life and to determine if there are any areas of question, concern, confusion, or misunderstanding.

SESSION II: TELLING THE STORY

To provide an opportunity for each child in the group to tell where they were when they first learned about their significant person's death—how they found out—and how they felt at that time.

SESSION III: GRIEVING THE LOSS—FEELING THE FEELINGS

To increase understanding and learn how people commonly feel and behave when someone or something they care about dies. To acknowledge that the feelings related to loss may be varied and difficult to have and/or to share.

SESSION IV: TAMING THE WILD THINGS

To understand that anger, fear, guilt, and worry are natural responses when we lose someone or something special. To learn how to safely and creatively access and express uncomfortable feelings.

SESSION V: FAREWELL RITUALS AND UNFINISHED BUSINESS

To provide the opportunity for each participant to express and complete any unfinished business they may have around their significant person.

SESSION VI: COMMEMORATION

To provide the child with an opportunity to affirm the value of the life of the person who died.

SESSION VII: THE JEWELS WITHIN—TREASURING OURSELVES

To remind the children that they are strong and powerful—each unique in their own way—with wise and creative resources that can be called forth when needed.

SESSION VIII: THE HARVEST CEREMONY

To honor and witness all that has been done during the HEALS sessions, both individually and as a group. To remind the children that the techniques and skills they learned in The HEALS Program may be used at any time in the future when their feelings need to be safely expressed. To receive permission to go on.

The Psychological Tasks of Grief

Grief is love not wanting to let go.
— Earl Grollman

∿ **Grief**: a normal and natural response to the variety of losses that humans experience universally (i.e. death, divorce, separation, chronic illness, physical limitation, retirement). Grief affects our entire being, and it has a strong <u>emotional impact</u> on how we are able to perceive and function in the world.

∿ **Mourning**: the psychological period of time or <u>process</u> following a death when the acute reactions of grief are felt and expressed. The goal or purpose of this part of the grieving process is to integrate that which binds the survivor to the loss or one who has died.

∿ **Bereavement**: the <u>complex series of reactions</u> resulting from a state of being deprived or torn apart by loss through a death. Bereavement includes grief and mourning.

The following is a compilation of the stages, according to major theories, that bereaved children and adults commonly experience on their journey through grief. Although these phases are written in a linear fashion, they are by no means experienced that way. Waves from any phase may wash over us, or crash unexpectedly at any given time, and are not subject to linear order. To complicate matters, a loss that occurs in one phase of life may reappear at a later developmental phase needing to be regrieved and reintegrated, often with new understanding and meaning. Awareness of our own symptoms and patterns of grief will help us to navigate the rougher waters when they arise. It should also be noted here that grief may look very different, depending upon one's culture. Signs and symptoms that are normal in one culture may be considered pathological in another. When working with a culture other than your own, make sure to conduct some cultural research and seek appropriate consultations.

The Grieving Process

Loss: An event or loss occurs such as a death, divorce, separation, abandonment, illness, or other major life change or transition.

Protest: During this acute phase one may resist the fact that the loss has occurred. The bereaved may experience the following emotions and difficulties with cognitive and intellectual functioning:

↔ numbness	↔ disbelief
↔ confusion	↔ need for safety
↔ anger	↔ loss of control
↔ forgetfulness	↔ denial
↔ guilt	↔ mystical experiences
↔ preoccupation with the loss	↔ hallucinations or dreams

Physical symptoms of this phase might include:

⭢ crying	⭢ sighing
⭢ tightness in throat	⭢ aching
⭢ chest pain	⭢ nausea
⭢ dry mouth	⭢ insomnia
⭢ shortness of breath	⭢ loss of appetite
⭢ headaches	⭢ excessive appetite

Tremendous energy is often required in this phase just to survive and move through the motions of everyday life. Decisions are very difficult to make while in this phase.

Despair: This phase is often accompanied by deep pain from the growing awareness that the loss is real. Many feel that the heart has been torn open by this experience. In this phase, feelings begin to move, and the process of weaving the tangled shreds of the heart back together slowly begins.

Having to adjust to life without the deceased can spark feelings of:

⭢ resentment and anger	⭢ sadness and depression	⭢ irritability
⭢ anxiety	⭢ searching and yearning	⭢ pain

Cognitive behaviors demonstrated by this phase might include:

⭢ disorganization	⭢ inability to concentrate	⭢ restlessness
⭢ feeling detached	⭢ loss of interest in activities	⭢ apathy

Spiritual questions or affirmations often arise in this phase and can include:

⭢ questioning or renewing of one's spiritual beliefs
⭢ interest in and wonder about what happens after death
⭢ quest for spiritual beliefs and existence of soul
⭢ deep need to find closure—if there is none

The griefwork during this phase still utilizes a vast amount of energy, often leaving the survivor feeling drained and tired. During these times it can be helpful to talk about the loss over and over again.

Reorganization & Acceptance: During the reorganization phase one begins to accept the reality of the loss and begins to adjust to the environment without the person who died.

⭢ become involved in life again	⭢ reinvest in old friendships	⊚ begin new friendships
⭢ create new life plans	⭢ plan new adventures	

There is a lessening of the emotional and physical aspects of the grieving process as the heart begins to heal itself—drawing its torn strands into itself (this may be the longest period).

Integration: The heart's healing process continues as integration takes place. Finding meaning in the loss is often helpful as a spiritual way to integrate the loss into one's own personal, cultural, or religious philosophy. The person usually begins to redefine how life will be lived without the loved one or significant person.

∾ acknowledgment   ∾ acceptance   ∾ energy returned with renewed strength

When the fibers of the heart are strengthened, the effects of grief dwindle. The journey into the darkness of pain can allow for the possibility of yet another phase in the process. This state of awareness goes beyond the limits of ordinary experience:

Transcendence: The intense journey of grief can provide fertile ground for movement into a heightened awareness of the spiritual quality of life and death.

∾ experience of a greater love	∾ ability to perceive the "bigger picture" of life
∾ gain in awareness that although the body is gone, love is eternal!	

The survivor may savor and value life as a sacred gift to hold and honor while celebrating and acknowledging death as another aspect of life.

Positive Aspects of Griefwork

By fully experiencing the various phases of grief one can:

∾ Gain a new sense of balance, strength, acceptance, and empowerment

∾ Gain a new sense of energy

∾ Gain new perspectives

∾ Recognize one's values

∾ Discover ways to cope that can help in personal growth and spiritual awareness

∾ Appreciate what was learned or gained in one's relationship with the deceased

Children's Developmental Concepts & Responses Around Death

I know Jamin died, but when is he gonna come back?
—Preschooler, Mistwood Montessori School

Children's ability to understand the concept of death is often affected by their age and level of development. When a death has occurred adults can help children by providing them with honest information appropriate for their developmental stage of understanding . The following are some general guidelines to keep in mind when supporting grieving children. Please be mindful that each child is an individual and will respond as such to the unique experiences that shape his/her particular life.

Age: Under 2

Concepts:

- Is aware of emotional changes in caretaker's environment
- Is aware of change in physical environment
- Does not understand the concept of death
- Can perceive loss and abandonment.

Behavioral Responses:

- Cries frequently
- Is crabby, fussy
- Clings, fears separation
- Exhibits regressive behaviors (wants bottle, diaper, etc.)

Interventions:

∾ Keep baby's routine as normal as possible (eating, bathing, sleeping, etc.)

∾ If possible, keep the baby in its home with consistent caretakers

∾ Give extra cuddling which provides reassurance

∾ Talk, sing, and play with the child; these provide soothing and reassurance

∾ Create a memory box for the young child with mementos and pictures of the deceased so they can learn about this family member later

Ages: 3-5

Concepts:

- Has undeveloped sense of space and time, cause and effect
- Has limited concept of "dead," perceives death as temporary and reversible (may associate death with sleep)
- Needs consistent routines and structure (eating, sleeping, bathing, etc.)
- Feels sadness, but only for short periods, may escape into play
- Easily able to misinterpret actions and words intrinsically involved with death, i.e., someone died in the hospital—therefore it is not a safe place to go; "kill" the lights; grandpa went to "sleep"; "Jesus took your cat today"—anger, fear of Jesus

- May have difficulties with intangible concepts such as heaven, soul, spirit
- May not remember the person who died
- May see death as accidental, but not natural

Behavioral Responses:

- Shows regressive behaviors (thumbsucking, clingy, etc.)
- Exhibits aggression towards others
- Has nightmares
- Acts out, is non-compliant

Interventions:

∾ Be honest about the death of a loved one

∾ Use appropriate words such as <u>death</u>, <u>dead</u>, and <u>died</u>

∾ Be prepared for the child's repetitive questioning as they grapple with the concept of death—provide explanations in clear, simple words appropriate to their level

∾ Explain what death is and some of the feelings the child may experience

∾ Help the child to understand that they did not cause the death (power of wishful thinking)

∾ Acknowledge that they may cry one moment and play the next, and it is okay

∾ Allow the child to be involved as much as possible in the funeral or memorial arrangements, if they desire

∾ Let the child know that they are safe and will be cared for

∾ Allow the child to have memento/s of the person who died to help remember them

<u>Ages: 6-9</u>

Concepts:

- Understands the finality of death
- Has heightened interest in what causes death (sometimes to the point of preoccupation) —in the later stages children want to know what happens after death
- May feel guilty and blame self for the death (remnants of magical thinking stage)
- May develop fears about death and sleep ("Now I lay me down to sleep…")
- Is able to accept the reality of death, but not their own or their loved ones
- Tendency to interpret death as a person (i.e. the grim reaper, bogeyman, ghost, skeleton)
- May demonstrate a profound sensitivity to creating rituals and ceremonies for dead animals (such as birds, fish, or a guinea pig)

Behavioral Responses:

- Tends to caretake, grow up fast
- Shows possessiveness
- Develops phobias
- Exhibits aggression towards others/self
- Has headaches, stomach aches
- Is non-compliant, openly defiant

Interventions:

- ∾ Ask what they understand about death, work from their questions and fears(accept their feelings about death)
- ∾ Use appropriate language (<u>death</u>, <u>dead</u>, <u>dying</u>)
- ∾ Talk about and role model feelings that may come, and explain that other children experience those feelings too
- ∾ Admit that you do not have all the answers
- ∾ Maintain a routine
- ∾ Reassure children about their fears or guilt
- ∾ Involve the child as a participant in funerals and memorials, if they desire
- ∾ Be prepared that the topic of "death" may be prevalent in a child's play and art
- ∾ Even though the child may feel "too old," they may need more physical attention, provide them with them cuddles, hugs, and allow them to crawl into bed with a parent when they feel scared.

Ages 10-12

Concepts:

- Able to understand that death is final and irreversible
- Is curious about the biological components or "gory" details of the death process
- Has moral sense of right and wrong—death may be seen as a punishment
- Fears abandonment, being left behind

Behavioral Responses:

- Shows aggression
- May experience anger at deceased
- Has headaches, stomach aches
- Tends to caretake, grow up fast
- May avoid discussion of death
- Shows possessiveness
- Develops phobias
- Shows defiance, non-compliance

Interventions:

- ∾ Use appropriate language (<u>death</u>, <u>dead</u>, <u>dying</u>)
- ∾ If the child requests details of the death, provide them, but admit when you do not know answers
- ∾ Talk about feelings that may come, and explain that other children experience those feelings too
- ∾ Allow them to have a memento of the deceased
- ∾ Reassure them they did not cause the death, and could not have prevented it (in most circumstances)
- ∾ Involve them in funerals and memorials, if they desire
- ∾ Even though they feel "too old," they may need more physical attention, provide them with them hugs, and allow them to crawl into bed with a parent when they feel upset

13

~ Provide a journal for them to write down their thoughts and feelings

~ Offer love, support and opportunities to share memories

<u>Ages: 13-18</u>

Concepts:

- Has a sense of immortality, death happens to others not me, my friends, or my family
- Able to understand that death is an inevitable outcome of life, adult perception
- Has moral sense of right and wrong—death may be seen as a punishment

Behavioral Responses:

• Has sense of immortality shattered	• Shows possessiveness
• May tend to ruminate about own death	• Exhibits aggression
• May feel anger towards God, question beliefs	• May avoid discussion of death
• Is vulnerable to feeling "different" from peers	• Shows defiance, non- compliance
• May experience anger at deceased	• Shows increased risk-taking
• May increase drug experimentation	• Has headaches and stomach aches
• Need to grieve with peers	• Exhibits increased sexual activity
• Tends to caretake, grow up fast	• May experience suicidal ideation

Interventions:

~ Use appropriate language (<u>death</u>, <u>dead</u>, <u>dying</u>)

~ Talk about feelings they may experience, and share your feelings

~ Reassure them they are not responsible

~ Involve them in funerals and memorials, if they desire

~ Provide them with some form of touch and connectedness through hugs, pats,

~ Give them permission to cry, and let them know it is okay for you to cry too

~ Provide "warm fuzzies" in the form of compliments and verbal appreciation

Emotional and Cognitive Effects of Grief in Children

Children in all the groups above may experience emotional or cognitive difficulties in the following areas, which can affect them socially and academically:

- Inability to concentrate, focus
- Irritability
- Anxiety/Worry
- Lowered self-esteem
- Depression/Moodiness
- Problems with school
- Inability to follow directions
- Numbness

- Distractibility
- Feelings of rejection
- Fear or withdrawal
- Hypersensitivity
- Yearning/searching for deceased
- Shock, disbelief
- Inability to play, apathy
- Blaming death on others

- Disorganization
- Mystical experiences \
- Big Man/Big Woman role taking
- Idealization of deceased
- Forgetfulness

Physical Effects of Grief in Children

These are some of the physical manifestations or changes a child in grief may experience, which can impact their performance in many areas of their life.

- Tiredness, lack of energy
- Lack of or excessive appetite
- Headaches, tummy aches
- Sleeping too much or not enough
- Tightness in throat
- Clumsiness
- Hyperactivity, restlessness
- General nervousness
- Shortness of breath
- Crying
- Skin rashes
- Nausea

Most of these signs are regarded as normal grief expressions in children and adolescents. Some of the more benign ones, such as the regressive symptoms, may be tolerated and indulged as they will usually decrease with time and expression. If symptoms tend to manifest for a prolonged period of time, or are extremely intense of disruptive, they may be regarded as complicated grieving, and professional help or counseling for the child should be sought.

All children and teens need to have assurance that their needs will be met during times of loss. Providing extra love and attention is not only reassuring and soothing for children, but also for care-takers as well. If grief is minimized or avoided, children and teens may develop self-soothing behaviors that can be harmful, excessive, and habit-forming and may lead to addiction.

Throughout childhood, middle years, and into old age, human beings continue to change and modify their views about death throughout life, as the meaning of death changes for them. Earl Grollman sums it up aptly with this quote:

"The meaning of death shifts as the quality of life shifts."

Social Emotional Learning

All we are given are possibilities—
to make ourselves one thing or another.

—Jose Ortega y Gasset

Emotional Intelligence

In 1994, four years after the birth of The HEALS Program, Howard Gardner offered a theoretical framework called "multiple intelligences." His theory identifies seven major areas of performance and competency used to solve problems or create products. Only two of these intelligences, logical-mathematical, and verbal, are given due emphasis in traditional school settings. The HEALS Program focuses on the development of two of the other intelligences. These "personal intelligences" are:

- **Intrapersonal intelligence**—the ability to know one's own feelings and inner experiences, and manage them well. We will use the term <u>emotional intelligence</u> or <u>emotional literacy</u> for this domain.

- **Interpersonal intelligence**—the capacity for handling relationships skillfully. This domain we will refer to as <u>social competency</u> or <u>social literacy</u>.

The term "emotional intelligence" came into the literature in 1995 when Daniel Goleman introduced his insightful emotional literacy work. According to Goleman, emotional intelligence encompasses the experience of self-awareness, self-discipline, self-motivation, self-responsibility, impulse control, delay of gratification, patience, persistence, empathy, altruism, compassion, and social deftness. We believe that emotional literacy is of key importance in creating a happier and healthier world in which to live.

Social Emotional Literacy (SEL) programs similar to The HEALS Program are springing up across the nation. Forward-thinking educators are embracing these programs to undergird their academic curriculums and counseling programs. They understand the importance of children being able to identify and label feelings, express feelings safely, assess the intensity of their feelings, recognize the difference between feelings and actions, and learn how to manage feelings as highly desirable outcomes of the educational process. It is our hope that in the future, emotional literacy will be an integral part of progressive school curriculums, reaching all children, rather than the exceptional, outside, specialized program coming in, serving only a small population.

Social Competence

The other component of an emotional literacy program is social competency. Prevention models like The HEALS Program recognize the central role relationships play in the academic and social success of children. Decision-making, problem-solving, and conflict resolution skills define self-control, group participation, and social awareness. Opportunities to exercise these skills are integrated throughout the HEALS curriculum giving children opportunities to practice critical, interpersonal skills in the safety of a small group setting.

After running school-based groups for eleven years, our facilitators are noticing significant changes in the children who have repeated our program. Children who had behavior issues in their first series of sessions became noticeably calmer, in greater control of themselves, more responsible, empathic, and helpful in future sessions. While several causative factors for this dramatic change in behaviors could be considered, the notable changes among repeat participants signal the importance of these group experiences to the social and emotional development of children. More rigorous research studies are currently being developed to focus on these behavioral changes in our program.

Additionally, informal follow-ups with past participants are providing us with growing case histories showing that HEALS participants are using the information they learned for many years after the group has ended.

Eight-year-old Sarah attended one of our groups five years after the death of her father. Her family was unable to discuss this loss. Sarah created and used a Memory Box dedicated to her father to help her cope on the anniversary of his death. It was reported that Sarah used her Memory Box as a ritual on her father's next death anniversary, one year after she graduated from The HEALS Program.

Citing another case, a mother reported that her son, Aaron, now a senior in high school, keeps his grandfather's Memory Box in a special place along with other materials he created as a 5th grader while participating in a HEALS group.

Through playful, expressive arts activities in the HEALS curriculum, grieving children are given the opportunity to try out new ways to express themselves in a safe and creative environment. These children have ample opportunities to:

- practice listening skills
- learn tolerance and respect for other's thoughts and feelings
- learn that one can move through emotions, particularly the more difficult ones
- recognize patterns in their own or others' behaviors
- learn that they have the power to make choices to change their behaviors
- learn to practice confidentiality and to respect another's privacy
- learn how to go deeper within themselves and to feel the suffering of another's pain

Within the boundaries of a group of peers, HEALS children face one of the toughest challenges life offers—learning how to cope with the loss of a loved one (or significant person) while mastering important social and emotional skills (self-knowledge) that will serve them well through inevitable future losses and transitions. The mastery of those skills, coupled with an open heart, can help some children to experience compassion—a quality more precious than gold.

Preparing for the Ebb and Flow of Life: SEL

The position statement of the Collaborative for the Advancement of Social and Emotional

Learning (CASEL) sums up our HEALS curriculum quite well:

> *It is CASEL's position that all children benefit from programs and practices that promote social and emotional growth. Although many children live in extreme conditions and must cope with poverty, violence, substance abuse, and homelessness as a part of everyday life, many more also live in stressful situations which tax their capacity to learn. It is the rare child who is not affected by today's fast pace of modern life, by rapid changes in society and technology, and by media images and forms of entertainment that push them more quickly than ever into adulthood. As our economy becomes more service-centered and our work-force more diverse, social and emotional skills and capacities become increasingly important. If we are to prepare our young people for life in the next century, we must address these issues now, while they are still flexible enough to respond. CASEL believes that social and emotional programming should be implemented as part of every school curriculum and that every child should have equal access to experiences that foster optimal academic, social, and emotional development.*

Whether a child has been emotionally wounded or not, schooling the heart along with the head is essential in order to move our children toward becoming more holistic human beings.

Educational Support Group Vs. Therapy

The prepared or one-pointed mind
is open to creative insight because
it bypasses thinking.
—Joseph Chilton Pearce, <u>Magical Child</u>

The HEALS Program is designed as an educational support program that creates a unique and safe environment where children in grief come together to share and learn. The HEALS expressive arts curriculum may have therapeutic effects; however, it is not intended as therapy which has an altogether different approach. If the significant differences between these two kinds of groups are not considered by the facilitators at the outset, the group could be harmful to the participants and have adverse effects on the integrity of the program. For the most successful educational support group experience for yourself and the children, it is critical to consider and be mindful of the following elements that distinguish these two groups.

Anatomy of Educational Support Groups

Educational support groups provide **general support** with a focus on **curriculum-based activities** which are the heart or **content.** These activities combine information and experiences that zero in upon **practical lifeskills** that will be **useful to the group as a whole.** The thrust of the **group focus** can be maintained by the facilitator's ability to frame most questions so they are applicable to all members. For an example, a HEALS facilitator might ask, "Can each of you share what you usually do when you feel angry?" Another example is, "Okay, let's hear what other members of our group think happens when someone dies?"

Additionally, the psychological environment of an educational support group is usually **supportive and nurturing** with a heavy emphasis placed on the **modeling of healthy behaviors. Confidentiality** is very important to continually build trust and safety for all members.

In educational support groups, the **role of the leader is that of facilitator.** The facilitator's primary task is to find the most effective way to present the curriculum that meets the developmental level and learning styles of the group participants. Specialized workshops, trainings, or internships are encouraged, but **no licensure is required** to be a facilitator.

When problems arise, such as complicated grief issues or severe behavior problems, **referrals are made for assessment**. It is not the facilitator's responsibility to interpret or assess problems, but it is their responsibility to make a referral.

Lastly, educational support groups are **time limited** with the duration of the time being the same for all members, such as 8 weeks for a HEALS group. However, children are allowed to repeat a HEALS group, if space is available.

Anatomy of Therapy Groups

The purpose of a therapy group is to **resolve personal problems.** The primary importance of therapy groups is to focus on each individual's particular problems, even though they are in a group setting. Individuals in these groups each have a **treatment plan,** which the therapist attempts to focus on during the group. Rather than being content-based, **the therapy group is process-oriented** and attempts are made to **solve individual problems** within the group. A therapy group is supportive and nurturing but has the added element of direct **confrontation of its members** and their issues. **Confidentiality** is essential for group members to feel safe, to trust the group, the therapist, and the group process.

The leader of a therapy group is usually a **licensed therapist,** who has completed the training and educational requirements for licensure. The role of the therapist is to look at individual members' behaviors and their origins, and conduct tactical interventions to help the individual become aware of and resolve problems. They may phrase questions that dig and probe such as, "Are there other times in your life when you have experienced these feelings?" Therapists are trained to **assess and recommend individual treatment** on an **ongoing basis.** The therapy group may also be ongoing, depending upon the kind of group and the individual needs of its members.

Multicultural Grieving Differences and Ethnic Variations

As we do our own work of softening and opening....
the world softens and opens around us!
—Anne Black

When working with grieving children, it is essential to keep in mind that people from different cultures grieve differently. What is considered healthy grieving in one culture may be regarded as unhealthy in another. For most people, their beliefs about death and the soul's fate after death are sacred—beliefs that give meaning to life. Due to strong ideologies, it is very common for people from traditions other than the dominant tradition of an area not to share their religious beliefs and rituals, fearful that their practices may be criticized or ridiculed. There is a verse in the Bible that says, "Don't cast your pearls before swine!" Beliefs are precious and it is imperative that we hold another's "pearls" with reverence and respect.

For many parents coming from other countries with rooted death, dying and grieving legacies, there is a strong desire to pass their cultural traditions on to their children. Unfortunately, as their children become more and more acculturated by mainstream American ways of grieving (or not grieving), it becomes harder and harder to maintain the purity of their traditions.

Within any given culture there can be variations. If someone comes from Laos, for example, they may have Hmong beliefs rather than Buddhist—and every religious tradition has its own sets of practices that differ from one another. Similarly, the Hispanic community, which is primarily Roman Catholic, has a broad range of differing practices depending on whether their traditions have been influenced by Mayan or Inca rituals or by Spain, following the Spanish Inquisition. Socioeconomic levels and the education of individuals also contribute to how people grieve.

What a gift it is for children coming to us with their unique set of beliefs to find themselves within a HEALS group that has done the research and understands the child's grieving rituals and practices—and has perhaps even woven some of these customs into the curriculum. It is highly recommended to learn from the family and determine if they are receptive to incorporate some of their practices into their child's HEALS group. The parents will likely reach their decision based on their trust in the sincerity of your approach. If the green light is given by the parent, extra work will be involved, but the extra effort holds the potential to create an enriching opportunity for everyone in the group to grow, learn and heal together.

Each time someone shares their culture with us, it may be helpful to view this gift as a journey into an exotic, new world. Make an attempt to enter into learning about another belief system from the perspective of a curious being who truly cares about another human who has been acculturated in a way different from your own. It may be helpful to realize that had your soul been born into their culture that you would believe and practice as they do. We wanted to briefly discuss the uniqueness of customs and rituals in hopes that one never use a cookie cutter to define the edges of any one ethnic group or set of beliefs, and instead remain within the wonderment of discovery.

A Humanitarian Tone of Humility

When we allow ourselves to move into the unfamiliar and be stretched, perhaps the following statements can help remind us to constantly push the boundaries of our own limitations so that we can become more conscious, more receptive and more open to others:

More and more…I am opening my mind and heart to those who have beliefs different from mine….and as I honor and respect those customs and traditions that bring others comfort, hope and continuity…I give comfort, hope and continuity to myself…

Just for today…I accept where I am…knowing that as I let go of the judgments I hold of another human being who sees the world in different ways than I…that I feel freer within myself…and tensions melt away…

More and more…I long to come into a more genuine, purer harmony with others…to move beneath my mind, personality and ego…and to reach out from my soul that knows no separation…

More and more…I forgive myself for the times I criticized another and so tenaciously embraced my position that I created prison walls in my mind and around my heart….and now I move toward letting these mental barriers drop away….and as I breathe freely into the open spaces…I feel an expansiveness being created in my mind and in my heart…

And for now…I acknowledge that I, too, am a traveler in a complex world…and that the greatest gift I can offer humanity is to open the flower of my heart…petal by petal…and that as I do…I offer this unique blossom of my being…and I give from the deepest part of myself that I am able to access…in this moment…

How priceless it is to experience the grace of opening to embrace another being exactly where they are. When this convergence occurs, it can be likened to entering the shared garden of two souls. These times have an essence and flavor all their own. Soul connections are some of the purest treasures of humanity and most frequently occur when we "let go" and truly surrender, without an agenda, to the moment of encounter.

Complicated Grief

Everyone takes the limits of his own vision
for the limits of the world.
—Arthur Schopenhauer

What do we mean by complicated grief as it relates to The HEALS Program? Sometimes there are children who react to the changes occurring in their lives in ways that require more than our educational support group can offer. As soon as possible, refer these children for professional counseling or therapy. Utmost care and profound respect is required to communicate with all parties involved that the child is not yet ready for a HEALS group experience. The communication of this decision must not shame or belittle the child in any way. This is very important! Help everyone understand that there simply are pieces that need to be sorted out and processed before the child is ready to participate in a HEALS group.

How does complicated grief differ from a normal grief reaction? The most noticeable indicator of complicated grief is a significant change in the child's normal behavior and mood for a prolonged period of time. These symptoms may look like depression, morbidity, or behaviors that put children at risk of hurting themselves or someone else. Because the emotional pain is so great, these children frequently pull inward and simultaneously push people away. It takes a very special, non-judgmental person who can hold the container for these children and understand their unusual cry for love.

Here are some indicators of complicated grief:

- Continued denial of the reality for many months (after about the developmental age of 6-7 years)
- Extended period of depression and loss of interest in usual activities, chronic fatigue
- Prolonged physical complaints (i.e. inability to sleep or too much sleep, somatic complaints)
- Withdrawal from friends
- Unreasonable or extreme fear, panic, or frenzy
- Extended feelings of guilt
- Loss of appetite
- Decline in school performance or attendance
- Loss of self-esteem and self-trust
- Complete absence of mourning
- Preoccupation with morbid ideas
- Pervasive and prolonged sense of hopelessness
- Suicidal thoughts (i.e., wish to die and join the deceased)
- Engaging in high-risk behaviors
- Chronic defiance of rules, routines, and rights of others
- Excessive conflict with peers, brothers and sisters, parents, and/or other adults
- Promiscuity
- Experimentation with mood altering chemicals or drugs
- Escapist behaviors, including running away
- Disturbances in bodily regulation such as self-care, weight regulation, problems with bowels or bladder control
- Maturation and development difficulties

If a child is exhibiting any of the preceding symptoms for a prolonged period, a referral should be made to the school counselor to access additional support. Early interventions can minimize the long-term and serious effects of complicated grief.

What factors can cause complicated grief? A variety of circumstances can contribute to a child's predisposition or risk of exhibiting complicated grief. In her book, *Treatment of Complicated Mourning,* Terese Rando lists seven high-risk factors that can increase the level of trauma and add to complicated grief. These include:

- A sudden unanticipated death, especially when it is traumatic, violent, mutilating, or random
- Death from an overly lengthy illness
- The mourner's perception of preventability
- A relationship with the deceased that was markedly hostile, abusive, ambivalent, or dependent
- The mourner's prior mental health problems
- Multiple losses or unresolved earlier losses and stresses
- The mourner's perceived lack of social support

Children demonstrating complicated grief are at risk of becoming covered over by layers of pain, unworthiness, self-judgment, depression, and a general disappointment in life. As the precious souls of children are layered with unexpressed feelings and pain, they and everyone in their sphere, become more and more distanced from who this child truly is. When the layering process occurs, false behaviors and characteristics take the place of their authentic self. Hopefully, with some effective therapy, children can be helped to unravel some of these protective layers so that you and the child will have greater access to who they truly are when they participate in a HEALS group.

Keeping Memories Alive

"I begin at the beginning, examining each frame of memory. Images of another time rage in my stormy awareness, and I am jolted with searing sprays of inescapable reality. As hurt washes over me, I am tempted to abandon this cruel immersion. But I stay here, shivering, clinging to understanding that is still raw, believing that my very presence in these cold waters of remembrance will soon turn them warm and soothing."

—Molly Fumia

Finding tangible connections with the deceased following a death can be a very important part of the grieving process. Many people find comfort in being able to look at, touch, smell, or hold objects or wear articles that belonged to the deceased. Memories are a normal and natural part of the process. Even the smallest of things may carry strong, emotional significance as one wades through sorrow.

Naturally, photographs may soothe some of the yearning to be close to the departed at various times. If the deceased suffered a long debilitating illness or deforming accident, if possible it can be helpful to also provide earlier photos and memories of healthier times.

Children often express concerns and fears that they will forget the deceased, particularly a parent. The child may need extra help finding ways to remember a loved one. Making memory books and boxes filled with pictures, stories, and mementos of the deceased are excellent ways to help children remember and memorialize. Family and friends may share stories of the deceased and record them on a tape that can be played over and over again. These kinds of *aid d'memoirs* may help the child to independently explore and grieve in their own time.

Additionally, many children are keenly sensitive to the feelings of other family members and do not want to make them sad—they may avoid their own grief in order to maintain stability in the family. Having access to the kinds of transitional objects mentioned above can play an important role in the child's healing process.

The bonds of love continue long after a body drops away. These precious connections of the heart, while internally centered, can be brought forward and sustained for longer periods of time by using the tangible objects and visual reminders of loved ones. Our work is constantly committed to helping children connect with their hearts, because the longing they feel is the love.

Listening to Children

Listen in deep silence. Be very still and open your mind...
Sink deep into the peace that waits for you
beyond the frantic, riotous thoughts and sights and sounds
of this insane world.
—ACIM

Pre-Group Facilitator Preparation

It is a rare person who can automatically shift into a heart space, and facilitate a group of children, without using some sort of centering mechanism. For some, a centering or relaxation technique might include taking slow, deep breaths or spending a few minutes in silence to clear the mind of agitation, to provide a deeper sense of calm, to sharper concentration, to achieve a high level of intuitive understanding and to enhance their ability to truly hear what the children are saying. Another way to access this calm state is by doing a "let go" dance or some active, physical movements to a robust piece of music. As a facilitator shakes off and releases any nervousness, turbulence or other interfering energies, calmness will follow. We highly recommend you take sufficient time to release any tensions and become calm before the children arrive.

On Being An Empathic Listener

The ideal listener is, first of all, empathic. To listen empathically to a child means to listen to what he is saying, understand how his world seems to him, sense the emotional flavor it has for him, and see its personal meaning for him. This is no simple matter as our own judgments and beliefs may suddenly come creeping in to contaminate what the child is saying, and our good intentions may want to come crashing in to offer some of our pearls of wisdom in order to "correct" his beliefs and help him restate his experience.

If you are not naturally an empathic listener, it's something that can be learned. It is not a skill one is "born with." The best way to learn it is from empathic persons in an empathic climate.

Empathic listening may be passive, in that one listens in relative silence, or it may be active, in that the listener puts his/her understanding of what was said (and the feelings perceived beyond the verbal statement) into his/her own words and repeats it to the child for verification and clarification.

Listening in depth is difficult. We feel we must say something. There is a tendency to think that if we do not have a sage response that it means we are not competent. You will notice that some people prefer you to give answers and will even prod you to do so. If you can sit quietly without reacting defensively when they apply the pressure, they will withdraw it and let the talk flow.

Both ways of listening are **Active Listening** and communicate a willingness to hear, to understand, and to have empathy with the child. Many children are isolated and struggling to be heard. When children experience empathy, it gives them the needed confirmation that they do exist as a separate, valued person with an identity.

Active Listening requires that we:

- Be fully present
- Take the time
- Wish to be helpful
- Be able to accept the child's feelings and values
- Believe in the child's ability to find his/her own solutions to the problems if given the opportunity
- Avoid focusing on our own problems and concerns
- Avoid projecting our own values, needs, feelings, and prior experiences onto the situation we are hearing about.

Summary of guidelines:

- Listen to the basic message.
- Restate to the child a simple, concise summary of the basic content and/or feelings of the message.
- Look for a cue, or ask for a response to confirm your accuracy and understanding of the related message.
- Allow the child to correct your perceptions, if inaccurate.

Many people learn while they talk. Children may say things that sound awful to you, and which you do not agree with, but while they are saying them, their anger and frustration levels are shrinking. They are forming new insights about their situation. We can never really know what another is truly thinking and feeling deep down in their soul. In listening to children, we offer a chance for them to explore and work out their feelings.

Active Listening fosters catharsis and can help a child to identify and ultimately accept difficult feelings. It is a process that encourages independent thinking; demonstrates openness and acceptance; and communicates belief in and respect for the individual child and his/her potential for self-discovery.

Special Listening Tools: Talking Sticks

Respectful listening should be given to whoever holds the special object or talking stick. As a child shares his/her experience, it is essential that the other children and adults give the child their full attention. This is one of the most important treasures that can be offered to a child in grief. They want compassionate witnesses to hear their story and their pain, and they will withhold their reminiscences if they do not feel adequate trust and safety.

Suggested objects for use as talking sticks:

Velvet Heart	Koosh Ball	Decorated Talking Stick	Flower
Heart Stone	Magic Sphere	Wand	Feather
Beautiful Stone	Teddy Bear	Beaver Stick	Shell
Rain Stick	Stress Ball	Scepter	Star

Western culture trains us more in how to talk than how to listen. The old adage, "We were given two ears and one mouth for a reason" is a valuable mantra for us to keep in mind when we are working with children in bereavement.

Listening & The Expressive Arts

Using the expressive arts with children requires another level of listening skills from both the facilitator and group participants. The variety of ways to express oneself without words—through movement, sound, and art—requires listening skills that are more reflective in nature. In order for each group participant to feel heard, an emotional listening tool called "mirroring" is commonly used. Mirroring occurs when the whole group (or dyads) are asked to mimic a movement, a sound, or an art image made by one of the members. In this way the entire group is able to experience much more deeply by connecting the feeling through their own body. Daniel Goleman refers to mirroring as being able to "capture not just the thought but also the feelings that go with it. The effect of being mirrored accurately is not just feeling understood, but having the added sense of being in emotional attunement." (1999). Having others step into your emotional shoes can be a powerful, joyful experience. Mirroring, when used effectively, can increase group cohesiveness, build empathy amongst participants, and foster a sense of belonging.

Fostering An Optimum Listening Environment

- Form the group in a circle so all group members may have direct eye contact with one another. A circle provides a sense of security and warmth.

- Control your level of active listening responses. Modeling active listening more frequently at the beginning of the series of sessions helps children feel more comfortable about sharing. Reduce modeling as needed, particularly if children tend to respond directly to you all of the time.

- If group members tend to defocus onto other topics, be aware that your active listening response level may not be high enough to keep them focused.

- Promote group cohesiveness by engaging all the group members.

In conclusion, whether it is empathic or active, intuitive-listening is a complex art—and an art worthy of ample rehearsal time to refine. Effective listening doesn't magically happen. It involves being aware of the personal patterns that can get in the way of our ability to listen. Probably the greatest obstacle to becoming an effective listener is a mind that has its own agenda and chatter. For this reason, we highly recommend the facilitator of a HEALS session do whatever it takes to come into a calm, centered place before the beginning of a group. When the mind is quiet, we are more able to drop into a stillness that allows us to be present with each child while maintaining an awareness of the session objectives so we can gracefully step into the openings the children will create—and access the teachable opportunities. Learning to be in the "listening zone" takes practice and keen consciousness, but its fruits are well worth the effort as listening brings with it the precious gift of a child feeling truly heard.

The Expressive Arts

When you ask me how I feel, I'm the only one
who can tell you. And I like that!
—A Kindergarten student

Swirling With Grief

The expressive arts we use in The HEALS Program include movement, art, sound, and writing. These art forms are valuable tools to assist grieving children in both accessing and releasing the strong and varied emotions that occur following the death of a family member, friend, or pet. Attempting to describe their internal world with words alone can prove frustrating to children whose vocabulary and life experience have not nurtured and encouraged their verbal ability to identify and articulate the more than eighty different emotions that are inherent to our human species.

All unexpressed fear, anger, sadness, and guilt, as well as joy and love are carried inside a child's emotional and physical body. These intense emotions swirl together in a dance that can be both overwhelming and confusing to the vast majority of children; the only way most children know how to ask for help is to "act out," get sick, or withdraw into themselves, hoping that a caring adult will notice and help them lighten the emotional burden they carry. It is a very rare and fortunate child who is able to be sufficiently in touch with their grief process to describe their feelings to an empathic adult and then feel validated and supported. The adult with whom the child most needs to process feelings is too often engulfed in their own grief and accompanying pain to adequately be present with the grieving child. A lot of the child's grief, therefore, gets pushed down and is left unresolved and unexpressed.

Since the verbal articulation of emotion is difficult for many children, we have found that using the body in a non-verbal manner to feel and express these emotions is easier for children while allowing them direct access to their feelings.

The Creative Connection

An expressive arts approach, developed by Natalie Rogers, called "The Creative Connection" has proved helpful in our work with grieving children by making links between the body, the emotions, and the child's essential spirit. When we began using this sequence with children, we discovered that as they moved their bodies, the movement helped them begin to focus on the areas where they were holding tension and emotions. As this awareness was used as the source from which to do art, the children felt both connected and energized to put their feelings on paper or into clay. When the children ultimately put their experiences into the written word and/or verbally shared their inner content, it was quite powerful for them (and us) to discover a whole new way for them to be with their inner environment. Thus, we discovered that an interesting relationship exists between moving, drawing, sounding, and writing in working with children in grief (what we call The Creative Healing Approach).

When grieving children move with awareness, their minds become quieter as they open to profound feelings which can be a source from which to create in the form of art. The use of guided imagination between the movement and the art helps create the space for some of these children to "see" images, colors, and forms which surface from the child's emotional world. When children write immediately after movement and art, they have been amazed at their ability to find a new way to describe what they are living with inside their bodies. Their writing, often in the form of poetry, seems to "fly" out, permitting them to witness their own insights and truth.

It is important to remember that some children may feel inhibited, shy, or blocked when it comes to utilizing certain art materials, using their bodies to move, doing any form of "performance," or even expressing themselves through writing. Remind them often that no one else knows or can express what they are feeling—not the greatest artist, singer, or dancer. Each child has powerful truths to express and share with others. No one else can paint their picture or dance their dance. Let the children know that they are being given an opportunity to allow feelings to come out of their bodies and whatever comes out is okay. A child's feelings are the source from which their expression can be channeled into movement—or art—or sounding—or writing. For example, if a child is feeling confused, s/he can dance or draw the confusion. Even if s/he is tired, the tiredness can be danced. And if a child is happy or sad, colors can be chosen to draw those feelings, or a poem can be written to express the feelings. Happiness, too, can be sung or danced or drawn. Any emotion can be expressed through movement, art, sound, or writing.

The Creative Healing Approach

These exercises, particularly movement, can stir up many feelings in children. Guard against rushing in too soon and interrupting a child's process. It is much more helpful to ask the child what they are needing from the group in the moment, allowing them to be with the richness and scope of their emotions, or guide them into putting their feeling(s) into one of the expressive arts. If it seems appropriate, one of the facilitators may work privately with a child while the rest of the group resumes. As these waves of emotion wash over the children, teaching them to draw them—or sound them—or write about them—or express them through movement will be giving them very powerful tools to release their feelings which can serve them well throughout their lives.

The expressive arts portion of the HEALS program can be designed to use the arts in a sequence one after another or several of the mediums can occur simultaneously to put children in direct touch with how they are feeling in the moment. For our purposes, however, we tend to use The Creative Healing Approach to progress from movement, to art and/or sounding, and finally to writing. It is not necessary to always use this approach. This is merely a suggestion, and each facilitator is encouraged to experiment with the expressive arts and find what works the best for him or her.

Our hope is that as children continue to experience the arts that they will have a growing awareness of how they can more easily identify what is going on inside their bodies in order to congruently express their feelings. As they become more able to navigate the up and down terrains of their own inner landscapes, they will tend to move along better with the ebb and flow of life in general while not remaining stuck in any one place. As children become more adept at letting feelings come and go, they will have a greater zest for life and see the "WOW!"

The way a child perceives the outside world is a direct projection of how he feels inside his own body. Therefore, as we work toward facilitating more peacefulness in the internal world of a child, we work toward a more peaceful planet.

In the following sections we will discuss movement, sound, art, and writing as modalities for expression and explain how to use Imaginary Journeys to gently move deeper into the exploration of loss and feelings through the expressive arts.

Movement as Expression

The best way to get out of our heads,
is to move our bodies.

—Gabrielle Roth

Connecting Movement with Emotions

Children move their bodies all of the time. It is difficult for them to sit or stand perfectly still for very long. Their bodies tend to be in perpetual motion, and they demonstrate how natural it is to move and experiment with the hundreds of different ways their bodies can express the feelings they are experiencing in the moment.

Remember that childrens' bodies and minds are in a continual state of rapid growth and change. Movement forms a central foundation to build self-awareness. What is often unconscious within makes itself conscious through our muscle structures. "We do not know what is happening in us until our face, body muscles, and breathing muscles arrange themselves into patterns that we recognize as fear, anger, ecstasy, joy, and other feelings. It requires but an infinitesimal amount of time for our muscle structure to rearrange itself in response to an internal state, but we all know it is possible to inhibit our feelings before they become visible to others. We then become aware of such muscle changes. These changes are what most of us can immediately feel. "(The Centering Book, 1975). Development of this essential tool for self-awareness through movement is of key importance in developing social and emotional literacy skills.

The Grieving Body

Children who are mourning the loss of a loved one, significant person, or pet may have an emotional range anywhere from having extreme difficulty attending to a focused task because of their agitated internal state to appearing lifeless, withdrawn, and far away. The child who is extremely active generally relishes the opportunity to express feelings through movement to the beat of a drum or other instrument. Children who are kinesthetically inclined thrive on movement and when they are allowed to connect specific emotions with movement, tend to request this activity over and over again, because the movement helps them to feel alive and comfortable in their bodies. For those children who are quiet and withdrawn, however, movement is more of a chore, and they need to begin by waking up their sleepy bodies and feelings. When childrens' emotions get identified, and they move with awareness, the numbness they have been experiencing disappears, and they are visibly more able to tap into the connection between their body and their emotions. Movement has a magical quality to calm and relax the active child as it stimulates and awakens the "sleeping" child.

In The HEALS Program we use movement to:

- gain awareness of the body as individual parts are identified and moved
- explore the connection between a suggested emotion and the body

- allow the opportunity for children to playfully express themselves
- interact with peers through a technique called "Body Sculpting" (Body Sculpting is explained in the section on "Attunements")
- access anger
- release tension and stress, or excess energy

Dance & Movement: Waking The Body

Simple movements done with awareness can also be used to allow the children to spend some time with their bodies. This can be done to taped music as you invite them to move specified body parts, or you can ask the children to do some gentle, slow movements as you model the movement for them. We have found Gabrielle Roth's tribal-like music, "Body Jazz," to be an excellent tool as a warm-up to awaken the body.

For children who feel inhibited, self-conscious, or "too cool," we often use dancing scarves that can be tossed into the air and caught or thrown to one another as a game. Most children love to dress themselves up using the dancing scarves and move to music. Older children also enjoy wearing masks while dancing or moving, which gives them permission to try on new personas and to experiment with their changing bodies and movement within a less exposed structure. It is important to be able to have fun when working with the body. Movement is a wonderful way to release tension and stress while raising the endorphin levels which strengthen our immune systems.

Another way of engaging in movement, with older children particularly, is using small scarves for games such as juggling. With background music available, the body will tend to harmonize its movements with the rhythm.

Inviting the children to bring in their own music is another way to engage them in movement. (Be clear with them that the music they bring in must be approved in advance for appropriate language and content.) Experiment using a variety of expressive music with children, and explore the feelings called forth. When given the opportunity, most children know intuitively how to explore moving their grieving bodies in the ways that feel right for them.

Taming Wild Emotions

During the session called, "Taming The Wild Things," children are given the opportunity to release uncomfortable feelings, particularly anger, in safe ways through several movement activities: breaking sticks, kicking pillows, banging on a drum, dancing, etc..

Anger is usually expressed through one of three different pathways out of the body:
1. Mouth and Voice: screaming, yelling, or swearing
2. Hands/Fists and Arms: hitting, punching, or breaking things
3. Legs and Feet: kicking, stomping or running

When you invite children to choose one of the activities to express their anger, trust them to select the method that works best for them, and do not assume that all children should do it the same way. This can be a powerful and intense exercise, and many children ask to be permitted to experiment with all the different ways of feeling and releasing their anger. We suggest *practicing* these ways of releasing with children in a fun and exploratory way—before they are truly needed. If you have the time, this is a great gift to give to children. It should be noted that these activities need to be very carefully and safely structured. Children who have problems with self-restraint or have experienced violence or trauma may benefit by working with quieter release activities, such as painting your anger, creating angry clay sculptures, or constructing a Screaming Box.

Children, Movement & Yoga

Yoga is another very effective way to help children focus their awareness on their body. This centering process can be extremely calming and quieting for some children, and it can evoke giggles from children who have difficulty staying present with themselves and their bodies. These postures can be very simple and do not require a lot of time if you are planning an involved art project or activity. The success of using yoga does not depend upon the facilitator being trained or proficient in yoga. This is for anyone. There are many helpful yoga books designed for children which are easy to use. (Some of these books are listed under the *Movement and Children* section in the bibliography.)

Don't be frightened off by yoga if you have never tried it. Being a table or a bunny or a tree can be fun for you, too! Remember these postures can be very, very easy and are a wonderful resource to have in your repertoire. It is important to keep in mind that children need to move their bodies often, and yoga can be easily used to help you transition from one activity to another.

Setting the Stage for an Imaginary Journey

After the children have done physical movement such as dancing or connecting movement to a feeling, we might invite them to lie down or sit in a comfortable position for an Imaginary Journey. During this experience, we direct the children's attention to focus their awareness on each isolated part of their body in an attempt to be fully present with any tension they may be holding in that region. The children are then invited to relax into the area as they continue breathing. It is always gratifying to us as we observe their hands relaxing and their breath deepening. By doing imagery after the movement, the children are encouraged to be fully present in and with their bodies—the dwelling they will be living in for their entire life.

Sound as Expression

*(Spontaneous) sounds . . . come to open us,
to soothe us, to create new forms within us,
to reunite us with primary material which lies
between us and our origins.*
—Greenwell

The Voice As An Instrument

The voice is a very powerful instrument that we too seldom use in grief work. Historically, certain cultures would wail and scream to release the pain that accompanies the loss of loved ones, but unfortunately, this custom has been eliminated and viewed as too uncivilized for our mainstreamed American way of life. Children rarely have adult models who are able to access their grief in a vocal, primitive way. We, as adults at our best, tend to cry and then verbally explain what we are feeling. This is a start, and there is more which can take us to deeper levels of expression.

During our HEALS sessions, we use sounding in the following ways:
- to express what the children are feeling in the moment
- to access anger through screaming
- to experiment with a variety of vocal sounds
- to experiment with an assortment of instruments

We give the children permission to scream if strong emotions surface and they wish to expel the energy that can build up inside their bodies. This can be a very intense experience, and some children want to have witnesses and feel the support of a group while others prefer getting their screams out with only one trusted adult. It is respectful to ask the child what his or her preference is rather than making that decision. Have a place in mind should such a request be made. Find an environment that is as private as possible where a minimum amount of sound will travel into the school or where other children could hear. Screaming into a pillow, towel, blanket, thick coat, or a Scream Box are options should a more private location be unavailable. Children can be taught to use a scream towel with one end of the towel held securely against the throat to protect the vocal chords and the other end over the mouth. Screaming from the diaphragm into the towel effectively relieves strong emotions with less noise!

Sometimes children want to scream but are fearful of what may happen if they do, or the child may simply be shy and self-conscious. In such a case, they often feel reassured if the entire group screams with them. This can be done standing in a circle but not touching each other to allow each person to experience the power of their own scream. It feels energizing to engage the breath in accessing the depths of our being. Often the children discover how good this feels, and they may ask to do it again and again. Trust your instincts to know when to end. You may wish to have a final group scream while holding hands in a supportive circle; this will help the children feel connected and more grounded. If a child really gets into screaming and is in direct contact with strong emotions of anger, it is not uncommon for them to move into crying or sobbing. Do not rush in too quickly, but remind them that you are there for them and ask them how you can best support them. When they are finished, you can ask them if they would like a hug. Respect their wishes.

A multitude of sounds—screams, grunts, groans, wails, laughter—are stuck inside our bodies. These sounds got stifled there because we learned from society that it was not appropriate or acceptable to let the sounds out in response to many situations. Children carry these unexpressed sounds in their bodies where they are recorded in their body tissues. During a HEALS session we attempt to give them access to these sounds by inviting them to attach sounds to feelings when we attune at the beginning and end of the group. Sounding can be dramatically transformative for children who have found themselves in victim situations as it opens them to their power and strength while clearing out some of the feelings of abuse.

Another way to express feelings through sound is to use a technique called **gibberish**. Gibberish is the production of sounds that are unintelligible and pre-verbal which are allowed to spring up from the "imagination" or whatever you want to call the "unknown." This is great fun plus being an excellent tool to explore feelings, especially when children are invited to "dialogue" in pairs while they express a specified emotion together.

Musical Instruments

Instruments are a wonderful way for children to express their feelings. Drums in all sizes permit access to the strong and powerful emotions. Children often are magnetically attracted to drums through what appears a deep and instinctual drive. Perhaps the drums' ability to capture the gentle rhythms of a heartbeat to releasing the furor of an angry volcano lends the drum an ancient and primal quality. Wooden blocks, triangles, tambourines, shakers, cymbals, bells, simple flutes, and anything else that can produce sounds, may be used to express an emotional state. For children who are reluctant to make loud vocal sounds, the instruments are a safer less threatening means to vicariously feel as if the sound is being generated from within them.

It may feel at times that the "music" the children are creating is chaotically wild and causing you to feel crazy. In this situation, you may wish to invite the group to express some more gentle emotions with their instrument, such as making the sound of what love or peacefulness feels like in their body. Left to their own devices children can get carried away with the instruments. A skillful facilitator permits free expression while knowing when to help children gain control of their wildness. Keeping control of the group process is essential. Integrating the structure of the *Freeze/Flow Technique* is a way to allow freedom of sound, movement, and music within a structured framework. (Refer to *Creative Mind Activities.*)

Art as Expression

What is art? Art grows out of grief and joy,
but mainly grief. It is born of people's lives.
—Edvard Munch

Retrieving Art as Play

Young children are comfortable with the language of art as they play with various mediums, engrossed in the process of discovery. They are not concerned with how the picture will look or how others will feel about it. They explore freely. During the middle grammar school years, however, many children start looking for approval, imitating others, and becoming concerned with the product. As early as age seven, a child's playful, inner child may have retreated to a place of safety, and the outer child, the one they project to the world, no longer has access to the deeper resources of pure self-expression. As we work with these children during our HEALS sessions, we have found it necessary to frequently remind them not to be concerned with the product, but instead to put their attention on telling their story or expressing their feelings.

Since we generally have a limited amount of time in which to "work" (play), and nothing much more than a quick sketch to express a feeling or situation is available, this makes it easier for the children to understand that nothing too detailed is being asked of them.

Children who have been criticized and have felt ashamed of their art will often be hesitant to begin to use art materials. Be watchful for these children and reassure them that they will not be graded or hear any unkind comments about artwork that is produced by them or any other student. Remind them that in this group we respect and support each other with kind words, and that each student's artwork is a precious expression from inside of them.

Artist's Rights

Three important ARTIST RIGHTS to communicate are:

1. The right to have their art work treated as a valuable expression which will be respected by others
2. The assurance that their art work may be touched only with permission
3. The right to pass if they do not choose to tell about their picture

Each Art Medium Has Its Own Asset

• Clay allows us to have the feeling and to kinesthetically experience it

- Drawing helps us to discover that which is hidden
- Working in a 3-D project allows us to bring together parts in the creation of the whole

Creating a safe atmosphere where children can re-experience direct communication with line and form is essential. Playing relaxing music can soothe many children and make it easier for them to filter out the external distractions, so that they can be more present with themselves and what they are feeling.

Helpful Ways to View a Child's Art

- When you are witnessing a child's drawing, look at the position of the elements in the picture. This will give you some valuable information about the relationship of the parts.

- Ask yourself: "What is missing in this picture?"

- When you observe an area of a picture which is very dark or where the child has obviously drawn intensively, you can ask: "Can you tell me about this place in your picture?"

- Remember to respond with your feelings. If a child draws a scary picture, you may choose to say: "Stephen, this drawing feels very scary to me. Can you tell me what you were feeling as you drew this?"

- When a child draws on a horizontally held piece of paper, it often means that they are telling a story; and a vertically drawn picture often means that they are making a statement.

- We do not advocate giving universal meaning to the colors children decide to use or analyzing their work. That is not our role in this support setting.

Note: There are differing opinions as to whether or not it is advisable for a facilitator to do their own art while the children are engaged in theirs. In The HEALS Program, we are of the belief that since we are sharing members of the group, it is important for us to draw or sculpt or create right along with the children. While you do your art, however, please remember to focus your peripheral attention on the children and do not get lost in your own process. Stay present with their processes and what is happening with them. We have found that it is beneficial for facilitators to take care of themselves later in the day by completing activities they were unable to finish or give full attention due to their role as group leader.

Imaging

Throughout time humans have used art to dialogue and communicate their pre-conscious and mental images into form, color, movement, sound, or words. Symbols, imagery, and dreams have the ability and power to connect to the deeper sense of self, making the unknown known or the unconscious conscious. By exploring and dialoguing with these symbols and images, we come to know ourselves, involving a broadening and deepening of our consciousness as well as providing spiritual nurturance and guidance (Jacobi, 1942).

In The HEALS Program, grieving children are usually quite comfortable working with spontaneous imagery and symbols to express themselves. It seems there is a *universal need to express oneself* (Gregg Furth, 1988), and because children have not fully developed their abstract thinking abilities, the modalities of the arts are perfect venues for self-expression and being educated in the emotional realms.

The Power of Symbols & Image-Making

When art is allowed to speak from the pre-conscious or unconscious, it may contain information from the psyche that the "artist" is not ready to face or may not be able to understand at their stage of development. The relationship between the "artist" and their symbols appears to be a non-verbal dialogue that prepares the individual, perhaps on multiple levels for change, growth or healing. This can be witnessed in the symbols that dying children use in their imagery that often relays a certain knowingness about their condition and the journey they are about to take. The power of the symbol is best explained by Gregg Furth (1988):

> *A symbol refers to something so deep and complex that consciousness, limited as it is, cannot grasp it all at once. In this way, the symbol always carries an element of the unknown and the inexplicable, that which is not amenable to words, and which often has numinous quality. Yet the very fact the symbol exists tells us that at some level we know or feel the meaning behind the symbol. In this tension between knowing and not-knowing, between conscious and unconscious, there is a great deal of psychic energy.*

> *Consciousness is analogous to focusing the eye. The area of peripheral vision is the unconscious which needs to be brought to consciousness. The symbol is a vehicle for bringing peripheral vision into focus, aiding the movement of psychic content from an unconscious level to consciousness. This potential for consciousness is what makes human beings different from other animals, for with this potential we can understand ourselves, even at the deepest levels, and make conscious decisions about our actions and the direction of our lives.*

In the foreword of the Gregg Furth's book, *The Secret World of Drawings* (1988), Elizabeth Kübler-Ross discusses the uses of art and image-making as "preventive psychiatry." A well-trained analyst, art therapist, dance-movement therapist or expressive arts therapist may be able to use various modalities as effective diagnostic tools when working with their clients. While HEALS facilitators are not concerned with the *interpretation* of children's art, they do need to be aware of the signs of trauma and complicated grief, and to be able to assess when a referral for therapeutic support might be advisable. (Refer to *Complicated Grief* in the *Backbone* segment.)

Writing as Expression

I can recapture everything when I write, my thoughts, my ideals and my fantasies.

—Anne Frank, <u>Diary of a Young Girl</u>

Spontaneous Writing

When children have freely moved and drawn, they are in a very receptive place to do creative writing. "Free writing" or "spontaneous writing" or "automatic writing" is a simple exercise that takes only ten minutes. It helps children to know themselves in a way that is spiritually, mentally, and physically beneficial as it allows them to tap into their optimistic and hopeful inner resources.

Spontaneous Writing Instructions

1. Write for ten minutes.

2. Do not stop writing.

3. Do not worry about spelling, punctuation, neatness, complete sentences, or logic.

4. If nothing comes to your mind, write, "I can't think of anything to say," over and over again until you do think of something.

5. Do not read over what you have written (at least for awhile).

Writing "I Statements"

There are other writing approaches which can be tried as well. Following an art experience, children can be invited to write five or more **"I Statements"** on the back of their paper, such as "I am feeling lonely" or "I am awkward and unsure" or "I am flying high." This helps the child to own their picture and to go deeper, rather than casually dismissing it and moving on to the next activity. These feeling statements, in keeping with the HEALS philosophy, may be shared with the group, may be shared privately with the facilitator, or may be held in confidence. This ability to decide what works for the child allows them to feel empowered and to take care of themselves.

Non-Dominant Hand Writing

Non-Dominant Hand Writing is a technique we learned from Lucia Capacchione and is explained in her book, <u>The Power of the Other Hand</u>. It has been discovered that our non-dominant hand is a direct channel to the untapped potential of the brain's right hemisphere. In Lucia's approach, we are instructed to pick up a pen/pencil/colored marker with our "other" hand (the hand we don't normally write with) and write whatever comes. The two hands can dialogue or the dominant hand can ask questions of the non-dominant hand. As we continue to write with the non-dominant hand, the awkwardness eventually lessens and this writing style can allow a new world of insight and information to unfold. This technique is also valuable following the completion of art work. The children are instructed to ask the piece of art what it wants to say and then allow the non-dominant hand to respond.

Creative Journal-Keeping

We often use Creative Journal-Keeping in The HEALS Program. Each child is given a journal with unlined drawing paper inside where they can:

- express feelings and thoughts
- play with new mediums of expression (color, images, symbols)
- sort out the experiences of their life
- record memories and dreams
- discover a deeper meaning for their life

We encourage children to use their journal to discover themselves and their ability to express their feelings, and to trust their own process of self-expression. These journals are used for both art and writing that the children create during a session and are safely kept by the HEALS facilitators. On the final session, the journals are honored as a sacred account of their journey to date, and the children are encouraged to continue to draw and write as they are inspired and/or need to express their feelings.

You need both kinds of knowing—
the logical and intuitive.
Let the two come together.
They were never meant to be apart.

—Lucia Capacchione,
The Power of the Other Hand

Imaginary Journeys

Imagination is more important than knowledge.
—Albert Einstein

Promoting Relaxation and Stillness

Guided imagery, or what we call "Imaginary Journeys," is a technique we use during a HEALS session to help children:

- to become aware of their body in order to relax the individual parts
- to provide stillness and space for children to remember their past experiences with the significant person or pet who has died
- to assist children to connect with their feelings and to allow time for creative impulses to occur in order to express those feelings

When we facilitate an Imaginary Journey during a bereavement session, we generally invite the children to get comfortable in a sitting position or lying down with a pillow(s) while quiet, peaceful music is playing in the background. We also encourage the children to close their eyes as they begin to relax, but for some children this is uncomfortable and they become agitated. If it becomes apparent that this is the situation for any children in your group, you may invite them to keep their eyes open, suggest that they pick a spot somewhere in the room, and maintain a "soft focus" on their spot as they listen to your voice and suggestions. Transition time is important as you prepare for the Imaginary Journey to allow the children to begin the relaxation process. As you slow down the speed with which you speak, the children's breathing will deepen, and they will soon be ready to follow your instructions.

Slowing The Brain Waves

As we relax during Imaginary Journey into an alpha state, our brainwave patterns slow down. Listed below are the various brainwave states:

- High beta—revved up, increased anxiety or hyper responses and thinking
- Beta—alert behavior and concentrated mental activity
- **Alpha—relaxed wakefulness when the brain is not actively engaged in any specific mental or emotional activity**
- Theta—drowsiness, dreaming, which can also have periods of alertness with sudden insight or recognition of events from memory
- Delta—deeper states of sleep. These are the slowest waves.

As a child matures from birth to adolescence, their predominant brainwave patterns develop as follows:

- Infants function primarily in a delta state
- Toddlers are in a theta state
- Elementary school age children are predominantly at the alpha level (actively getting programmed)
- After puberty children have full access to their critical capacities and begin to function predominantly at the beta level (except when watching TV)

For our purposes, we are attempting to relax a child into an alpha state. Since this alpha state resides between beta and theta, it is composed of the characteristics of each and is therefore very powerful. It can be both active and receptive, simultaneously. The alpha state is the threshold between inner and outer consciousness. Children past puberty welcome the opportunity to be in an alpha state, and frequently request guided imagery exercises. Imaginary Journeys can be a disappointing experience for a facilitator with younger children, since some of them have difficulty settling down and being still. Each group is different. Each child is different.

As you begin to guide the children with your voice, strive to keep your voice soft and slow. Ideally, your words should be spoken at a pace to match your heartbeat, and your phrases should match the length of your breath. The timing of your words is vitally important. Give enough time for the children to do their inner work, but not so much time that they fall asleep!

When leading an Imaginary Journey, attempt to present your ideas in an orderly sequence that flows smoothly from one suggestion to the next. Make logical transitions from step to step; and be careful not to do or say anything that would jar or upset a child while they are in this relaxed state. Example: suggesting that there is a cat with three heads could be very disorienting. Make certain the room is warm enough because as our bodies relax, our body temperature drops.

Remember to trust your intuition during this process. Being connected to your intent while being sensitive to the group is imperative for a successful Imaginary Journey experience. Remember to BREATHE!

Cautious Reflections on Anger

We boil at different degrees.
　　　　　—Ralph Waldo Emerson

All of us are unique individuals who require nurturing and need tender loving care in order to grow into our fullest potentials as human beings. When children are denied certain needs or opportunities in their lives, or are oppressed or abused, this uniqueness and ability to thrive is often thwarted. Feelings may bubble up that are uncomfortable, and can affect behaviors and decision-making. Additionally, losses experienced through bereavement can make a child feel guilty for feeling anger, resentment or 'perceived' abandonment by the person who died. Uncomfortable feelings are the ones we most often minimize or deny, and for good reason! But the price we pay in avoiding our true feelings is a loss of being able to be fully alive, present and spontaneous. Holding onto feelings of anger or resentment can affect how our mind and body function. Feelings do not disappear. We just move the feelings away from the focus of our current attention—for a while. But hidden feelings have a way of seeping out and coloring the lens in which we view the world, and ourselves. Unless they are taken out and given a good airing, an uneasiness often develops.

One story we love to use with children to talk about uncomfortable feelings is a great little book called *There's No Such Thing As a Dragon* by Jack Kent. In that story children and adults learn through metaphor that when we deny feelings, they can grow themselves into very unmanageable monsters. The moral of the story is simple: all feelings just want to be noticed, even our most uncomfortable ones. In order to flourish—even when we are faced with great challenges—it is extremely important that we acknowledge all our feelings and learn to navigate them.

The Second Most Important Emotion

Love surely must be at the top of the list for *the most* important feeling a human can experience. Conversely, anger must be the second most important emotion since, when in its most intense or brutal state it can hurt or destroy living things. For this reason it is also the scariest emotion for humans to handle. Every day our culture, especially the visual media, models *unsafe* and *uncontrolled* images of expressing anger. At the same time, we have been taught that it is *not okay* for us to feel or express our anger. But we *do* feel it! Anger is a normal human response to losses of any kind—including loss of power, control, or injustice. And because it is such a powerful emotion, it is one of the most important for us learn about. This is why we have devoted one entire session in our curriculum to explore and learn to dance with our anger.

Our "Anger Philosophy"

The topic of anger is one we, and our facilitators, have struggled with for many years when teaching emotional literacy skills. We live in such a violent culture, and many of us worry that teaching children how to release anger physically is only perpetuating more violence. After much thought and research, we have developed a philosophical approach to address this complex topic. The goal of this segment of our curriculum, *Taming The Wild Things,* is to learn about the ranges of anger many of us experience on a continuum from mild to intense, and to find creative ways to deal with all of them. Some of our more overt physical release activities are helpful when we feel ourselves getting out of control, when our temperature has reached the boiling point. However, by learning our own unique *early warning signs* of anger, there are plenty of interventions that have proven useful to defuse feelings before we get to that stage—and get ourselves into hot water.

We have included many activities we have found valuable to help children learn to release anger in safe and appropriate ways all the way along the continuum. When we engage in these activities, such as stick breaking, or paper ripping, we create structured guidelines, and encourage the activity to be done in a playful state of mind—maybe *pretending* to be angry. This exploration allows children to learn physical ways to release intense feelings while in a state of mind that is conscious of safety guidelines. Creating and practicing a variety of structured activities to manage uncomfortable feelings is a very important part of learning about self-control and responsibility. All feelings are okay, but it is our responsibility to learn to express those feelings safely and at appropriate times.

Planning a Session on Anger

We want to encourage you to be especially sensitive when designing Session IV. Some children may have experienced trauma or violence that can make them uncomfortable when in the presence of others releasing intense feelings. If you do not know the group of children well enough, we advise staying away from some overtly physical anger release activities (such as stick breaking, temper tantrums, or Nerf bats, etc.). In addition to children who may have trauma histories, there are some children who have more difficulty with impulse-control and may be unable to calm themselves down, or even keep themselves safe, once they get wound up. For this reason, we caution you to know your children and carefully choose activities that are appropriate for them for *Taming The Wild Things.*

Follow Anger Release Activities with Reflective Time!

When using anger release techniques with children, be sure to allow some reflective time afterwards to discuss how they felt. Explore some of the following ideas with them:

- Which activities worked well for different children? Why?

- Which of the three Pathways of Anger did the activity use? (Mouth, hands/arms, or legs/feet?)

- Review a list of safe anger release activities. Have the children evaluate them for effectiveness, and when it might or might not be appropriate to do certain activities. Which activities would be appropriate at school? Home? Bedroom? Why?

- Can the children share ways in the past in which they have expressed their feelings of anger that got them into trouble or were ineffective for them?

- Can the children talk about angry behaviors they have seen in others, and how it made them feel at the time? (no names, please!).

In The HEALS Program, we approach anger with a sense of play and adventure as a way to get to know it, to lessen our fear, and to "make friends" with it rather than repress it. We are always amazed at the feelings of relief and renewed vitality and peace we experience after releasing anger. The children's exclamations of joy and wonder after creating an angry dance, or angry and ugly drawing or sculpture informs us how very freeing those activities are for them, and us! It is a giant step in learning to transform one of the most difficult feelings that seem to plague the world we live in.

The Continuum of Anger Release & Transformation

Suggestions for safe anger release are divided into two segments. The first segment focuses upon the more physical and overt release of anger. The second segment focuses upon gentler, quieter ways of coping and transforming anger. It is important to know or learn skills from both categories, since we may find ourselves in situations where it necessary to release anger in quieter ways.

Physical Release

The following suggestions are offered to help a frustrated or angry child learn to physically release feelings in safe and creative ways. As a parent or facilitator, please build safety structures into these activities to minimize any possibility of danger (i.e. marshmallows are not to be thrown too hard **or** in someone's face, temper tantrums should be thrown on a soft base such as a thick mat, a futon, or mattress, etc.). It is a good idea to practice many of these activities in a playful way first before they are needed for true anger release.

Running	Screaming into a pillow
Breaking sticks	Stomping
Digging in dirt	Hitting a punching bag
Pounding a drum	Skimming stones in a pond
Ripping old newspapers	Kicking a ball
Dancing wildly	Creating Angry Art Sculptures
Balloon Bopping	Marshmallow Flinging
Dancing wildly	Playing sports
Throwing Nerf Balls	Throwing a temper tantrum
Recycling glass bins	Pounding nails (w/ adult guidance)
Imaginary Anger Ball Throw	Releasing of Negativity (T'ai Chi)
Stomping	Throwing snowballs
Skateboarding	Bouncing on trampoline

Transforming Anger Peacefully

Here are some quieter, more peaceful ways of coping with and transforming feelings of anger and frustration.

Talking it out	Focusing on breathing, slowly and deeply
Wringing a towel with two hands	Playing with clay
Writing feelings out	Swimming or hottubbing
Writing/drawing in journal	Writing a letter to the person, ripping it up
Walking in nature	Choosing peace or conflict
Sitting or walking meditation	Creating an Imaginary Journey tape
Sitting and listening to nature	Releasing Negativity (T'ai Chi)
Creating a group rainstorm	Sitting in a peaceful place
Listening to beautiful music	Blowing bubbles
Rubbing a Worry Stone or	Using Worry Beads or Worry Dolls
Focusing on "Belly Breathing" (Yoga)	Kneading and rolling a kneaded eraser

- Practice consciously replacing anger with warm and loving intentions for yourself and others.

- Whenever the anger arises, imagine it dissolving and leaving your body and being replaced with a golden ball of glowing love in the area where the anger was held.

"One of the secrets of a long and fruitful life is to forgive everybody—everything—every night before you go to bed."

—Ann Landers

Forgiveness and Anger

The ultimate transformation of anger is the powerful act of forgiving whomever or whatever is perceived as making one angry. While in the stages of grief, anger or resentment is often a natural part of the process, so it is not unusual for a child to feel anger as part of their grieving process. But when anger is prolonged after a death loss, there may be more issues at stake that need to be dealt with such as any unfinished business, abuse, or neglect issues. It is helpful to seek support (through counseling or therapy) to release the feelings that can become stuck, affecting the body-mind-spirit of a child.

Remember that anger is just an emotion that requires a tremendous amount of energy for the body and mind to suppress. Over time, the suppression of anger can lead to "dis-ease." Once we learn how to release anger in safe ways, more energy is available to us for a healthy and productive life. By incorporating stress release techniques into our lives, we may lessen, and even prevent, the need for chemicals and substances to help us cope when uncomfortable feelings arise.

❦

"Anger is one letter away from danger."
—Eleanor Roosevelt

Section II: The Heartbeat

Program Delivery System

The HEALS Program Coordinator Packet

This packet contains the critical information The HEALS Program Coordinator needs to liaise with schools and supervise facilitators.

HEALS Program Coordinator Responsibilities outlines, in a sequential manner, the coordinator's roles and responsibilities as the primary liaison with the schools and The HEALS Program facilitators.

Promoting HEALS Programs in Schools Sequence explains the most effective times of the year in which to contact and coordinate school support groups.

The Introductory Letter to School Counselors describes the HEALS Program being offered and any other details that might be helpful for school counselors such as brochures, testimonials, etc.

The Follow-up Letter to School Counselors is a reminder that includes a postcard for counselors to return indicating an estimation of what semester of the school year they might like to have a HEALS Program including potential times, days and grade levels to be served.

HEALS Coordinator Responsibilities

The HEALS Coordinator is responsible for the overall community education, administrative management, facilitator supervision and support concerning The HEALS Programs for children in grief. The HEALS Coordinator is a valuable resource for HEALS facilitators to provide ongoing support, supervision, evaluation and growth opportunities. The role and responsibilities of this position follow.

Initial School Liaison

The HEALS Coordinator functions as the initial liaison with schools to establish the contracts for services taking the following steps:

A. Educate school counselors and communities about The HEALS Program and how to identify children in grief. This may include an introductory letter, presentation to school staff, and/or other promotional materials, such as newsletters and brochures

B. Once a school expresses a need for a group, the HEALS Coordinator will send them a School Counselor Packet, which includes information about their role and responsibilities and contains a contract for services.

C. Once the contract has been signed and returned, the HEALS Coordinator contracts with two HEALS facilitators to provide the children's support services.

D. The Lead Facilitator is given a Facilitator Packet which includes all forms needed for one entire group series. At this point the Lead Facilitator becomes the primary liaison and is responsible for providing the service.

Supervision and Continuing Education of Facilitators

The HEALS Coordinator is a valuable resource for HEALS facilitators to provide ongoing support, supervision, evaluation and growth opportunities. This support includes:

A. Assures that all materials, supplies and budgets for HEALS kits are ready and available for facilitators to check out;

B. Provides weekly Lead Facilitator support and monthly group supervision and support of the all HEALS facilitators;

C. Provides supervision for facilitator's performance of housekeeping and administrative tasks, teamwork, and performance as a facilitator representing the agency and program;

D. Provides troubleshooting and mediation support between facilitators, if necessary;

E. Maintains supplies, oversees facilitator paperwork and reporting requirements;

F. Provides quarterly opportunities for additional trainings and in-services;

G. Oversees the evaluation process, provides program analysis, and collects data needed for research and funding purposes

Promoting HEALS in Schools Sequence

(Outline for HEALS Program Coordinator)

Introductory Letter to Schools

A. In the Spring a letter is sent to all school counselors in early April (before Spring Break). The letter describes The HEALS Program, and includes a postcard for counselors to return, indicating which quarter they would like a group, and estimate what time, day, and grade levelsthe group might be. An Autumn follow-up letter or phone call to confirm the school's interest in groups and a letter are other options, if needed. Letters for Winter/ Spring groups should be mailed in October.

B. Once the postcard is returned, the HEALS Coordinator informs the school counselor of their role, responsibility and timeline prior to beginning a group. A School Counselor Packet is provided with all pertinent information, including a contract agreement which must be signed and returned.

C. Once the above has been completed, the HEALS Coordinator assigns and contracts with the HEALS facilitators who will provide the groups. The Lead Facilitator then becomes the primary liaison with the school.

The HEALS Program

Sample Introductory Letter to School Counselors

To: School Guidance Counselors
From: The HEALS Program Coordinator
Date:

Dear School Counselor,

This letter is to inform you that a special expressive arts loss support group for grieving children, called The HEALS Program, is available. Participation is open to any child who has experienced a death or loss in their family. HEALS Groups consist of approximately eight children and are led by two trained HEALS Facilitators who have led groups for children in many other schools.

The purpose of the group will be to provide an opportunity for children to explore feelings through the expressive arts and help them develop skills to deal with their grief in safe and healthy ways. Important social and emotional literacy skills are integrated into the curriculum to help the children learn about respect, empathy for others, listening and sharing skills and appropriate and safe self-expression—social skills that are much needed in the world today. The HEALS Program believes that if children are supported surrounding issues of loss, and strengthened with knowledge of coping strategies as soon as possible following a death, they will be better prepared for future losses, will have a reduced risk of emotional acting out, and be less likely to abuse substances and foods to deaden feelings of grief.

I am excited about this opportunity for the children in your school to experience this creative healing approach. If you would like more information on how to get The HEALS Program into your school, please feel free to contact me.

Sincerely,

HEALS Program Coordinator

 The HEALS Program

Follow Up Letter to School Counselors

To: School Guidance Counselors
From: The HEALS Program Coordinator
Date:

Hello!

You recently received a letter with the description and objectives of The HEALS Program for children in grief that will be available for area children during the coming school year. We hope you have been able to identify youth that you think would be appropriate for this social emotional learning support group. We understand that some of your decisions may be a bit tentative at this point, but it would be very helpful in our planning if we could hear from you this spring. Enclosed is a post card on which you may indicate interest in a group/s. After we have received your postcard, we will contact you to discuss plans for next school year.
We ask that you consider the following time-line in planning groups with us:

- 1 to 2 months prior to start date of group: identify children to be in group

- 1 month prior: talk to parents of identified children

- 1 month prior: find a space and time for group (coordinate with HEALS staff)

- 3 weeks prior: send permission slips out

- 1 to 2 weeks prior: permission slips come back in

Thank you so much. We look forward to a full schedule next year! If you need more information on any group, please do not hesitate to call, and one of our staff will gladly get back to you.

Sincerely,

HEALS Program Coordinator

The HEALS Program School Counselor Packet

The following list contains the descriptions of the forms school counselors are responsible for providing to The HEALS Program and to perspective group members' parents or guardians. The parent forms need to be filled out and signed by a parent or guardian prior to acceptance into the group. Samples of each form or letter follow.

The HEALS Contract & Agreement must be signed by the school counselor as a representative of the school for HEALS Program services.

The Sample Letter to Parents Form is completed by the school counselor and given to each parent of a perspective HEALS group member. The Parental Permission Form accompanies this letter.

The Parental Permission Form is sent to each parent by the school counselor and is to be completed, signed, and returned to the school counselor prior to the first HEALS session.

Consent Artwork or Photos Form is a form which is signed by the student artist, his/her parent or guardian, and the HEALS facilitator giving The HEALS Program permission to use the student's artwork for educational displays. The artist may request to have their name included with the artwork or remain anonymous. It is suggested that this form be used only if you wish to retain a copy of the student's artwork for future use.

HEALS Group Roster contains the names, ages, grades, addresses, and specific loss of each group member. Any other pertinent information should be included here such as allergies, special needs or medications facilitators should be aware of prior to group. This form is usually filled out in the first meeting between the HEALS Facilitators and the School Counselor.

The HEALS Program Evaluation Form is a simple way for the students to give us feedback. Through this feedback we learn how the children currently feel and also how they experienced the various components of The HEALS Program. We ask the students to complete this evaluation form during their final HEALS session.

The HEALS Program Delivery System

Role of The School Counselor

The following school counselor responsibilities are necessary to organize and provide a successful HEALS Program in a school:

Pre-Group Preparation

☐ Sign the "HEALS Contract and Agreement" with The HEALS Coordinator School prior to group
☐ Announce the group via letter, school newsletter, classroom presentations, etc.
☐ Send permission forms to parents/guardian
☐ Secure signed permission forms two weeks prior to group for all children
☐ Organize children and schedules for each program
☐ Meet with HEALS facilitators two weeks prior to group to talk about implementation of the program (provide facilitators with permission slips, discuss individual children's losses and needs, possible group dynamic issues, view meeting space, give special instructions, etc.)

While Group is in Progress

☐ Gather children for group each week
☐ Consult with the HEALS facilitators prior to each session about issues, absences, feedback from school staff and parents to the HEALS facilitators as needed
☐ Should any behavior issues arise, allow the HEALS facilitators to cope with them following our HEALS Behavior Management Plan. Speaking with the child about any issues that occur within the group, without the permission of the HEALS Facilitators, can undermine or damage the important trusting relationship building between the facilitators and children.

Post-Group Responsibilities

☐ Meet with HEALS facilitators for debriefing of program
☐ Parental follow-up meeting (optional)
☐ Write a brief end-of-program evaluation with your impressions the program, our facilitators, and submit to the HEALS Program Coordinator (see sample School Counselor HEALS Program Evaluation)

The HEALS Program

CONTRACT FOR SERVICES

Type of group: _____ Date: _____

Number of sessions: _____ Cost: _____

Location of group: _____

Room: _____

Dates/time of group: _____

Funding source/s: _____

The school also agrees to provide signed parent permissions forms and a roster of children in the group **prior** to the first session.

_____
(School Counselor signature)

Sample Letter to Parents About HEALS Groups

(on school letterhead)

Date

Dear Parent or Guardian:

This letter is to inform you that a special expressive arts loss support group for children, called The HEALS Program, will be offered at our school. Participation is open to any child who has experienced a death or loss in their family, but spaces are limited. The purpose of the group will be to provide an opportunity for children to explore feelings through the expressive arts and help them develop skills to deal with their grief in safe and healthy ways. The HEALS Program believes that if children are supported during of loss, and strengthened by learning available coping strategies as soon as possible following a death, they will be better prepared for future losses, will have a reduced risk of emotional acting out, and be less likely to abuse substances and foods to deaden the feelings of grief.

The HEALS Group will consist of approximately eight children and will be led by two trained HEALS Facilitators who have led groups for children in many other schools. The HEALS Program encourages respect for one another, empathic listening skills, and confidentiality. The group will meet on eight consecutive (days & time) at the school.

As the school counselor at the (name of school), I am aware that your child has experienced a family death or loss in the past. I am excited about this opportunity for children at this school to experience this creative healing approach, and I believe that your child would greatly benefit from participating in this group.

If you would like your child to participate, please fill out the enclosed Parental Permission Form and checklist, and return by .

If you have any questions, please feel free to contact me. Thank you for your support.

Sincerely,

School Counselor

The HEALS Program

Parental Permission Form

I give permission for my child to participate in The HEALS Program for children in grief.

Child'sName_____ Date of Birth _____
School_____ Grade _____
Home Address_____
City _____ State_____ Zip_____
Home Phone _____ Parents' Work_____
Parents'/Guardians' Names _____
Emergency Phone Number _____
Name of deceased person(s) and relationship to the child _____
Does the child know the exact cause of death? _____
How did s/he find out, and who told her/him? _____
Date of Death(s)_____
Circumstances_____
_____
_____

Has your child received any professional psychological assistance relative to the death
(i.e. therapist, counselor, psychiatrist) outside of the school? _____
     If yes, please specify_____

Is your child on any medications, or are there any special needs of which we should be
aware?_____

I understand that the information shared in this support group is confidential and will not be
released to anyone outside The HEALS Program unless it involves the safety of my child.

Parent/Guardian Signature_____ Date_____

Signs of Grief—Parental Checklist

Place a check mark in the box next to any feelings or symptoms you observe your child exhibiting since the loss.

Emotional:

☐ Disbelief/Numbness
☐ Disorganization/Panic
☐ Feeling out of control
☐ Fear or worry
☐ Loss/Emptiness/Sadness
☐ Feeling need to take care of others
☐ Feeling guilty when having fun

☐ Lack of Feelings
☐ Physical pain
☐ Feeling powerless
☐ Guilt/Self-Blame
☐ Acceptance
☐ Wanting to be an innocent young child again

Physical:

☐ Tiredness, Lack of energy
☐ Wanting to sleep more
☐ Shortness of breath
☐ Tightness in throat, Screaming
☐ Headaches
☐ Skin rashes
☐ Inability to concentrate

☐ Difficulty with sleeping
☐ Lack of appetite
☐ Excessive appetite
☐ General nervousness
☐ Stomach pains
☐ Hyperactivity/Restlessness

Behavioral:

☐ Needing parent/s more
☐ Not wanting to separate from parents
☐ Not wanting to go to school
☐ Feeling sick more often

☐ Desiring to sleep with parent
☐ Arguments and fights with friends
☐ Needing a little extra help with tasks normally done alone

The above are all normal reactions which may be experienced after losing a loved one. Please complete both sides of this form and return to your school counselor.

HEALS Group Registration Roster

School _____

Dates of Group _____

Child's Name	Age/Grade	Teacher	Loss/es	Caregiver Name/Address
1.				
2.				
3.				
4.				
5.				
6.				
7.				
8.				

The HEALS Program

Teacher Information Form

Facilitators from *(name of organization)* will be running an expressive arts bereavement group called *The HEALS Program* for some of our children. Here is the information you will need to know about the group:

Teacher/s: _____

Class: _____

Day of Week & Time of day group will meet: _____

Dates of group:_____
(If field trips are scheduled on any of the dates targeted above, please let the school counselor know immediately).

Group facilitators: _____

_____

Children in group: _____

_____

_____

_____

_____

_____

_____

The HEALS Facilitator Packet

The HEALS Facilitator Packet consists of forms addressing personal commitment, facilitator responsibility, and being a representative in the community for The HEALS Program. The specific forms are:

❧ **Facilitator Information Form** is a questionnaire to determine the facilitator's geographical limitations, availability, and a variety of other preferences.

❧ **Facilitator Commitment Form** are the principles for facilitators to keep in mind to assure help them maintain a clear view of their role while working with children.

❧ **Co-Facilitator Commitment Form** provides the guidelines to foster mutual respect between co-facilitators and is a key factor in implementing a successful group experiences.

❧ **Facilitator Code of Ethics** lays the foundation for the facilitator's commitment to The HEALS Program and its protocols.

❧ **Role of Lead Facilitator** describes the responsibilities of that position.

❧ **Role of Assistant Facilitator** lists that position's responsibilities.

❧ **The Facilitator Evaluation form** is used as a helpful tool to assess facilitator skills and can be used for interns, co-facilitator, and for self-assessment.

❧ **Giving & Receiving Feedback** provides gentle process guidelines and agreements for giving and receiving feedback and evaluations.

❧ **Reporting Suspected Abuse** explains the protocol to be used in the event that a HEALS facilitator suspects some kind of child abuse has occurred to a group member.

❧ **Report of Suspected Abuse Form** is the form for reporting suspected child abuse.

The HEALS Program

Facilitator Information Sheet

Name_____

Address_____

Phone #'s_____

Email _____

- In what geographical areas do you prefer to work?
- How far are you prepared to travel?
- Would you travel farther if you were reimbursed for fuel?
- What days and times are you available to work with children?
- Would you prefer to work with : ☐ groups or ☐ individuals
- With which age group do you feel you would most like to work? Feel free to circle several!

  ☐ Preschool   ☐ K-2nd   ☐ 3rd-6th   ☐ 7th-8th   ☐ 9th-12th   ☐ Adults

- Are there any particular areas within the expressive arts that you are interested in exploring further?

- Is there an activity or topic you would like to share/present to your peers at an in-service?

- Would you be interested in giving talks/presentations about The HEALS Program to groups, schools, and organizations in your area? If you are interested, we suggest that you co-present with another facilitator to get the feel for it. Please comment:

The HEALS Program

Facilitator Commitment

When working with an individual child or group, I will strive to keep the following principles in mind to assure program uniformity and to help me maintain a clear view of my role when working with children.

- I will set aside my personal "stuff" when I am working with children in bereavement. If something arises during a session, I will take care of my issues following the session with my co-facilitator, program coordinator, a trusted friend, a therapist, or by myself.

- I will strive to trust my intuition and be flexible. It is more important to connect with a child than to accomplish what is spelled out on my session objectives.

- I am not expected to "fix" each and every situation. I will do my best to recognize that I am in the position of providing educational support, not as therapist or an expert, but a caring support person. Being a good listener and asking carefully chosen questions are always more valuable than preaching.

- I will look for opportunities to empower children, helping them to make their own choices, and find their own solutions and answers.

- I will follow The HEALS Framework when planning each session. I will ask for feedback from the Program Coordinator if I wish to pursue a different course or create a new activity.

- I will stay in touch with my inner child and maintain a sense of playfulness.

- I will offer a gentle approach to the children in my group.

The HEALS Program

Co-Facilitator Commitment

All HEALS facilitators are expected to provide a dependable, respectful, and nurturing environment not only for the children, but for one another. The HEALS Program requires a Lead Facilitator and an Assistant Facilitator for each program with specific responsibilities. Mutual respect between co-facilitators is a key factor to implement a successful group. Any discord will be felt by the children and will affect the group as a whole. Please keep the following co-facilitation tips in mind to maintain your commitment and to create a caring and effective working relationship:

- Clarify roles and responsibilities for the group as a whole and before each group meeting

- Arrive at all meetings on time

- Honor all commitments made to each other

- Apologize sincerely if you fail to meet an obligation

- Respect one another's time—agree on planning time available and stick to it

- Allow ample time for group set-up and clean-up each week

- Know your session's goals, objectives and materials well and be prepared. Designate on planning session sheet which facilitator will prepare and bring specific materials.

- Provide empathy and support for one another after a difficult session, discuss new ideas for handling the same situation in the future

- When leading a group, being responsible for staying alert to distractions and handling behavior issues

- Remember that the group's needs come first

- Be willing to alternate and share the group leader role

- Understand the division of roles and responsibilities clearly, and always plan far enough in advance for each facilitator's comfort level

- Be willing to provide and receive constructive feedback on work

- Help one another recognize transference or counter-transference reactions

- Communicate directly via telephone with your co-facilitator about any last minute changes—do not depend on assumptions or email communications!

If an illness or emergency occurs, call co-facilitator immediately to cancel meeting. Lead Facilitators are responsible for notifying School Counselor that a group must be canceled.

The HEALS Program
Facilitator Code of Ethics Agreement

🕊 I understand the private nature of the HEALS work and will maintain client confidentiality at all times.

🕊 I will participate in ongoing training and support groups with my peers as offered during the year.

🕊 I will contact a HEALS Program Coordinator as needed regarding the group I am facilitating to insure good planning and communication.

🕊 I will attend group supervision meetings as needed or requested.

🕊 I will make available to the supervisor all curriculum lesson plans for each session.

🕊 I will keep the supervisor informed of any changes or limitations in my ability to volunteer.

🕊 I understand and will adhere to the policies and procedures set up for each program.

🕊 I will report any suspected abuse of a child to the school counselor, and my supervisor.

🕊 I understand that when I am working in the community I am a representative of The HEALS Program and commit to be mindful and respectful of that position.

🕊 I respect the limits of my role and am committed to the safety and well-being of all children in my care as well as my co-facilitator.

🕊 I agree to maintain both personal and professional boundaries in my work.

🕊 I will not transport children in my car unless I have written permission from their guardian/s.

As a facilitator for The HEALS Program, I have read the Facilitator Code of Ethics above and agree to abide by them:

_____ _____
Facilitator Signature   Date

The HEALS Program Delivery System
Lead Facilitator Role

The primary focus of The HEALS Program is to provide educational support groups for children in bereavement within school systems. The role of the Lead HEALS Facilitator is to:

Pre-Group Preparation
☐ Be responsible to the HEALS Program Coordinator

☐ Be the primary liaison with the school once the contract has been completed

☐ Provide classroom presentations for child self-referral recruitment, if applicable

☐ Coordinate with the school counselor and co-facilitator the days and times

☐ Meet with School Counselor and co-facilitator two weeks prior to group to talk about implementation of program (provide facilitators with permission slips, discuss individual children's losses and needs, possible group dynamic issues, view meeting space, etc.)

☐ When assigned, act as a supervisor for HEALS interns

☐ Adhere to The HEALS Program policies and represent the agency to the school in your capacity as a HEALS facilitator.

While Group is in Progress
☐ Be responsible for implementation of The HEALS Program curriculum for group members

☐ Conduct pre and post-group evaluations with group participants

☐ Take attendance at each group or have children sign in

☐ Assess each weekly session upon completion with the school counselor and co- facilitator and plan the following session

☐ Communicate weekly with a HEALS Program supervisor for support

☐ Attend monthly HEALS facilitator support meetings and quarterly HEALS Connections (in-services)

☐ Consult with school counselor about any concerns or red-flags you observe among individuals in the group—remind school staff to allow the HEALS Facilitators to cope with problem behaviors following the HEALS Behavior Management Plan before seeking the outside help of the school counselor, principal or parents

☐ Follow the Suspected Abuse Reporting procedures and protocol if a facilitator suspects a child is being or has been abused

☐ Maintain confidentiality at all times regarding the people HEALS serves

Post-Group Responsibilities
☐ Meet with School Counselor to debrief, ask them to fill out evaluation form

☐ Provide parental follow-up meeting (optional)

☐ Lead Facilitator provides main office with pre and post-group participant evaluations

☐ Submit invoice for hours with materials receipts attached(if contracted)

☐ Provide a written evaluation of your own and you co-facilitator's performance

☐ Meet with HEALS Coordinator to discuss your performance, strengths as well as areas of growth

☐ Turn in all required paperwork—in a timely fashion within two weeks after the end of the very last session

The HEALS Program Delivery System
Assistant Facilitator Role

The primary focus of The HEALS Program is to provide educational support groups for children in bereavement within school systems. The Assistant Facilitator is responsible for the implementation and co-facilitation of a HEALS group. This person is accountable to the Lead Facilitator. Other responsibilities- ties include:

Pre-Group Preparation
- ☐ Co-facilitate classroom presentations for child self-referral recruitment, if applicable
- ☐ Meet with School Counselor and co-facilitator two weeks prior to group to talk about implementation of program (discuss individual children's losses and needs, group dynamic issues, preview meeting space, etc.)
- ☐ Design curriculum plan and materials preparation with Lead Facilitator

While Group is in Progress
- ☐ Take responsibility for implementation of The HEALS Program curriculum for group members
- ☐ Record weekly participation, or have children sign in
- ☐ Assess each weekly session upon completion with the school counselor and co-facilitator and plan the following session
- ☐ Attend monthly HEALS facilitator support meetings and quarterly HEALS Connections (in-services). Communicate about group's concerns and/or achievements
- ☐ Consult with school counselor about any concerns or red-flags you observe among individuals in the group—remind school staff to allow the HEALS Facilitators to cope with problem behaviors following the HEALS Behavior Management Plan before seeking the outside help of the school counselor, principal or parents
- ☐ Follow Suspected Abuse Report procedures as provided and notify The HEALS Program Supervisor
- ☐ Turn in all paperwork in a timely fashion
- ☐ Maintain confidentiality at all times regarding the people HEALS serves
- ☐ Adhere to The HEALS Program policies and represent the agency to the school in your capacity as a HEALS facilitator.

Post-Group Responsibilities
- ☐ Meet with School Counselor to debrief
- ☐ Provide parental follow-up meeting (optional)
- ☐ Assist Lead Facilitator in written Group Summary Report stating "personality" of group, challenges, what worked well, what did not work so well, and other observations
- ☐ Provide a written evaluation of your own and your co-facilitator's performance
- ☐ Meet with Lead Facilitator to discuss your performance, strengths as well as areas of growth
- ☐ Turn in all required paperwork—in a timely fashion within two weeks after the end of the very last session

The HEALS Program
Facilitator/Intern Evaluation

NAME: _____

GROUP: _____

DATE: _____

	See Comments	Meets Expectations	Could Use Improvement	No Opportunity To Observe
General				
Begins and ends group on time				
Attends at least 60% of facilitator support meetings				
Performs paperwork in a timely fashion				
Open to feedback from supervisor and co-facilitators				
Communicates with co-facilitator/supervisor about group concerns				
Collaborates with co-facilitators				
Individual Skills				
Establishes group rapport				
Nonjudgemental, respectful of children				
Communicates warmth and support				
Reflects feelings—helps children identify & express				
Communicates empathy and understanding				
Demonstrates creativity in planning activities				
Effective in handling children's behavior problems				
Guides children in problem-solving/decision-making				
Makes referrals when appropriate				
Self-discloses appropriately—does not dominate group				
Encourages participation of children				

The HEALS Facilitator Evaluation pg.2 *

	See Comments	Meets Expectations	Could Use Improvement	No Opportunity To Observe
Group Structure & Process				
Posts and reviews group guidelines				
Encourages children to help each other				
Moves group along—helps children stay on topic				
Completes communication with one child before moving on to another or the whole group				
Identifies commonalities among group members				
Models communication skills				
Able to identify needs of the group and modify group plan as needed				
The HEALS Program Educational Support Model				
Demonstrates familiarity w/ HEALS curriculum & grief				
Helps maintain positive image of the agency				
Educational				
Communicates to children at children's level				
Does not plan too little material for group				
Does not implement too much material for group				
Presents information with consideration for all learning styles—auditory, visual, and kinesthetic				

Comments

Location: _____ Date: _____

Evaluator: _____

Co-facilitation and Our Growing Edge:
Giving and Receiving Feedback

Guidelines for Providing Feedback to Your Co-facilitator

Due to differences in facilitator styles and perceptions, difficulties may arise between co-facilitators. When a difficulty arises, it is best to be gentle, open, and as direct as possible. Here are some helpful ideas for giving feedback to your co-facilitator. Agreement on the process for giving and receiving feedback as you enter the co-facilitation relationship is very valuable and states your openness for continual growth.

1. **Choose a private place.** Allow time to be able to process and reflect. Feedback can sometimes be uncomfortable to receive. Allow time to work through the emotions.

2. **Prepare yourself and what you want to say.** Consider your co-facilitator's personality and how s/he might best receive feedback when planning what to say and how to say it.

3. **Use "I" statements**. State your perceptions and how you or the children might have felt in a specific situation such as, "I felt that when Shannon tried to share how she felt, you cut her off rather abruptly and didn't let her finish. I think it is very important to allow children to finish their statements."

4. **Provide clear and concrete suggestions for improvement.** It is easier to grow when we are given ideas that are conducive for change in performance. A statement such as, "I feel stressed because you consistently arrive a few minutes before our group. I would appreciate if you could plan to arrive a half hour earlier to help me set-up."

5. **Be open for an exchange of his/her ideas or perceptions.** It may be that your co-facilitator has legitimate reasons for their behavior, which may help you, shift your perceptions if you can maintain an open mind. (Of course, anything that involves safety or boundaries should be reported to the supervisor.) If approached with an open mind, both facilitators may end up with a deeper understanding of one another.

Tips for Receiving Feedback

Being on the receiving end of feedback can be very uncomfortable. Here are some helpful on opening to receive feedback:

1. **Focus on what is being said—not how.** Your co-facilitator may be very nervous, gruff or angry which can affect the delivery of the message. Maintaining your focus on the message is necessary in order to learn.

2. **Clarify and accept the information and perspective of the person giving feedback.** Use active listening skills to nondefensively clarify the message. Once the message is clear, explain that you hear what they are saying and will consider or think about it.

3. **Maintain a positive attitude.** Keeping an open mind and positive attitude when offered opportunities to grow will help you to listen better and learn new skills.

4. **Seek constructive and concrete suggestions for improvement.** In order to improve, you must be given specific ideas on how to change your behavior or attitude. For example, a suggestion of, "You should be warmer with intruders in front of the children" is not very helpful. You might ask, "What are alternative ways to ask intruders to not interrupt our group?"

5. **Summarize the feedback you receive.** To show that you understand the ideas discussed in the feedback conversation, summarize the main points. This is also helpful in reminding yourself what you have learned.

We always encourage facilitators to work out differences or problems when they arise between themselves. However, if either facilitator feels that further support or mediation is needed, contact your HEALS supervisor for assistance, who is responsible for helping co-facilitators successfully work and grow together.

Protocol for Reporting Suspected Abuse

*To all of you, for your courage and for putting your careers
on the line that fateful day, March 5, 1973.
You saved my life.*
—Dave Pelzer

If information is revealed in one of the group sessions that could potentially endanger the student's life or well-being or someone else's—or if you learn that the student is being abused physically, sexually or emotionally, it is important to abide by the following guidelines:

- notify HEALS co-facilitator and supervisor
- notify School Counselor as soon as possible
- provide a written report to document what was said or observed for school officials and for HEALS supervisor (See Suspected Abuse Reporting Form)

Talking With a Child About Suspected Abuse

If a child voluntarily reveals, or you suspect, abuse of some kind, it is important to remain a calm and stabilizing factor for the child, regardless of what is revealed. Make sure to find a safe, non-threatening, private place away from the group to talk about what might have happened. It is of primary importance to **let the child know that you believe him or her.** Let the child know that part of your job is to make sure that children are safe, letting them know the seriousness of what they shared. Ask the child if they have shared the information with anyone else. Sometimes a child may talk about an abuse that occurred in the past that was handled by the authorities. Gently inquire to assess if the abuse is still continuing, or not, and report this to the school counselor.

Be sure to document whatever the child reports and describe any physical injuries they report, including the date and time of their disclosure. Note any physical or behavioral signs of abuse. It is not necessary to see an injury to make a report. If a child reports an injury and wants to show you, be sure that you have your co-facilitator as a witness.

Reporting to School Counselors

Make sure that the school counselor is informed as soon as possible. If you are in a situation that requires more consultation with your co-facilitator or school counselor, you may request the counselor not talk with the child until you have had an opportunity to explain to the child your position on confidentiality and reporting and getting help. You have just become a trusted adult in this child's life. Seek support from the school counselor to not jeopardize this important relationship.

Informing The Child About Reporting Procedures

Remind the child about the group confidentiality agreement and the only exception to that rule is if you suspect a child is not safe. Safety is every child's right. It is important to assure the child that they are not in trouble, they have not done anything wrong, and whatever happened to them is not their fault. Your role is to support the child. Let them know you will support and get help for them. Avoid further questioning and or investigation. To maximize safety for the child and yourself, never confront the possible perpetrator yourself.

*Child abuse has a domino effect that spreads to
all who touch the family. It takes its greatest toll on the child...*
—Dave Pelzer

The HEALS Program
Reporting Suspected Abuse Form

Reporter:

Your Name_____

Address _____ Phone _____

Organization_____ Phone _____

Address _____

Child's Name _____

Child's School _____

Name of suspected abuser: _____

Suspected abuser's relationship to child: _____

Time and date alleged incidents occurred: _____

Place/s where alleged incidents occurred: _____

A description of the alleged incident/s as described by the child:

A description of any corroborating information or evidence:

Any description the child gave of what precipitated the incident:

Signature_____ Date _____

Setting the Stage for a HEALS Session

The Physical Environment

The spaces which schools provide for our HEALS Programs can vary considerably from large, well-equipped kindergarten classrooms to small, cramped closets. Ask to accompany the school counselor or principal when looking at the available spaces prior to the first session. If at all possible, attempt to find a room that:

- has natural lighting
- is cheerful with enough space to do movement and art
- has a sink for cleaning up after art projects
- is private and will receive no disruptions while in session
- has few distractions

Since you travel to the school with your HEALS materials, ample time is needed to bring things into the meeting facility, set up and have a few quiet moments to center and prepare for the children's arrival. Prepare the room in advance so that as the children come in they get the message that this is a place to explore, try something new, and be playful. Be ready to welcome the children as they arrive, have them sign in and chat or draw together on the Graffiti Welcome Mural until all group members are assembled.

Feel free to express your own style when setting up the classroom, with permission from the teacher or staff who use the room, of course! If you find your space to be full of distractions, find ways to minimize them as a much as possible. To avoid distractions from windows and passersby, close the curtains or cover them with paper during the sessions. This will greatly aid in reducing potential behavior problems. (Also, see segment on Behavior Management). It is fun to create an atmosphere that is unique to you. The following are suggestions to show what can be brought to establish the tone of the session:

1. **A Centerpiece** which can be a decorated piece of colored felt, a scarf, a tie-died sheet, a small round tablecloth, etc.
2. **A Flowering Plant or Bouquet,** or if the facility allows, a candle in a holder which offers protection from an exposed flame
3. **A Teddy Bear** or other soft, cuddly animals for each child
4. **A Treasure Box** which is visually appealing and contains smooth stones, crystals, trinkets, shells, natural things that represent centeredness, fantasy, and wonderment
5. **A Koosh Ball or Talking Stick** which is held by the person speaking
6. **The HEALS Agreement Poster** which states the intentions of the group
7. **The HEALS Rights and Guidelines** which promote fun and safety
8. **A Tape/CD Player** for movement or background music
9. Enough **Pillows** for each participant to sit upon
10. **Graffiti Welcome Mural** to draw on until all group members arrive

It is recommended that the same centerpiece items remain constant from week to week to establish a reassuring continuity of tone for what happens in the group. Additional expressive arts materials will be included as needed in each session.

The seating in most HEALS groups consists of enough small individual pillows and a bear for each person. The facilitators should agree on their particular seating in advance so they are not side by side. Strategically place yourselves for ease of presentation materials and/or sitting next to or in-between any children that are easily distracted.

The Social/Emotional Climate

As the children enter the room the centerpiece will attract their attention and their natural curiosity will bring them toward you. Having pillows arranged around the centerpiece invites them to claim a specific spot and to get comfortable in this new adventure. Do all within your ability to be relaxed. Even though you may be nervous and afraid, remember to breathe to help you center and focus on your purpose and on the children. Convey a spirit of welcome, safety, understanding, and support. Allow the children some time to explore what you have set out in the room as you maintain awareness of their interactions and responses. Permit yourself to feel comfortable "hanging out" with the group for awhile, recognizing that they need some time to make the shift from their left-brain classroom world to the inner world of emotion.

When the session officially begins, introduce yourself in a personal and natural way. Don't rush or try to say too much at this point. You are establishing the tone of your group as you begin, and it is helpful to talk in a way that lets the children know you as a real person. You may choose to ask the children if they know why they are here. This provides valuable information, and you will begin to get a sense of how openly and honestly the death of the significant person in their life has been addressed.

Talk briefly about why you are there and what The HEALS Program is. After you explain that this expressive arts program will give them many new ideas and ways to communicate their feelings and take care of themselves, you might want to invite them to put how they are feeling about being in the group into a movement. Always model for the children, using your own feelings as a source for your expression, before you expect them to try something that may be very new for them.

When providing HEALS support these principles are invaluable:

**Show up
Be aware
Say what's true
And don't be attached to the results!**

Planning a HEALS Session

In planning a session, the HEALS Framework will be helpful in assisting you as you progress through the bereavement process. References will be made to <u>attunements</u>, <u>groundings</u>, or <u>centering</u> <u>exercises</u> as we discuss the planning, so let's begin by defining those terms. (More in-depth information and ideas for each of these topics can be located in *Section III: The Creative Mind.)*

An **attunement** is an invitation to identify a feeling being experienced in the moment and to then translate that feeling into an expressive art form. An attunement gives you a window into where each child is as you "check-in" at the start of the session and reconnect at the close of a session.

A **grounding or centering** exercise is valuable to use when a group or an individual has experienced a particularly deep level of inner awareness and reports feeling "floaty" or light-headed. This technique allows the individual to reconnect with his/her body in external reality. It is not a good idea to send a child back to the classroom or out into the world until they have made that shift. Therefore, having several grounding or centering techniques in your repertoire is valuable to help children return to the present.

Most grieving children respond well to a moderately consistent structure as they progress from session to session). For example: we may use a familiar exercise and introduce a variation. This accomplishes two goals: 1) It gives the child a sense of security with what is familiar and 2) helps them explore new opportunities). At the very end of each session our facilitators provide a group **Circle Closure**. This allows the members of the HEALS group to fully prepare for transitioning from the bereavement group to their next activity. HEALS Circle Closures offer the children an opportunity to connect with one another in a playful way, return to present time, and say good-bye to the group for the week.

Suggested Steps:
1. Determine the Framework session.
2. Select a Framework activity(s) to correspond with the session.
3. Choose two attunements for the session—one for the beginning and one for the end of the session.
4. Make a list of all the materials you will need to bring to the group.
5. Include ample opportunities for the children to stretch or move.
6. Have a grounding or centering exercise in reserve in the event one is needed.
7. Provide a Circle Closure as a transition activity to help the group say good-bye to one another.

The HEALS Program
Curriculum Plan

Session # _____
Date _____

School: _____ Grade/s: _____ #: _____
(# of children)

Name of School Counselor: _____

Names of Facilitators: _____

Title of Session Title: _____

Materials: teddy bears, pillows, centerpiece, HEALS Rights Poster, HEALS Learning Agreement Poster, markers

I. Welcome & Introduction:	Today's Group Evaulation
II. Attunement:	**What worked?**
III. Session Activity:	
	What didn't work?
IV. Centering Exercise:	
V. Closing Circle:	**Unique Challenges?**
VI. Notes & Reminders:	

The HEALS Learning Agreement and Rights

The following HEALS Learning Agreement may be used at the beginning of each session to help the group focus on intent and promote safety:

> **"This is a special group. While we are here, we will share our feelings and listen to each other's experiences without criticizing. We will support each other with kind words and understanding. We know our group is confidential. This means we will share with no one else the personal stories of others shared here—unless it involves the safety of a group member."**

We are stating in this agreement that we will not discuss what has been shared by others. **If the children want to talk about their own story outside of the group—that is perfectly fine.** But confidentiality means we do not share other people's stories without their permission. This agreement can be printed on individual cards or put on a large piece of paper or posterboard to be read aloud by the entire group. It is a good idea to laminate the cards and/or poster to protect them from wear and tear.

The HEALS Rights for Group Members

We have found that a group is much more meaningful for children if they are able to create their own rights or guidelines, and the facilitators can add their own ideas, too! Below is a list of the guidelines we generally encourage in our groups. Children may create similar ones using their own words. Remember to keep the guidelines stated in positive phrases. For example one 5th/6th grade group wanted to add "No Put-Downs" to their list. The facilitator asked them if there was a different way to describe what kind of behaviors they wanted rather than didn't want to encourage. After the group discussed it, they rephrased the guideline to say "Only Put-Ups Allowed Here." They were then able to focus on the things they wanted to create for themselves in the group with a richer, more expansive, positive attitude. Imagine if you were a child agreeing to either of those group rights. Can you feel the amazing difference in your mind and heart? Here is a sampling of rights to keep in mind when developing your group rights with children:

- The right to confidentiality, respect one another's stories
- The right to privacy
- The right to say "no" or "pass" to any activity
- The right to cry and express your feelings.
- The right to have your art work treated as a valuable expression of yourself which may be touched only with permission
- The right to ask one of the adults to talk privately following a session.

HEALS Questionnaire about Death Experiences

Name_____ Age_____ Grade_____

1. My first experience with death happened when I was _____ years old.
   It was the death of my _____named _____.
   This person/pet died of _____.

2. My most recent experience of death was _____.
   How long ago? _____ days _____ months ____ years

3. I know someone who is dying. This person is _____.

4. I have been present at the moment of someone's death.   Yes   No
   The person or animal was _____.

5. I felt _____.

6. I believe that the following happens after we die: _____
   _____
   _____
   _____

Please use separate pieces of drawing paper for the following:

7. Draw a picture of death.

8. Draw a picture of your life before the death.

9. Draw a picture of what your life looks like now.

Signs of Grief—Student Checklist

Place a check mark in the box next to any feelings or symptoms you have been feeling since your loss.

Emotional:

☐ Disbelief/Numbness
☐ Disorganization/Panic
☐ Feeling out of control
☐ Fear or worry
☐ Loss/Emptiness/Sadness
☐ Feeling need to take care of others
☐ Feeling guilty when having fun

☐ Lack of Feelings
☐ Physical pain
☐ Feeling powerless
☐ Guilt/Self-Blame
☐ Acceptance
☐ Wanting to be an innocent young
   child again

Physical:

☐ Tiredness, Lack of energy
☐ Wanting to sleep more
☐ Shortness of breath
☐ Tightness in throat, Screaming
☐ Headaches
☐ Skin rashes
☐ Inability to concentrate

☐ Difficulty with sleeping
☐ Lack of appetite
☐ Excessive appetite
☐ General nervousness
☐ Stomach pains
☐ Hyperactivity/Restlessness

Behavioral:

☐ Needing parent/s more
☐ Not wanting to separate from
   parents
☐ Not wanting to go to school
☐ Feeling sick more often

☐ Desiring to sleep with parent
☐ Arguments and fights with
   friends
☐ Needing a little extra help with
   tasks normally done alone

The above are all normal reactions which may be experienced after losing a loved one. It is okay to ask those around your for extra support, help, and understanding during this time. This process of grief is love not wanting to let go. Be very gentle with yourself. ☺

Form Pre-K (Post)

The HEALS Program
Before Group Thoughts
(Youngers)

1. My thoughts and feelings are important.   Yes   Maybe   No   Not Sure??

2. When someone dies, people   Yes   Maybe   No   Not Sure??
   experience many different feelings.

3. Is it okay to talk about death?   Yes   Maybe   No   Not Sure??

4. I think the death was my fault or   Yes   Maybe   No   Not Sure??
   I did something wrong.

5. Can you name 2 people you can talk to about your worries?

_____

6. Draw a picture of your family.

Form Pre-K (Post)

The HEALS Program
Post Group Thoughts
(Youngers)

1. My thoughts and feelings are important. Yes Maybe No Not Sure??

2. When someone dies, people
   experience many different feelings. Yes Maybe No Not Sure??

3. Is it okay to talk about death? Yes Maybe No Not Sure??

4. I think the death was my fault or
   I did something wrong. Yes Maybe No Not Sure??

5. Can you name 2 people you can talk to about your worries?

   _____

97

6. Draw a picture of your family.

The HEALS Program
Before Group Thoughts

First Name_____ Age_____ Grade_____

When someone close to us dies, it is natural to experience many different feelings in our hearts, minds and bodies. By answering these questions you are helping The HEALS Program understand how to best support you.

Scale: 1 = Never   2 = Rarely   3 Sometimes   4 = Usually   5 = Always

1. I am afraid to talk about death.   1 2 3 4 5

2. I feel like the death was my fault or I did something wrong. 1 2 3 4 5

3. I think my thoughts and feelings are important.   1 2 3 4 5

4. I am looking forward to the future.   1 2 3 4 5

5. I can be happy even though this person died.   1 2 3 4 5

6. When I am feeling sad or mad, I know "safe" things   1 2 3 4 5
    to do to help myself feel better.

Multiple Choice Questions

7. What do you do when you feel angry or upset?

    Check all that are true:
        ☐ a. I want to be alone.
        ☐ b. I talk with someone.
        ☐ c. I hurt, break or throw something.
        ☐ d. I find something I like to do.

8. I can talk about death with

       ☐ a. My family

       ☐ b. My friends.

       ☐ c. No one

Many children experience some of the following grief reactions when someone close to them has died. Please check the answers that apply for you.

9. Lately I:

☐ a. have stomach aches	☐ h. have headaches
☐ b. sleep too much	☐ i. am not hungry very much
☐ c. have trouble sleeping	☐ j. visit school nurse alot
☐ d. eat too much	☐ k. need to be with a parent/caregiver more
☐ e. want to be alone alot	☐ l. don't want to go to school
☐ f. fight and argue more	☐ m. need help with things I normally do alone

10. I often feel:

☐ a. short of breath	☐ e. tired	☐ i. lonely	☐ m. confused
☐ b. unable to concentrate	☐ f. nervous	☐ j. fearful	☐ n. guilty
☐ c. hyper/restless	☐ g. sadness	☐ k. numb	☐ o. worried
☐ d. a tightness in my throat	☐ h. ignored	☐ l. empty inside	

Draw a picture of death or what you think happens after we die.

The HEALS Program
Before Group Thoughts

Date_____

First Name_____ Age_____ Grade_____

When someone close to us dies, it is natural to experience many different feelings in our hearts, minds and bodies. By answering these questions you are helping The HEALS Program understand how to best support you.

Scale:　1 = Never　2 = Rarely　3 Sometimes　4 = Usually　5 = Always

1. I am afraid to talk about death.　　　　　　　　　1　2　3　4　5

2. I feel like the death was my fault or I did something wrong.　1　2　3　4　5

3. I think my thoughts and feelings are important.　　1　2　3　4　5

4. I am looking forward to the future.　　　　　　　1　2　3　4　5

5. I can be happy even though this person died.　　　1　2　3　4　5

6. When I am feeling sad or mad, I know "safe" things　1　2　3　4　5
   to do to help myself feel better.

<u>Multiple Choice Questions</u>

7. What do you do when you feel angry or upset?

    Check all that are true:
        ☐ a. I want to be alone.

        ☐ b. I talk with someone.

        ☐ c. I hurt, break or throw something.

        ☐ d. I find something I like to do.

8. I can talk about death with

☐ a. My family

☐ b. My friends.

☐ c. No one

Many children experience some of the following grief reactions when someone close to them has died. Please check the answers that apply for you.

9. Lately I:

☐ a. have stomach aches   ☐ h. have headaches

☐ b. sleep too much   ☐ i. am not hungry very much

☐ c. have trouble sleeping   ☐ j. visit school nurse alot

☐ d. eat too much   ☐ k. need to be with a parent/caregiver more

☐ e. want to be alone alot   ☐ l. don't want to go to school

☐ f. fight and argue more   ☐ m. need help with things I normally do alone

10. I often feel:

☐ a. short of breath   ☐ e. tired   ☐ i. lonely   ☐ m. confused

☐ b. unable to concentrate ☐ f. nervous   ☐ j. fearful   ☐ n. guilty

☐ c. hyper/restless   ☐ g. sadness   ☐ k. numb   ☐ o. worried

☐ d. a tightness in my throat ☐ h. ignored   ☐ l. empty inside

Draw a picture of death or what you think happens after we die.

The HEALS Program

Group Summary Report

Please provide a brief overview of your HEALS Group. You may comment on the personality of the group, what worked well and not so well, the challenges, and any other observations that will help others in providing future groups at this school.

School: _____ Grade level: _____ # _____ (# of children)

School Counselor_____Months/Dates: _____

Lead Facilitator:_____ Co-facilitator:_____

Brief Overview: _____
_____
_____
_____
_____
_____
_____
_____
_____
_____
_____
_____
_____
_____
_____
_____
_____
_____
_____
_____
_____
_____
_____

Facilitator Signature:_____Date_____

The HEALS Program

Post-Group Letter to Parents

(Date)

Dear Parents/Guardians,

It is hard to believe that the eight weeks of The HEALS Program have come to an end. We have enjoyed having your children in our bereavement group and hope they leave with fond memories and useful tools for dealing with loss. We have enclosed a bibliography both for children and adults that we hope you will find beneficial. We welcome feedback from all and messages can be forwarded to us through The HEALS Program.

Wishing you and your child the best.

Respectfully,

(HEALS Program Facilitators name)   &   (HEALS Program Facilitators name)

HEALS Program Facilitators

The HEALS Program

Consent To Use Artwork

I hereby give my consent for The HEALS Program to use the artwork or writings by _____ for displays and community educational or fundraising purposes for The HEALS Program.

Please check one of the following:

☐ I would like my name to be included with my artwork

☐ I would prefer to remain anonymous.

_____Date_____
(Child's signature)

_____Date_____
(Parent or Guardian)

_____Date_____
(HEALS Facilitator)

Behavior Management

The Physical Environment

Preparation of the environment is a key component in anticipating potential distractions for children in your group. Thoughtful planning ahead of time can go a long way toward reducing behavior problems. If your room has many distractions, try to minimize them as much as possible. For instance, blocking off areas where children can hide, closing the piano lid, or removing items that attract too much attention is strongly recommended. If windows pose a distraction from the inside, or the outside, we recommend closing the curtains or covering them with paper during the sessions.

Sometimes the seating arrangements need to be structured to minimize behavior problems and to split "cliques" that can be distracting. Occasionally you may run into a group that is "behaviorally challenged." We have found that seating them at tables with chairs provides more structure than pillows. The make-up or "chemistry" of each group is different and may require tailored accommodations for a successful experience.

The Social/Emotional Climate

As discussed previously in the segment Listening to Children, the importance of the physical and mental preparation of the facilitators play a key role in setting the stage for the group. Remember that this may be one of the few places in their lives where children feel safe, cared for and respected. Managing the behaviors within the group will promote a general atmosphere of respect and safety for all group members.

Transitioning From One Activity to Another

There are children who appear to have more difficulty during transitions, or moving from one activity to another. It is vital to prepare them ahead of time, and structure the transitions by being very clear what is expected. When designing the curriculum for a session, be thinking about all the transition periods during the session and how best to structure them. Instructions need to be short, clear and aimed at the appropriate developmental level of the children you are working with, regardless of their chronological age. Thinking about the possible challenges ahead of time can help your group run as smoothly as possible.

Respecting The HEALS Rights

You will quickly discover that some children may test your limits. As a facilitator you should be extremely alert to this because the safe atmosphere being provided is at stake once the ground rules are tested and broken. It is important to discuss with the school counselor their school's routine for dealing with misbehavior. For example: Do teachers typically send kids to the office? Can and should facilitators call the office from the room, and the school counselor or someone will come to assist? Does the school use "time outs?" These are important points to know about each school's particular "culture." Some children may have their defenses up for good reason, and this should be explored. Groups may not be appropriate for all children.

Be prepared ahead of time with a plan of action for "testing." The HEALS Rights can help you to maintain a safe physical and psychological climate with confidence. We suggest the following technique we call the "Three Chances Plan." It is important to share this with the school counselor in advance to make sure they will support the behavioral management plan:

The Three Chances Plan

1st Chance: The "testing" child is given a verbal warning that one of the rights has been forgotten or overlooked. The facilitator or counselor restates The HEALS Right and asks that it be respected for the comfort and safety of all the members of the group.

2nd Chance: Same as above, reminding the child that this is the second time The HEALS Right has been brought to their attention. This is a good time to make sure the child fully understands the right.

3rd Chance: This time speak privately with the child, reminding them that this is the third time they have jeopardized the other children's sense of security within the group. The child needs to make a choice between a behavior change or leaving the group. Writing out a Contract (see next page) that outlines what the child needs to do in order to continue in the group empowers the child to make this decision. If the child decides not to return, do not view yourself as a failure. Most likely this child is dealing with multiple losses and is in need of something more than a bereavement support group. It will be helpful to process such a situation with the school counselor or psychologist if such a situation arises.

As a HEALS facilitator you are working as a team member with the counselor and perhaps another co-facilitator. It is vital that all the adults be alert to violations of The HEALS Rights and consistent in requiring their respect. If you are the adult nearest a disruptive child you should take the initiative in helping the child understand The HEALS Rights with more clarity. This will provide valuable support for all the members in your HEALS group.

Contractual Agreement

Between _____ and _____.
(Student's Name)   (Facilitator's Name)

I, _____, will be able to remain in the HEALS group if I follow these ground rules:

1. I will make no unkind comments to any group member.

2. I will listen to others and say nothing unless it is my turn to speak.

3. I will not throw anything or do anything with my body that disrupts the group.

If I break this agreement:

- <u>1st Time</u>: **WARNING**

- <u>2nd Time</u>: **WARNING**....And....then....

I will be asked to leave the group for 10 min.

- <u>3rd Time</u>: I will be requested to permanently

        LEAVE THE GROUP..... ⟹

I understand this contract and agree to abide by it; and I want to remain in the HEALS group.

_____   _____
(Student's Signature)   (Date)   (Facilitator's Signature)   (Date)

The Art of Healing Childhood Grief

Section III: The Creative Mind
The HEALS Curriculum

The following pages contain the essential program elements used in designing a HEALS session followed by sample HEALS session plans for three separate age-level groups which may be used as is or as reference points. Each sample segment is followed by a list of other suggested activities and materials that can be used as alternatives for each of the eight sessions.

We encourage you to tap into your own creative juices and to allow your intuition to guide you in planning your sessions as you take into consideration the group you are supporting.

Important Note: Sometimes people may die leaving rather painful memories for children, particularly if they were abusive or violent. In such cases, the HEALS curriculum or language may need to be adjusted. For this reason we have carefully alternated using the words "special person" or "significant person" with "loved one" throughout the curriculum to remind us to be aware of the possible complex feelings children may have with the person who died.

The HEALS Program Framework & Objectives

Based on the work of Sandra Fox, founder of the Good Grief Program, and expanded by Anne Black and Penelope Simpson for The HEALS Program.

SESSION I: WE ARE NOT ALONE WITH OUR LOSS
To acknowledge that each member in the group has experienced a loss. To allow for the opportunity to share the death of the significant person in their life and to determine if there are any areas of question, concern, confusion, or misunderstanding.

SESSION II: TELLING THE STORY
To provide an opportunity of each child in the group to tell where they were when they first learned about their significant person's death—how they found out—and how they felt at that time.

SESSION III: GRIEVING THE LOSS—FEELING THE FEELINGS
To increase understanding of how people commonly feel and behave when someone or something they care about dies. To acknowledge that the feelings related to loss may be varied and difficult to have and/or to share.

SESSION IV: TAMING THE WILD THINGS
To understand that anger, fear, guilt and worry are natural responses when we lose someone or something special. To learn how to safely and creatively access and express uncomfortable feelings.

SESSION V: FAREWELL RITUALS AND UNFINISHED BUSINESS
To provide the opportunity for each participant to express and complete any unfinished business they may have with their significant person.

SESSION VI: COMMEMORATION
To provide the child with an opportunity to affirm the value of the life of the person who died.

SESSION VII: THE JEWELS WITHIN: TREASURING OURSELVES
To remind the children that they are strong and powerful—each unique in their own way—with wise and creative resources that can be called forth when needed.

SESSION VIII: THE HARVEST CEREMONY
To honor and witness all that has been done during the HEALS sessions, both individually and as a group. To remind the children that the techniques and skills they learned in The HEALS Program may be used at any time in the future when their feelings need to be safely expressed. To receive permission to go on.

HEALS Group Facilitation Tips

The following ideas help create a group that runs more smoothly, stays more focused and fosters respectfulness and participation among group members.

∼ Mementos

We highly encourage children to bring a memento of the person who died, such as a picture, a special object or perhaps something that belonged to that person. We place these treasures in the center of the circle. In most of our groups, it is very difficult to ask the children to wait until the activity to share their mementos, so we often allow them to share at the beginning of the session. Some children choose to keep the memento on the centerpiece the entire eight weeks while others may not be able to do that, for a variety of reasons. Having these special mementos not only helps group members learn more about the person who died, and also helps keep the group focused on the sacredness of why they are gathered together each week. It is important to keep these mementos in a *very* safe place between sessions.

∼ Timing and Creating Smooth Transitions

Facilitators working with groups must become wizards at pacing and the timekeepers of activities. Working within a school system is even more challenging because the time allotted for groups is generally rather short. Occasionally, you may experience magical times when everyone is so entirely involved that timeshifting seems to occur. Sometimes the clock appears to stand still and an amazing amount gets accomplished. Savor these times, for they are truly gifts of being totally present in the moment with a group.

When the children are involved in any expressive arts activity it is important to prepare them for transition into the next part of an activity by notifying them several minutes ahead of time, and again when there is only one minute left. This psychologically allows them time to begin disengaging with their art which may be communicating with their psyche on many different and deep levels.

∼ Talking Sticks:
Most groups function more smoothly when a talking stick or object is held by whoever is speaking. Introduction of the talking stick concept is important in the beginning of the very first session. For more details on talking sticks, please refer to our segment "On Listening To Children."

∼ Modeling:
We have found that adult modeling of attunements, sharing time/length in circle and certain expressive arts activities ensures a better understanding of procedures desired by the group members. The first person to share or begin an activity usually sets the tone and pace which can have quite an impact on the objectives of an activity. For example, during the sharing circle, if the first child passes (for whatever reason) a precedent may be set that results in a large percentage of children passing. For an expressive arts activity, verbal instructions followed by adult role modeling accommodates two of the three learning styles—auditory and visual. When these are followed by the group engaging in the kinesthetic or actual activity itself, all three learning styles are optimized.

Freeze/Flow Technique: The Freeze/Flow Technique is used when first introducing a group to some kind of movement, sound, or experiential activity that will involve stopping in the midst of whatever they are doing on cue. It takes some practice and conducting the Freeze/Flow Technique allows a facilitator to make sure the group understands the cue before the actual activity begins. For example:

> To the beat of a drum, encourage the children to move freely around the room expressing a particular feeling using sound and movement with the caveat that they will *Freeze* as soon as the signal occurs (i.e. the signal might be the drum stops, the music or light turns off, a scarf or flag is raised, whatever signal facilitators decide to use).

Children love to take turns at being in control of the whole group in this way. This activity fosters a sense of control, promotes decision-making and can be very empowering for grieving children who may feel little control in their lives.

Parent Information: Prior to or during the group it is helpful to send informational handouts to parents on the topics and/or activities the group will be covering. Useful educational handouts can be found in the Appendix.

If a facilitator is aware that a child is planning to take something home and seeks to involve the parent in some way (ex. burning a sealed envelope of unfinished business), the HEALS facilitator may call the parent to pave the way, sharing background information, perceptions and observations of the child.

Name Games

In the very first couple of sessions of a HEALS group it is important to immediately begin to build group cohesion. One effective way to help individuals become part of a group is by getting to know one another in a playful, non-threatening way. New participants may be nervous—and laughter is a wonderful way to relax everyone and become acquainted. Here are some fun ideas to warm up a group while learning everyone's names.

❧ **Alphabet Fun Name Game:** (best for older children) Explain to the children that they will be playing a name game. Mention no specific instructions. Group members listen to the example and then raise their hand to volunteer to go next. Each noun (or verb) in the statement should begin with the letter of the person's name. For Example: "I am **J**ack. I drive a **J**eep. I'm from **J**apan."

❧ **Ball Toss Name Game:** The leader begins by holding a ball and saying his or her name, then says the name of someone in the group and tosses the ball to him or her. If the child does not know someone's name they may ask, "Can you tell me your name, please?" Do this several times until all group members names have been spoken and everyone feels they have a fairly good idea of one another's names. **Variations: a) Pattern Ball Toss**: Begin the name game in the same way as above, but create a pattern that stays the same. Try to make the ball go faster and faster for each round. Some groups may time it and try to beat that time in following sessions; **b) Multiple Balls Pattern Toss**: Same as above, but add two or three balls to increase the difficulty (and the laughter!); **c) Thank You _____ Ball Toss**: Again, same as above, but this time once the ball is moving well around the circle, ask the person catching the ball to say "Thank you" and include the name of the person who threw the ball. ("Thank you, Jill!"); **d) Wacky Toss**: Use different size balls or strange stuffed or rubber objects or creatures; and **e) Rolling Names**: For younger children who may have trouble catching the ball, have them sit with their toes touching their neighbors and roll the ball to each other practicing saying their names.

❧ **Name Drumming:** Have a small drum and drumstick that is passed around the circle allowing each person to beat the rhythm of their name on the drum. If there are enough drums, the entire group can repeat the person's name on their own drums.

❧ **Name and Movement:** Have each person say their name with a movement that expresses how they feel. **Variations: a) Name, Movement & Mirroring**: The rest of the group mirrors the person by repeating each person's name and movement as closely as they can; **b) I Am _____**: Say your name and something significant about yourself or a quality you have. Example: I am Fred and I love soccer!

Attunement Ideas

Since an attunement is an opportunity for the group to become aware of what each participant is feeling, we begin by having the group members take a few quiet moments to check in with their body. If a child is asked, "What are you feeling?" they will often give you a blank stare and respond, "I don't know." This is an honest response to a perplexing and overwhelming question. We suggest providing a large chart like the sample drawing following these attunement ideas. This visual aid will allow the children to consider many feelings with an accompanying face in order to get in touch with which face and feeling matches what they are feeling.

For example:

> **Feelings Chart:** (see *Feelings Chart* in *Session III: Feel The Feelings.*) Directions are given for each person to think about how they are feeling in the moment and identify with a feeling on the Feelings Chart. Each group member, using the talking stick, shares that feeling.

Here are some Attunement ideas to use at the beginning and ending of each session. In choosing or designing attunements appropriately, always bear in mind the given ages, personalities and sex of the group members.

1. Body Sculpting: This attunement is done in pairs. Child "A" focuses his/her attention onto what s/he is feeling in the moment. After being granted permission to touch Child "B," the first child "sculpts" "B" into a position that best depicts the sculptor's feelings. To complete the exercise, reverse the process.

2. Animal: Think about how you are feeling right now. If you could turn it into an animal, what animal would you be?

3. Air Frame Portraits: Draw an imaginary picture frame in the air as large as your body, or however big a portrait you will be making. Step inside of it and freeze your body into a position that describes how you feel right now. **Variation**: Unfreeze and add movement that represents how you are feeling.

4. Art Museum Body Sculpture: Imagine yourself walking through an art museum…you are seeing lots of paintings hanging on the walls…Now you walk into a large circular room…in the center of the room is a life-sized statue of a person which has been sculpted by a famous artist…as you get closer to the statue and look at it carefully…you realize that it is a sculpture of you…it is positioned just the way you are feeling today…put your body into that sculpture to show what you are feeling now…share your feelings with the group, if you choose.

5. Bird: Take a moment to quietly go inside of yourself and think about how you are feeling at this very moment. If that feeling could turn into a bird, what kind of bird would you be?

6. Body Awareness: Move and direct awareness to all parts of the body beginning with fingers and palms, then whole arms, upper, middle, lower back, pelvis, buttocks, stomach, thighs, calves, shins, ankles, feet, toes. Breathe in and out top of head, relaxing whole body. Move scalp, eyebrows, chin, jaw, and neck. End with shaking and flapping the whole body and sounding. Follow with an attunement to help the children check in with their feelings in the present moment.

7. Body of water: What body of water depicts what you are feeling in the present moment? It can be any form of water. **Variation:** It can be any form of water and can include sounds and movement.

8. Circle Greeting: Everyone joins hands in a circle. Send your breath down into the ground… visualize your legs like taproots bringing earth energy up into your body…relax, rooted with your weight on the floor, rocking back and forth on your heels and toes, finding where your center is…breathe into your center…breathe the energy of the circle into yourself and send it out into the circle. We are calling on what is highest and deepest in us all. Now open your eyes and say hello with your eyes to everyone in the circle." Each person shares how s/he is feeling right now.

9. Clouds: Take a moment to quietly go inside of yourself and think about how you are feeling at this very moment. If that feeling could turn into a cloud, what kind of cloud would it be?

10. Color: Take a moment to quietly go inside of yourself and think about how you are feeling at this very moment. If that feeling could turn into a color, what color would it be?

11. Dancing Scarves & Feelings: a) Use a scarf to make a movement about how you are feeling right now. Steering the scarves **b)** Colorful Clouds: Each child becomes a colorful Cloud—let each cloud take turns leading the movement around the room, stating who is leading— "Red Cloud leads."

12. Dance Your Inner Landscape: Go into your center and view your inner landscape. Through movement, dance what you see. If you do not see anything, move what you are feeling. Note: This attunement is a bit "riskier" and we don't recommend it's use until the group has had many opportunities to experiment with the expressive arts. **Variation: a)** Use Dancing Scarves; and **b)** have group members "mirror" the dancer.

13. Elemental Feelings—Earth, Fire, Air, Water or Metal: Think about how you are presently feeling. From what element would that feeling be made—something of Earth, Fire, Air, Water or Metal? Why?

14. Energy: Using your hands, show how high or low your energy is at this moment.

15. Feelings Creatures: If you could take how you feel right now and turn into any kind of creature, what would you be?

16. **Feelings Flavors:** Share a flavor or taste that best describes what you are feeling in this moment.

17. **Feeling Hieroglyphics:** Draw a symbol/hieroglyphic showing what you are feeling at this very moment. Share the feeling and tell where it is in your body.

18. **Feeling Instruments:** Pass a musical instrument around the circle, allowing each participant a chance to let the instrument make sounds that resemble how they are feeling in the moment (drum or other percussion instruments, small keyboard, shakers, guitar, xylophone, thumb harp, etc.).

19. **Feeling Scale:** On a range of 1-10 (1 = very crummy and 10 = ecstatic) how are you feeling NOW? (See *Feelings Chart* in HEALS *Session III: Feel The Feelings.*)

20. **Flighty Feelings:** Using Dancing Scarves, the first person takes a moment to see how they are feeling. Then they imagine they can fly and move around the room with the scarf in a way that shows how they are feeling. **Variation:** Other group members follow, mirroring the same movements (and sounds if appropriate) with their scarves.

21. **Flying Pilots of Feelings** The children are asked to think about how they feel in the moment and then fly a pretend airplane that shows and sounds like how they feel (can also do aerobatics). **Variation: a) Integrate Dancing Scarves;** and **b) Group Members Mirror** lead pilot.

22. **Fragrance or Smell:** If you could be any fragrance or smell what would you be at this moment?

23. **Flower:** Take a moment to quietly go inside of yourself and think about how you are feeling at this very moment. If that feeling could turn into a flower, what flower would you be?

24. **Hands:** Close you eyes and be still. Say "hello" with your hands to the group. What are you feeling? Express that feeling with your hands (sadness, happiness, compassion, anger, etc.), and name the feeling, if you are willing.

25. **Insect:** Take a moment to quietly go inside of yourself and think about how you are feeling at this very moment. If that feeling could turn into an insect, what kind of insect would you be?

26. **Inside My House:** "Go inside your body and see how you are feeling in this moment. If you were to place your emotional feeling state inside an imaginary house, where would you find yourself in that house?"

27. **Inside Weather Scoop:** If you could take how you are feeling right now and turn it into weather, what kind of weather would you be?

28. **Invisible Paints:** In any position you choose, imagine you are painting a picture of yourself and how you feel right now. Use a variety of movements, motions, strokes, from large to small to express your feelings. **Variation**: Can also be integrated with the **Air Frame Portraits.**

29. **Land, Air or Sea Creatures:** Imagine you are a living thing that best represents how you feel right now. What are you and where are you most comfortable right now—on the land, air or in the sea?

30. **Machine**: If you could be any kind of machine, which machine would represent how you feel in this moment?

31. **Magical Feeling Fairies:** If you could be a Magic Feeling Fairy representing a particular feeling you have today which Feeling Fairy would you be? (i.e. The Mad Fairy, The Sad Fairy, The Confused Fairy, etc.).

32. **Musical instrument:** Which musical instrument would best help you to express what you are feeling right now?

33. **Name/Movement Mirroring:** Say your name with a movement that expresses how you feel.

34. **Native American Names**: Think of a color that describes how you are feeling right now. Next think of an animal that represents how you are feeling. Now say your name, the color, and then the animal. Example: *Emily Red Eagle.*

35. **Natural Environment:** Be still and imagine yourself in a natural environment that reflects how you are feeling right now. Name or describe that place in nature.

36. **Precious Stone:** As you do a feeling check inside, what precious stone best describes you in this very moment?

37. **Song:** Going inside of yourself, take a moment to see how you are feeling. Allow a song to percolate up that will express how you feel—you may also compose a new one in the moment.

38. **Sound:** While standing firmly on the ground let out a sound that expresses how you are feeling in the present moment.

39. **Snowman or Snowwoman:** Sculpt and freeze a facial expression that represents how you feel right now. **Variation**: **a)** Include your whole body in the frozen sculpture; and **b)** if you have an undesirable feeling, allow it to melt away either from your face and/or your body.

40. **Steering Wheel of Feelings:** Remind children that it can be dangerous to drive a car if you are experiencing very strong feelings. But we are going to *pretend* to sit in the driver's seat and drive a car in a way that expresses our feelings in the moment.

41. **Texture**: Take a moment to quietly go inside of yourself and think about how you are feeling. If that feeling could have a texture, describe the texture you feel in this moment?

42. **Tools**: If you could be any kind of a tool, what would you be at this moment? (hammer, screwdriver, chisel, saw, mallet, wrench, sander, scraper, clamp, vise, etc.)

43. **Touchstones:** Provide a bag of colorful stones or glass globules. Invite each child to take a colored stone that represents how they feel right now; describe their feeling; and put the stone or globule in a clear bowl or glass brick in the center of the circle. This can be used each week so the group members can see the bowl fill up with their colorful and varied feelings. **Variation: a) Waterstone Vase:** if circumstances allow, fill the container with water ***Option:** At the end of the group, each participant could be provided with a small stone or a small scoop of the feelings stones/glass globules from the Waterstone bowl.

44. **Tree**: If you could take how you feel at this moment and be any kind of tree, what kind of tree would you be?

45. **Wikki Stix:** Colorful, wax-colored string called "Wikki Stix" can be sculpted to show how you are feeling in the moment. **Variations: a) Glitter Bend Bands:** Use the same way as Wikki Stix to make a shape to show how you feel right now. Great for attunements or as an activity in the 1st-3rd sessions; and **b) Group Sculpture:** Have the group members express their feelings using Wikki Stix or Glitter Bands and connect them all together to create a group sculpture. This can be used as a centerpiece decoration.

Suggested books for young children learning to identify feelings:

My Many Colored Days by Dr. Seuss. After reading, allow group participants to answer the question: "What are you feeling and what color is your day so far?" with movement and sound. Option: other group members may mirror the movement/sounds.

Today I Feel Silly & Other Moods That Make My Day by Jamie Lee Curtis. We all have moods that change each day. This book helps kids explore, identify, and even have fun with their ever-changing moods. Includes a **Fun Wheel** at the end of the book that kids can use to describe how they feel today.

Memory Attunements
About The Person Who Died

These Memory Attunements help group members focus on memories they may have of their person who died. We find these memory "triggers" to be useful in particular sessions—such as Unfinished Business or Commemoration, to help the participants get more in touch with the person who died prior to the session's core art activities.

- **Favorite Colors:** What was your special person's favorite color? If you do not know, what color might you think he or she liked the most and why?

- **Favorite Food:** What was your special person's favorite food/s to eat?

- **Favorite Memory:** Think of a favorite memory you have of your special person and share it.

- **Hobbies:** What kind of hobbies or activities did your special person like to do?

- **Music:** Think about your special person—do you remember what kind of music they enjoyed?

- **Musical Instrument:** Is there a particular instrument that your special person liked or knew how to play?

- **Smell:** Begin by talking about our powerful sense of smell and how certain smells remind us of someone. Think of a smell that reminds you of the person who died.

- **Something Silly:** Think of something really silly you remember about your special person.

- **Sounds:** What sound comes to mind when you think of your special person? Why?

- **Things They Taught You:** Think of one thing your special person taught you.

HEALS Centering Exercises

Imagination is more important than knowledge.
—Albert Einstein

Following deep expressive arts work, it is possible for some children to find themselves feeling as if they are "floating" and not ready to resume their day to day activities. It may be helpful to provide the children with centering exercises in order to assist them in returning into their bodies and feeling more anchored. The following are suggestions:

A. Acorn Sprouts: "Curl up on the floor and pretend you are an acorn planted below the surface of the earth. You can feel the soft soil on top of you being watered by the rain and then warmed by the sun, causing your nutshell to soften so it can move as you begin to expand, and to unfold and to grow towards the light. You slowly uncurl and move upwards, moving beyond your shell, stretching your branches towards the sky. Take a moment to see how good it feels to have your roots deeply digging into the earth while your branches are reaching towards the sun." (If possible, give each child an acorn to keep as a memento).

Variation: **a) Stomping Trees:** When it is time to leave the circle, playfully pull your root out of the earth and quietly "stomp" around to say goodbye to one another; and **b) Flower Blossoms:** "Curl up on the floor and pretend you are a little flower seed planted just below the surface of the earth. Feel the soft earth on top of you being sprinkled by water and then warmed by sunlight. Keeping your chin near your chest begin to push up from the earth, green shoots (arms) growing towards the bright spring sunshine. As you stretch upwards begin to unfold your leaves and slowly show your beautiful, smiling blossom (face) to take in the world. Take a moment to enjoy this feeling of being rooted in the earth while shining your flower of light into the world. Seque into the Closure Circle by having the "flowers" hold one another's leaves (hands) and send their smile or a buzzing bee around the flower garden.

B. Calm Lake Centering: Imagine a Calm Lake in the center of our circle. Let all your anger melt, sinking down into the lake, into the calmness for now. Take a few quiet, deep breaths until you feel the calmness saturate or fill your mind and body.

C. Chi Energy Field: Partner A stands rooted on the floor with his/her eyes closed while Partner B claps his/her hands together and rubs them briskly to develop Chi energy. As Partner B begins to separate his/her hands they become aware of an energy force growing between the palms of their hands. It will feel like Partner B is rolling a ball of energy between his/her hands…Partner B stays in touch with this power and then gradually turns his/her palms toward Partner A's body and, maintaining a distance of four inches, surrounds Partner A's body with this energy. Partner B concludes by placing his/her hands on Partner A's feet and firmly holding them to the ground as Partner A breathes deeply. Change places and repeat the exercise for Partner B.

D. Old Oak Tree Grounding (shorter version of Maple Tree): Each group member is reminded that they have a wealth of inner strength and wisdom, like a strong Oak tree with roots that go way down deeply into the earth. During stressful times they can remember to draw on this inner strength to calm and soothe them. Invite them to imagine themselves firmly planted in the earth and sending down their tap root until they feel firmly rooted. Take a few silent minutes to let the peace from their strength and wisdom travel upwards and permeate their entire body and mind.

E. Rooted Palm Passing: Sitting in a circle, have all participants put their palms together for a quiet moment. Have them visualize that they are a tree sending a tap root deep into the earth. When they are centered or rooted, a designated person, A, begins passing this centeredness by turning towards his/her neighbor, B, and touching open palms together as a way of honoring and sharing being rooted together. Partner B then turns and passes this on to the next person and on around the circle. **Roots of Love Variation**: All group members are asked to stand very quietly, feeling their feet supported by the floor. Imagine the body sending a root down deeply into the earth. When the signal is given, the children may touch their palms with the neighbors on either side of them and send this supportive and grounded energy around the circle and then out into the world (raise branches outwards and up).

F. The Grounding Exercise/Press Feet: Divide the participants into dyads and have them take turns grounding one another's feet by Partner A places his/her hands on Partner B's feet and firmly presses them to the ground as Partner B breathes deeply. Change places and repeat the exercise for Partner A.

G. The Sugar Maple: The participants stand with their feet shoulder-width apart, their elbows at their sides, and their hands reaching upward. (Pause until everyone is ready.) The facilitator now begins with the guided imagery: "Close your eyes and imagine that you are a 125-year-old sugar maple tree…you are growing in a vast open field of colorful wildflowers…you have weathered many seasons and seen many things…you are endowed with strong, sturdy branches…your leaves are healthy green, and full of sap…you reach toward the sun…and receive the sun's energy and power into your body…feel the energy from the sun's rays trickling down your arm branches and into the trunk of your being…know that what you receive is powerful and full of vitality…now bring your awareness to your feet…you have been rooted in the ground for a long time now… You are of the earth…you are below the earth and above the earth…your roots are many…they provide you with support and the rich resources from under the ground…potassium…nitrogen… phosphorus…and many other nutrients to feed you…many of these roots are thick and powerfully strong…anchoring you solidly into the earth…these roots are dense with singleness of purpose… to feed and to hold you….feel the anchoring of the roots…all the roots…the taproots…as well as the webbed, dense, matted roots…as they hold you firmly on the earth….the roots and the energy from the sun meet…in the center of your body…and you can feel the energy of these two powers join and intermingle…as they work together to create the force that enables you to continue to grow….bask in the warmth of the sun and the rootedness of the soil beneath your feet…know that you are here…you belong here…you are welcomed here…you may open your eyes knowing that you will continue to feel anchored and grounded like the 125-year-old tree."

You may transition to a closure circle from here by inviting the children to take their "branches" (arms) and hold onto their neighbor's "branches," then pass a soft "buzzing" of life energy force around and through the maple forest. **Winds of Change Variation:** Allow the wind to blow through your branches, gently swaying your trunk, knowing that you can move gently, bending and adapting to the Winds of Change, always staying rooted or grounded.

H. The Velvet Goose: Explain to the children how sometimes our feelings of grief can "ruffle" us, like we have imaginary feathers. To calm ourselves and bring us back to our "center" we can do things like smoothing The Velvet Goose with feathers.

Partner A stands in a fixed pose while Partner B uses a large feather to smooth out Partner A's imaginary ruffled feathers from head to toe. (*Partner B must ask permission from Partner A to do the "Smoothing.") Any child has a right to pass. Partner B begins by holding the large feather over "A's" head for a moment to allow the child time to become accustomed to Partner B's presence. Now Partner B imagines that Partner A's entire body is covered with velvety-soft, white, downy feathers which have become ruffled. These feathers need to be gently and tenderly smoothed down. Partner B slowly flicks the large feather about 2-3 inches away from the body beginning from the head and going down Partner A's body to the shoulders, back, and on down to the heels. Then Partner B smoothes the imaginary feathers along both sides of the body and the front of Partner A's body.

After Partner A's "feathers" have been smoothed into place, Partner B kneels down in front of Partner A, and again asks permission to touch Partner A's feet. If permission is granted, Partner B places his/her hands over Partner A's feet, and gently presses the feet into the earth. Partner B holds this pressure for a minute or so. Repeat on the back of the heels. Change roles and repeat this procedure for Partner B.

HEALS Circle Closures

A. Dancing Scarves Circle Sculpture: Divide the group into an inner circle (4 people) and an outer circle 6 people). Persons in the inner circle face out towards the outer circle. Have each person in the outer circle hold one corner of a scarf and connect the opposite corner with a person in the inner circle using the corner of a scarf. Have the group untangle itself until it forms a circle without letting go of the scarves.

B. Dancing Scarf Painting: Have each of the group members take their dancing scarves (or Magic Carpets) and create a collective painting on the floor—using the scarves as their paint. When each person is finished adding their scarf to the "painting" invite them to take a few moments to admire it from different angles.

C. Drumming Rhythms: The participants dance to a drum beat placing the soles of their bare feet solidly onto the surface of the floor.

D. Group Sound, Chant, Song or Hum: Holding hands in a circle, standing up or sitting down, make or sing a favorite sound, chant, song or hum. **Variations**: Each person gets to lead the group in their personal sound, chant, song, or hum. Be creative and let ideas just happen, such as the sound of machines, or instruments, food cooking, emotions, etc.

E. Hand Drum Circle: Have all group members get on their hands and knees facing the center of the circle. Each person places their hands on the either side of their neighbor's hands with palms on the ground. The leader then chooses which direction the Hand Drum will pass and taps the ground with one hand. The drum tap must continue round the circle of hands. This is very silly and confusing, requiring a lot of concentration to get it right. (It is also a great circle closure for kids who do not like to hold hands or touch others.)

F. Independent—Interdependent Parts: Create a large body sculpture with all participants. Each person takes a turn to pull away from the group and become an independent self, observing the whole, perhaps moving to their own beat, or creating an individual sculpture. When the individual person is ready, he or she reintegrates back into the larger sculpture.

G. Machine Sculpture: Create a machine sculpture by adding people one at a time who will perform a certain movement and sound for the machine. **Variation**: Have the machine break and recreate itself into a new machine with new movements and sounds.

H. Massaging Hands: Divide into dyads and have the children take turns giving one another very gentle hand massages. **Variations**: shoulders, head, feet.

I. Pass The Squeeze: Have the group hold hands while standing or sitting in a circle. One person is designated to squeeze the hand of the person next to him/her, to their left. The second person passes the squeeze to the person on their left and on down the line until the squeeze returns to the original person. **Variations: a) Pass the Squeeze With Eyes Closed** or when you receive it give a little Hop, a Sound, a Beep, or an Electric Jolt; and **b) Pass the Squeeze Using Pinky** fingers only.

J. Rhythm Band: The entire group makes rhythmic music together using a variety of instruments (i.e. small drums or other percussion instruments, shakers, rhythm sticks, rainsticks, two stones, hands and knees, spoons, pots and pans, or anything that makes sound).

K. Roots of Love: All group members are asked to stand very quietly, feeling their feet supported by the floor. Imagine their body sending a root down deeply into the earth. When the signal is given, they may touch their palms with the neighbors on either side of them and send this supportive and grounded energy around the circle and then out into the world (raise branches outwards and up).

L. Rope Sculpture: Have all members hold onto a rope in a line or circle. Create a sculpture keeping everyone connected together.

M. Soothing Rainstick: To calm and quiet a group, pass a rainstick around allowing each person to turn it over once while everyone listens to the comforting sounds of rain. Ask them to keep the quietness inside as long as they can. Request that they depart the group silently or using whisper voices.

N. Transformative Sculpture: Divide the group in half. Invite group one to create a sculpture. with their bodies. The members of group two then replace each individual in group one's sculpture.

O. We Are All Thumbody Special: Standing closely together in a circle, have each group member hold up their right thumbs in the center of the circle. Then have them turn their thumb horizontally to the left, slipping it inside the closed fingers of the neighbor to their left. Everyone says. "We are all Thumbody Special!" Witness the beauty of the pattern their clasped thumbs make together in the center. (From *Circle of Prevention*, CAPSG, Minneapolis, MN). **Variations: a) Pinky Squeeze:** Do the same as above using only the pinky fingers; **b) Pass the Thumb or Pinky Squeeze** with eyes closed, or when you receive it give a little Hop, a Sound, a Beep, or a Hum.

The HEALS Program

Sample Sessions & Curriculum

Session I: We Are Not Alone With Our Loss

Objectives & Learning Concepts

Objectives:

- To acknowledge each member in the group has experienced a loss.

- To give each child an opportunity to share the death of the significant person in their life and to determine if there are any areas of confusion or misunderstanding.

- To give children an opportunity to ask any questions or voice concerns that they may have difficulty understanding.

Learning Concepts:

1. To understand that change, loss, and death are a natural and inevitable part of life.

2. To learn that grief is a natural response to the loss of someone or something that provided meaning or attachment.

3. To understand that when someone dies the physical body stops working.

4. To learn about different losses and deaths children encounter in their lives (nature, pets, separation, divorce, etc.). Silence only deprives the children of the opportunity to understand, share, and accommodate their feelings of grief.

5. To help school age children recognize and validate their losses and learn new skills to cope with, release or express the intense feelings of grief.

6. To understand that significant losses (parental death, sibling death, divorce, etc.) are often "regrieved" over the lifespan and may be reactivated by minor loss events that provoke memories or by new developmental tasks or events that would have involved that which was lost.

7. To help educational staff and parents understand how important it is to respect a child's need for emotional safety and privacy.

8. To understand that children are teachers, too. Adults need to listen to children to discover what meaning the loss has and what meaning they attach to the event. Remember: It's okay not to have all the answers.

Sample Session I: Preschool/Kindergarten

～ We Are Not Alone With Our Loss ～

Materials: centerpiece, flowers, bears, pillows, markers, paper, kooshball/talking stick, Learning Agreement and Guidelines paper, and Book: <u>The Dead Bird</u> by Margaret Wise Brown.
*Note: Encourage children to bring a memento of the deceased.

I. Introduction of Facilitators, The HEALS Program, and the Children: Ask the children if they understand why we are all here in this group. (We have all come together because we have each experienced the death of someone important in our lives.) Talk about how many times we will be meeting and any other pertinent information they will need to know.

II. Name and Loss: Introduce the Kooshball or Talking Stick and instruct them to pass it around the circle and have each person say their name and who the person was that died. Play a *Rolling Names (see* Name Games).

III. Read The HEALS Learning Agreement together and create **The HEALS Rights** or group guidelines together.

IV. Session Activity:

    A. Read the story <u>The Dead Bird</u>.

    B. Discuss the story with the children. What happened to the guinea pig and the turtle?
    Teaching concepts: A change occurred, the animal's bodies died. Everything eventually dies or changes. People have feelings when death/change happens.

    C. Movement: Move like various animals/characters in the story (even when they died).

    D. Art: Draw a picture about the story of **<u>The Dead Bird</u>.**

V. Sharing Circle: Each child is invited to share their picture and tell the group a little about what they drew. See if any of the children have questions about death and dying.

VI. Closure: From a "tickle place" play with the hands on either side of you just being silly. End by holding hands and sending a gentle hand squeeze around the circle. Thank the children for sharing their experiences with the group.

Reminder: Bring something special next week that reminds you of the person who died to share and put ito the circle

Sample Session I: 1st-3rd Grade

∽ We Are Not Alone With Our Loss ∽

Materials: centerpiece, candle or flowers, bears, pillows, cray-pas or markers, drawing paper, kooshball, Learning Agreement and Group Guidelines posters, and book: <u>Lifetimes: A Beautiful Way to Explain Death to Children</u> by Byron Mellonie and Robert Ingpen.

***Note:** Encourage school counselors to remind children to bring a memento of the person who died before the group starts.

I. Introduction of Facilitators, The HEALS Program, and the Children: Ask the children if they understand why we are all here. Explain that we have all come together because we have each experienced the death of someone important in our lives. **Introduce kooshball** and instruct them to pass it around the circle and have each person say their name and who the person was that died.

II. Name Game and Movement Mirroring Attunement: Using the kooshball, have each person go around and say their name and make some kind of movement to go with their name. Have the whole group repeat the name and mirror the movement all together. *Always have an adult model first!

III. Read The HEALS Learning Agreement together and create **The HEALS Rights** or group guidelines together.

IV. Session Activity:

> **A. Read <u>Lifetimes: The Beautiful Way to Explain Death to Children</u>** by Byron Mellonie and Robert Ingpen (see bibliography).

> **B. Art As Expression:** Invite the children to gather art materials and paper and find a quiet place in the room to draw a picture or images that remind them of the person who died. *Some children may have been too young to remember or may never actually have met the person. (Like a missing father, or an older sibling that died before they were born). In such cases, encourage the children to draw symbols or objects that remind them of the person, or maybe what they have heard others say about the person. When the art project is finished have the group bring their artwork back to the circle

V. Sharing Circle: Each participant is invited to share their picture and tell the group a little about the significant person who died. If the child brought a memento they may also share that at this time.

Thank the group for sharing and listening to one another so well. Remind the children there are seven more sessions and that they may bring mementos to any session. Check to see if anyone has any questions.

VI. Pass The Squeeze Circle Closure: End by holding hands and sending a gentle hand squeeze around the circle. Thank the children for sharing their experiences with the group.

Sample Session I: 4th-6th Grade

～ We Are Not Alone With Our Loss ～

Materials: centerpiece, candle or flowers, bears, pillows, cray-pas or markers, paper, kooshball, journals, Learning Agreement and Group Guidelines posters, and a ball.

*Note: Encourage children to bring a memento of the person who died, such as a picture, a special object, or perhaps something that belonged to that person. Place the mementos in the center of the circle.

I. Introduction of Facilitators, The HEALS Program, and the Children: Ask the participants if they understand why we are all here. Explain that we have all come together because we have each experienced the death of someone important in our lives.

II. Name Game: Introduce the kooshball and instruct the children to pass it around the circle and have each person say their name and who the person was that died. (Some facilitators prefer to allow the children who have brought mementos to share them at this time, as they are usually very keen to share). Then have them all stand and play the **Ball Toss Name Game** (see *Name Games* in *Section III: The Creative Mind*).

III. Read The HEALS Learning Agreement together and create **The HEALS Rights** or group guidelines together.

IV. Draw A Loss/Images Session Activity: Invite the participants to gather art materials and paper and find a quiet place in the room to draw images that remind them of the person who died. Let the children know how much time they will have to draw and gently help them prepare to transition to the next part of the activity by notifying them when there are only a few minutes left to finish their drawings. When they finish, they may return their art materials to the table and return to the circle with their picture.

V. Sharing Time: Each participant is invited to share their picture and tell the group a little about the significant person who died. *May share mementos at this time. Allow time to query the students about any areas that seem fuzzy and need more clarity before beginning closure.

VI. Closure: From a "tickle place," play with the hands on either side of you just being silly. End by holding hands and sending a gentle hand squeeze around the circle with eyes closed. Thank the children for sharing their experiences with the group.

Reminder: Bring something special next week that reminds you of the person who died to share and put into the centerpiece.

Session I: Additional Activities

∼ We Are Not Alone With Our Loss ∼

A. Before and After Pictures: Draw a picture showing how your special person looked before and during their illness. Finish by Drawing how you would like to remember them.

B. Draw a Loss: Invite the children to gather art materials and paper and find a quiet place in the room to convey in clay or draw a picture or images or that remind them of the person who died. *Note: Some children may have been too young to remember or may never actually have met the person. (Like a missing father, or an older sibling that died before they were born). In such cases, encourage them to draw symbols or objects that remind them of the person, or maybe what they have heard others say about the person. When finished have the group bring their artwork back to the circle.

C. Draw a Picture of Life and a Picture of Death: Suggest that the children draw a picture of what their perception of life looks like on one side of a piece of drawing paper or their journal. Then ask the children to draw what they think death might look like on the reverse side of the page.

D. HEALS Puppet Theatre Production: Barney's Feelings: This puppet show was written as an introduction to the expressive arts to help children access what they are feeling in the present moment. The script tells about a bear whose grandfather has died and how this loss is impacting on his relationships as well as his physical and emotional well-being. (Also appropriate for *Session III: Feel The Feelings.*)

E. My Loss Story—An Autobiography: Write about all the losses you have experienced in your life, starting at the beginning and going up to the present. You may integrate art and drawings for the events or write feelings about the events.

F. My Timeline of Life and Losses: Draw a timeline as shown with your birth date at the left side and the present year on the right end. (*Note: It does not necessarily have to be a straight line across the page—it could meander or move in a spiral.)

Birth———————————————————————————————————Present

Add lines in between to mark each birthday. Write and/or draw as many big and small losses that you can remember. This can be drawn on a long narrow sheet of paper that you roll up and tie in a scroll for safe keeping.

G. Paper Chain of Events: On strips of paper write down all the important losses you can remember in your life. Then link them together to make a paper chain.

Suggested Books to Use for Session I:

The Dead Bird by Margaret Wise Brown. Read the story and follow with discussion. Teaching concepts: Death is final; Everything eventually dies; People have feelings when death/change happens.

Lifetimes: The Beautiful Way to Explain Death to Children by Byron Mellonie and Robert Ingpen. Describes the cycles of life, beginnings and endings in plants, insects, animals and people. A touching book with lovely illustrations.

Session II: Telling the Story

Objectives & Learning Concepts

Objective:

• To give each child in the group an opportunity to tell where they were when they first learned about their significant person's death, how they found out, and how they felt at that time.

Learning Concepts:

1. To understand that death is a loss that is final and irreversible.

2. *To learn that change is a part of life, and that everything that lives also dies or transforms.*

3. To help children learn that everyones' life is different, and each person will die at their own time.

4. To recognize that death is a natural part of a life cycle.

5. To distinguish that feelings of grief may seem hard to bear because they may be very intense.

6. To learn that the degree of the intensity and duration of grief is individual and varies from person to person.

7. To understand that sometimes death comes to young people and may be difficult to accept but most people live to be older than the children's grandparents.

Sample Session II: Preschool/Kindergarten

∼ Telling the Story ∼

Materials: centerpiece, flowers, bears, pillows, markers, drawing paper, koosh ball, Learning Agreement and Group Guidelines posters, drum, dancing scarves, *Draw A Loss Imaginary Journey*, soft music and tape player.

I. Introduction: Read the **HEALS Learning Agreement** and review the **Group Guidelines.** Allow time for each participant to share a memento if they brought one. Encourage children to bring a memento to a future session. Introduce **Today's Topic:** We will be exploring our losses and learning more about the people who died and sharing our experiences surrounding their deaths.

II. Animal Attunement: Think about how you are feeling right now—if you could turn that feeling into an animal, what animal would you be? Move like that animal.

III. Session Activity: Imaginary Journey Draw a Loss (See *Imaginary Journey Draw a Loss* at the end of this segment) Invite the children to each take a scarf and walk/move around the room while the drum taps softly. When the drum stops, the children are invited to find a place to spread their scarves and make themselves comfortable upon them. Playing soft music, lead the group in a *Draw A Loss Imaginary Journey*. (Have the paper and art materials set up beforehand).

IV. Sharing Time: Each participant is invited to share their picture and tell the group the story about how their important person died. Allow time to query the students about any areas that seem fuzzy and need more clarity.

V. The Velvet Goose Centering Exercise: Explain to the children how sometimes our feelings of grief can "ruffle" us, like we have imaginary feathers. To calm ourselves and bring us back to our "center" we can do things like smoothing *The Velvet Goose's* feathers (see *Centering Exercises* in *Section III: The Creative Mind*).

VI. Pass The Squeeze Circle Closure: End by holding hands and sending a gentle hand squeeze around the circle. Thank the children for sharing their experiences with the group.

*Reminder: Bring something special next week that reminds you of the person who died. You will be invited to share and put your treasure into the centerpiece.

Sample HEALS Session II: 1st-3rd Grade

⁓ Telling the Story ⁓

Materials: centerpiece, koosh ball, candle or flowers, bears, pillows, Learning Agreement and Group Guidelines, drum, music, markers, modeling clay and plates, writing paper or journals, pens/pencils soft music and tape player, and 10 acorns (optional).

I. Introduction: Read the **HEALS Learning Agreement** together and review the **HEALS Rights.** Allow time for each participant to share a "memory object" which reminds them of the person who died. **Today's Topic:** We will be exploring our losses and learning more about the people who died and sharing our experiences surrounding their deaths.

II. Attunement: Say "hello" with your hands to the group. Then close your eyes and be still. What are you feeling? Express the feeling with your hands and name the feeling(s) if you choose. Then pass the koosh ball to the person on your right.

III. Movement as Expression: Using the drum, we will explore some playful feelings to develop a movement vocabulary.

> **A. Walk**—Be aware of your own body and feelings as you find your own path.
> **B. Walk with dignity**. How does your body change?
> **C. Walk angrily**. Maybe even have a temper tantrum.
> **D. Skip**—Now find someone to skip with. Notice the changes.
> **E. Walk—Now touch shoulders with someone**. Did you initiate or receive the contact?
> **F. Walk to the beat of the drum again.** Find your own path through the room and imagine that you are afraid.
> **G. Walk as if you are searching for a baby deer** in the woods.
>   Shake out all the feelings, then select a scarf (Magic Carpet) and find a place in the room that you feel comfortable, and lie down upon your scarf.

IV. Session Activity: Magic Carpet Imaginary Journey (See *Magic Carpet **Imaginary Journeys, 1st-3rd Grade,*** at the end of this segment). Use the Magic Carpet Imaginary Journey (with soft music) to guide the children through some brief relaxation and quieting exercises. Invite the children to visualize many details of the time they learned of their special person's death. Allow each member of the group to take a moment to be with those memories and feelings and then gently guide them into the art activity using modeling clay to tell their stories.

> **—Art as Expression:** Modeling clay on trays or paper plates.

V. Sharing Circle: Each participant is invited to share their art and story about the important person or loved one who died.

VI. Acorn Sprouts Centering Exercise: "Curl up on the floor and pretend you are an acorn planted below the surface of the earth. You can feel the soft soil on top of you being watered by the rain and then warmed by the sun, causing your nutshell to soften so it can move as you to begin to expand, to unfold and grow toward the light. You slowly uncurl and move upward, moving beyond your shell, stretching your branches toward the sky. Take a moment to see how good it feels to have your roots digging deeply into the earth while your branches are reaching toward the sun."

VII. Closure: Invite the children to take their "branches" (arms) and hold onto their neighbor's "branches," then pass a soft "buzzing" of life energy around and through the maple forest. (If possible, give each child an acorn to keep as a souvenir).

* May remind children they may bring a memento to future sessions if they have not done so.

Sample HEALS Session II: 4th-6th Grade

∼ Telling the Story ∼

Materials: centerpiece, koosh ball, candle or flowers, HEALS Learning Agreement and Group Guidelines, bears, pillows, drum, scarves, music, markers, modeling clay and plates, writing paper or journals, and pens/pencils.

I. Introduction: Read the **HEALS Learning Agreement** together and review the **HEALS Rights**. Allow time for each participant to share a memento which reminds them of the person who died, if appropriate. **Today's Topic:** We will be exploring our losses and learning more about the people who died and sharing our experiences surrounding their deaths.

II. Inside My House Attunement: Go inside your body and see how you are feeling in this moment. If you were to place your emotional feeling state inside an imaginary house, where would you find yourself in that house?

III. Session Activity: Floating Clouds Imaginary Journey *(Floating Clouds **Imaginary Journey, 4th-6th grades, at the end of this segment).*** Using your own or our sample Imaginary Journey, guide the children through some brief relaxation and quieting exercises. Then have the participants visualize many of the details of the time they learned of their special person's death. Allow the children to take a moment to quietly be with those memories and feelings and then gently guide them into the art activity (prepared ahead of time).

—Art as Expression: Use plasticine modeling clay. If the children have time they may write the story in their journal or on paper provided.

IV. Sharing Circle: Each participant is invited to share their picture and the story of how their important person or loved one died.

V. The Sugar Maple Centering Exercise: Use this exercise (see *Centering Exercises in Section III: The Creative Mind*) to help ground the children. Invite the participants to breathe in the fresh air and sunshine to help them come back to their center and rootedness.

VI. Closure: Invite the children to take their branches (arms) and hold the person's branch next to them and pass a soft "buzzing" of the energy of life around and through the maple forest.

*Reminder: The children can bring something special next week that reminds them of the person who died to share and put into the centerpiece, if they have not done so.

Session II: Additional Activities

∼ Telling the Story ∼

A. Draw a Loss: (See *Draw A Loss Imaginary Journeys* in *Section III: The Creative Mind.*) Invite the children to each take a scarf and walk/move around the room while the drum taps softly. When the drum stops, they are invited to find a place to spread their scarves and make themselves comfortable lying on them. Playing soft music, lead them in a *Draw A Loss Imaginary Journey*. (Have the paper and art materials set up beforehand).

B. Flannel Board Stories: Using a flannel board to encourage the child to tell their story. Ideas for objects: clouds, lightening bolt, sun, moon, rainbow, large water (pond or ocean), trees, house, sky (large blue piece), grass, religious symbols, cross, church, building, flowers, casket, urn, songbooks, umbrella, people (lots, in variety of colors and sizes & ages), shovel, tables, chairs, food, boat, cars, airplane, ambulance, police, baby and baby blanket, etc.

C. Magic Carpet or Floating Clouds: Invite the children to select a colored scarf, spread it out like a picnic blanket, and lie down on the carpet or cloud. Following an imaginary journey to relax the body, suggest that the children allow their memories to go back to when they first learned about the death of their significant person. Then draw a picture of the memory showing where they were, who was in the memory, and all the colors and things they can remember. The children may share their story with the group if they choose.

D. Paper Chain of Events I: On strips of paper write down all the important losses you can remember in your life.

E. Paper Chain of Events II: On strips of paper write down the chain of events that led up to the death of the significant person, breaking the events down into steps in how they occurred. (i.e. 1. Mom is sick. 2. I am scared. 3. The doctor had to operate on Mom. 4. Grandma came to stay with Bobby and me. 5. Mom had to have treatments and she lost her hair. 6. Mom has to wear a mask when Bobby or I get sick, because we can make her sick, etc.).

F. Paper Chain of Events III: (good for early intervention in classrooms, too): Have group participants use one particular color such as purple to represent themselves. Then invite them all to use another color to represent their significant persons/animals. Link together and display.

G. Plasticine Clay with Movable People and/or Objects: This exercise is similar to the *Magic Carpet* except that the children choose a specific color of clay to represent each person involved in the story. Each individual may be realistically formed or a symbol may be used to represent the person (using a symbol is often easier for children in that it can be quickly done rather than laboring over body details).The clay pieces may be placed on a paper which is decorated to show where the story takes place. Invite the children to tell their story with the group.

H. Sandtray Storytelling: Fill a large, shallow tray with sand and have available a variety of miniature people, animals, buildings, trinkets, natural objects and anything that a child could use to set the stage for telling the story about the death. Then have group members travel to each sandtray to witness each child's story. **Variation**: Using a large variety natural objects *only* from nature, invite the children to create their stories in small individual sandtrays.

Session III: Grieving The Loss—Feeling The Feelings

Objectives & Learning Concepts

Objectives:

- To increase understanding of how people commonly feel and behave when someone or something they care about dies.

- To acknowledge that the feelings related to loss may be varied and difficult to have or to share.

Learning Concepts:

1. To understand that all people of all ages grieve.

2. To learn that when a loss is significant, children's grief may be more intense or troublesome because they will act out what they do not understand.

3. To examine how children express grief differently from adults—through their art and play, they are able to release their feelings.

4. To explore that there are physical as well as emotional responses to loss.

5. To realize that grief is a natural and necessary response to a significant loss event.

6. To provide opportunities to learn that grief is accompanied by many intense feelings that children, as well as adults, may think are sick, silly, or bad and may wish to deny or avoid. In themselves feelings are neither "good" nor "bad."

7. To understand that grief may be encouraged or invited, but not pushed or demanded. It is acceptable to "pass" on any activities suggested in this or any other session.

8. To comprehend that children can learn to express feelings in constructive ways. Refer to framework activities.

9. To examine that no two people experience a loss in exactly the same way or grieve at the same rate or length of time, even those grieving the same loss.

10. To understand that grief is love not wanting to let go.

11. To explore that when someone or something we love dies, we have many feelings, and often feel lost and confused, and that is normal.

Sample Session III: Preschool/Kindergarten

∽ Grieving The Loss—Feeling The Feelings ∽

Materials: centerpiece, flowers, bears, pillows, cray-pas or markers, paper, koosh ball, drum, large table lined with paper, HEALS Learning Agreement and Group Guidelines. puppets and puppet scripts for Barney's Feelings, and graffiti mural on table or floor.

I. Introduction: Remember Why We are Here Today: To talk about how we feel when someone we care about dies. Review the **HEALS Learning Agreement** and **Group Guidelines.** Introduction to **Today's Topic**: When a person close to us dies we may experience a lot of feelings. In today's session we will explore a variety of feelings.

II. Attunement: Read *My Many Colored Days* book by Dr. Seuss. Allow group participants to answer the question: "What are you feeling and what color is *your* day so far?" with movement and sound. Option: Others may mirror the movement/sounds.

III. Session Activity: Brainstorm Feelings Brainstorm on a write n' wipe board or poster board the feelings people often have when someone dies (sad, mad, lonely, confused, worried). Add any other feelings the children know (happy, surprised, wild). Then explain that we are going to have a puppet show about a little bear who is learning about loss and feelings.

IV. Barney's Feelings Puppet Show: (see *Barney's Feelings Puppet Show at the end of this segment*) Facilitators provide the Barney's Feelings Puppet Show which integrates movement, sound and graffiti art using the feelings that the group has brainstormed.

V. Sharing Circle: Ask the group members to tell about their experiences of the feelings:

    1. Which feeling was the most fun to move, sound, or draw?
    2. Which feeling was the hardest to move, sound, or draw?
    3. Which feeling was the scariest for you?
    4. Which feeling made you feel the best after you had moved, sounded, or drawn it?
    5. Of all the ways we expressed our feelings, which way did you like doing it the most— moving the feeling, making sounds or drawing the feeling?

VI. Pass The Squeeze Circle Closure: Pass the squeeze around the circle with your eyes closed.

Sample HEALS Session III: 1st-3rd Grade

∿ Grieving The Loss—Feeling The Feelings ∿

Materials: centerpiece, flowers, treasure box, koosh ball, pillows, HEALS Learning Agreement and Group Rights, recorded soft music, tape player, roll of paper, scissors, tape, cray-pas or markers, dancing scarves, and paper/posterboard Planets of Emotions (Angry Planet, Sad Planet, Happy Planet, Worried Planet, Planet of Surprise, Planet of Confusion).

I. Introductions: Review last two sessions. Review the **HEALS Learning Agreement** and **Group Guidelines.** Allow opportunity for participants to share with the group anything brought as a remembrance of their significant person who died. Introduce to **Today's Topic**: When a person close to us dies we may have a lot of feelings. In today's session we will explore a variety of feelings.

II. Color & Sound Attunement: In a standing position, say a color and let out a sound that depicts how you are feeling at this very moment. Allow the group to mirror it back to the sounder. Continue around the circle in this way.

III. Session Activity: Journey to Planets of Emotion Imaginary Journey *(see Journey to Planets of Emotion Imaginary Journey at the end of this segment)* Have each child choose a colored dancing scarf and find a special place somewhere in the room to spread it out and lie upon it. After a brief relaxation period, guide the participants on a **Journey to Planets of Emotion** that are specified with large pieces of paper laid out in various parts of the room:

Upon arrival to the first planet, the Planet of Confusion (or whatever feelings you choose), invite the children to explore and express their feelings of confusion through movement and sound reflecting a drumbeat that is full of confusion. Then invite the children to draw that feeling with a color(s) to express that particular emotion. Now shake out that feeling and journey along to the next Feeling Planet, again moving and sounding followed by art expression. Other Feeling Planets might include the Planet of Anger, the Planet of Sadness, the Planet of Wildness, the Quiet Planet, the Proud Planet, the Planet of Joy and Happiness, etc. **Variation:** You may want to allow the children to share a time when they felt that way while visiting each planet after the movement and drawing segments.

Allow time for the children to tell about their experiences on the Planets of Emotion. You might ask the following questions:

1. Which feeling was the most fun to move, sound, or draw?

2. Which feeling was the hardest to move, sound, or draw?

3. Which feeling was the scariest for you?

4. Which feeling made you feel the best after you had moved, sounded, or drawn it?

5. Which feeling did you prefer today?

6. Of all the ways we expressed our feelings, which way did you prefer the most—moving the feeling, making sounds or drawing the feeling?

When finished, invite the group to lie down once more on their Magic Carpets and guide them back to planet Earth. As the carpets gently land, invite the children to feel their bodies sink softly into the earth, allowing the earth to cuddle them as they lie there quietly on their Magic Carpet. Remind the children that the feelings they have just experienced are rich and varied and there are many, many more feelings, some that do not even have names. None of the feelings are considered good or bad. We may enjoy some more than others, but they all play their part in the rhythm of life. Through experimenting with lots of feelings, we can learn to travel in and out of them, almost like dancing with these feelings. We did that today with our Magic Carpets—we flew in and out of a variety of emotions.

When we lose someone or something we love we may feel many emotions, some briefly—others for longer periods. Each of us may experience these emotions in our own way and in our own time, because we are each unique and different and that is okay, even desirable.

IV. Centering Exercise: Have the children divide up into dyads. One person lies their Magic Carpet overlapping the other's magic carpet and both stand upon them. Together they step off the Magic Carpets onto the land and welcome one another back to earth. Asking permission first, they may take turns pressing one another's feet and heels into the earth.

V. Feelings Circle Closure: As the koosh ball is passed around the circle, each person names a color that represents how they are feeling in the moment. Has anyone's feeling color changed within the hour?

End with a Passing-The-Squeeze Circle with eyes closed.

* Remind them that they are welcomed to bring special objects or mementos of their special person to a future session if they have not done so.

**Inform the group that we will be working on creating Memory Boxes in Session 6 and suggest that they begin looking for a special box or a box will be provided.

Sample HEALS Session III: 4th-6th Grade

∼ Grieving The Loss—Feeling The Feelings ∼

Materials: centerpiece, flowers, treasure box, koosh ball, pillows, bears, HEALS Learning Agreement and Group Guidelines, drum, write 'n wipe board or poster board, markers, roll of paper for graffiti mural, tape, and dancing scarves.

I. Introductions: Review last session. Review the **HEALS Learning Agreement** and **Group Guidelines.** Allow opportunity for participants to share with the group anything brought as a remembrance of the person who died. Introduce **Today's Topic**: When a person close to us dies we may experience a lot of feelings. In today's session we will explore a variety of feelings.

II. Inside Weather Scoop Attunement: If you could take how you are feeling right now and turn it into weather, what kind of weather would you be?

III. Session Activity: Feeling The Feelings

1. **Brainstorm Feelings on Board:** Have the children brainstorm the variety of feelings humans experience when someone special or a pet dies.

2. **Feelings Costumes, Movement & Art:** Invite the group to create costumes for themselves using the dancing scarves. Practice the Freeze/Flow technique a few times using a drum (see *Group Facilitation Tips*) and have the children move when the drum beats and freeze in whatever position they are in when it stops.

Invite the group members to move and make sounds that belong with the feeling word being drummed. After about 30 seconds, have them freeze. Instruct them to go to the Graffiti mural and choose a color that represents that feeling for them and draw an image/images of that feeling. Allow 30 seconds. Have them return to the circle and shake off that feeling. Continue in the same way with the list of feeling words using movement and art. You may allow the kids to take turns leading with the drum. (This can be a very empowering experience for children to lead a group of peers and adults in this way.)

IV. Sharing Circle: Allow the children to reflect about their experiences with the feelings: You might ask the following questions:

1. Which feeling was the most fun to move, sound, or draw?
2. Which feeling was the hardest to move, sound, or draw?
3. Which feeling was the scariest for you?
4. Which feeling made you feel the best after you had moved, sounded, or drawn it?
5. Which feeling did you prefer today?
6. Of all the ways we expressed our feelings, which way did you prefer the most—moving the feeling, making sounds or drawing the feeling?

When we lose someone or something we love we may feel many emotions, some briefly—others for longer periods. Each of us may experience these emotions in our own way and in our own time because we are each unique and different and that is okay, even desirable.

V. Pass The Squeeze & Sound Closure: Pass the Circle Squeeze making a sound as it is passed from each person.

*Remind them that they are always welcomed to bring special objects or mementos of the deceased to any of our HEALS sessions.

**Inform the group that we will be working on a Memory Boxes and suggest that they begin looking for a special box (unless they are being provided by the facilitators).

Session III: Additional Activities

～ Grieving The Loss—Feeling The Feelings ～

A. Body Drawings: After drawing a full sized body of the child, allow them to color the picture. Then have them put band-aids on any areas where they hurt due to the loss. Have them write what the pain is about (can actually be written on the band-aid itself).

B. Ceremonial Dress—Now: Right now—in this moment—if you were celebrating the life of your significant person—how would you like to dress for yourself, for others, for the essential spirit of your loved one, or any other reason. This is your opportunity to design your costume to creatively express some aspect of yourself.

C. Clay Worry Beads: (Requires two sessions, variation requires one session) Provide the children with a variety of colors of oven-fired or air dry clay. Invite the children to roll them into little beads, and use a wooden skewer to make holes. Harden as directed on clay instructions. String the beads together to use as worry beads. **Variation:** Have a variety of beads (plastic, glass, clay) available for children to choose and string to keep as worry beads.

D. Colored Bubbles: After some gentle relaxation or breathing exercises, invite the children to imagine that they are surrounded by a bubble that is a specific color of light. Have them imagine what kinds of feelings they are experiencing while surrounded by that particular color. Invite the group draw or write those feelings. Do different colors affect them differently when they are surrounded by it? How?

E. Dyad Art Dialogues: Group the children into pairs. Provide each pair with one piece of paper and a couple of markers. Have one children in each dyad draw an image or mark on the paper and have the second child respond to it by drawing. Encourage the children to take turns making images on the paper in response to one another without talking. When they have taken turns about 4-5 times, invite them to stop and take part in a reflective discussion. Ask the children how they felt doing this exercise. How did it feel to lead? To respond? Did any other feelings come up? **Variation**: 1) **Feelings List:** Show a list of possible other feelings they may have experienced. (ie. frustration, compassion, anger, silliness, empathy, nervousness, confusion, etc.) 2) **Triads:** Try varying the number of children into groups of three.

F. Emotional Body Sculptures: Build a large body sculpture with all members of the group. Instruct the group to be a machine that moves and sounds a particular emotion (i.e. a machine of anger; a scared machine; a happy machine; a machine of confusion, etc.)

G. Feelings Costumes, Movement & Art: Invite the group to create costumes for themselves using the dancing scarves. Practice the Freeze/Flow technique a few times using a drum (see *Group Facilitation Tips*) and have the children move when the drum beats and freeze in whatever position they are in when it stops. Then invite the group members to move and make sounds that belong with the feeling word being drummed. After about 30 seconds, invite the children to freeze. Instruct the group to go to the Graffiti mural and choose a color that represents that feeling for them and draw an image/images of that feeling. Allow 30 seconds. Invite the children to return to the circle and shake off that feeling. Continue in the same way with the list of feeling words using movement and art. You may allow the children to take turns leading with the drum. (This can be a very empowering experience for children to lead a group of peers and adults in this way.)

H. Feelings Bingo Bear Game: Pass out the Feelings Bingo Bear cards (numbered 1-12), one to each player and a handful of bingo markers (glass floral stones, pebbles, beads, etc.). Everyone places a marker on their Free spot. The first player takes a single feeling card from the basket and reads it out loud. Everyone places a marker on that feeling on their Bingo Bear Cards. The person who chose the card then shares a short story of a time when they felt that way in their life. They then pass the basket to the next person. When someone gets five feelings in a row they shout Feelings Bingo! Most groups we have worked with love to fill their entire cards up, where many group members are all winning and there are no losers.

I. Feelings Cards: Using feeling cards, each person draws a card of their choice and shares a time when they felt that way. **Variation**: Go around the circle and allow all group members to share a time when they felt the feeling chosen—such as the feeling word that Jordan picked. (This can take a long time and should only be done in very small groups).

J. Graffiti Feelings Mural: Practice Freeze/Flow Technique with the drum first. Using a list of feelings that have been brainstormed by the group, invite the children to move to a specific feeling using the drum for about 30 seconds. When the drum stops they group may go to the Graffiti table covered with white paper and do a scribble drawing or image that expresses that feeling.

Possible emotions to move and "dialogue" could be:

1. worry   5. confusion

2. love   6. excitement

3. sadness   7. lonely

4. angry   8. happy

*See *Feelings List,* which follows in a few pages, for a wider variety of emotions.

K. HEALS Puppet Theatre Production: Barney's Feelings: This puppet show was written as an introduction to help young children explore feelings using the expressive arts. The story is about a bear whose grandfather has died and how this loss is affecting his relationship with his best friend, because he has so many feelings. (This is also appropriate for Session I for young children.)

L. Imaginary Journey to Planets of Emotions: (see *Imaginary Journeys* at the end of this *Section III: The Creative Mind.*)

M. Inside Me, Outside Me: Many times when we have experienced loss, we act in ways that don't match what we are feeling inside. Invite the children to draw a picture of their body as others see them on the outside. Then draw a picture showing how they really feel on the inside. **Variation:** Using paper plates, write or glue feelings that you show to the world on one side. On the other side, write or glue the feelings you prefer to keep to yourself.

N. Little Feeling Faces on Sticks: Using circles cut from heavy paper, draw expressions of a variety of feelings: a happy face, an angry face, a wild face, a confused face, etc. Glue or tape the faces to popsicle sticks or tongue depressors so that they can be used as puppets. These can be decorated if time permits. (Age 3-5 years)

O. Mask Making: 1. Plaster Cast of a child's face to be made and then later decorated to show how they feel. This requires a great deal of sensitivity and thoughtfulness before attempting with children. Best to consult someone who has used this particular technique.
2. Paper mache mask   3. Paper bags or plate masks

P. Movement as Expression: Ceremonial Dress—Then Invite the participants to remember the funeral or memorial ceremony for their significant person. Using clothing from a dress-up trunk, dress in a manner that portrays how you appeared/felt that day. Walk around the room to the beat of the drum allowing your body to communicate how you were feeling at that period in your life.

Q. Movement and Gibberish: To the beat of a drum, invite the children to walk around the room until the drum beat ends and find a partner. Suggest an emotional state which the dyad will "discuss" using gibberish to express that feeling for 15-20 seconds until the drumming stops. Then tap the chime to cleanse the space. Allow the drum to beat at a regular heartbeat pace between feelings. Great to combine with the Feelings Mural below! **Variation: 1) Soundless Gibberish** (do the same as in Gibberish using body language to express feelings but try it without sound. Then add sound again. Discuss how it feels both ways.

R. My Body—My Self: Draw a picture of your body. Suggest the children color in the areas of their body where they are storing feelings at this moment. A guided visualization may help them relax and feel into isolated body parts.

S. Scarves and Art: A variation on the above theme is to use scarves to move and express designated emotions. This may be done individually or in dyads to a drumbeat or music that expresses a variety of feelings. These same emotions may then be expressed in art.

T. The Poetic Artist Within: Create a poem about the feelings one experiences when one loses someone special.

U. 3-D Sculpture Project created with wood, clay, found objects, beads wire, etc. that conveys how the sculptor is feeling.

Other Ideas to Incorporate:

A. Also add Reflective Questions to stimulate discussions...
>Which feeling was the most fun to move, to sound, to draw?
>Which feeling was the hardest?
>Which feeling was the scariest?
>Which feeling did you prefer?
>Which of these feelings have you had about your loss?

B. Emotional Vocabulary List (See at the end of this segment)

C. Student Signs of Grief Checklist: A checklist that children read and mark off any feelings or behaviors that they identify with, particularly in relation to their loss. This allows children understand how the death of someone close to us can affect our feelings physically, emotionally and behaviorally. (See *Student Signs of Grief Checklist* in *Section II: The Heartbeat*.)

Suggested Books to Use for Session III:
These books are great to use with young children as the precursor to an attunement at the beginning of this session.

My Many Colored Days by Dr. Seuss. After reading, allow group participants to answer the question: "What are you feeling and what color is your day so far?" with movement and sound. Option: other group members may mirror the movement/sounds. (Pre-K)

Today I Feel Silly & Other Moods That Make My Day by Jamie Lee Curtis. We all have moods that change each day. This book helps kids explore, identify, and even have fun with their ever-changing moods. Includes a **Fun Wheel** at the end of the book that kids can use to describe how they feel today.

List of Feelings Vocabulary

Confused	Worried	Proud	Upset
Embarrassed	Scared	Sad	Satisfied
Confident	Joy	Peaceful	Bored
Angry	Hurt	Stressed	Pleased
Loving	Guilty	Mad	Shocked
Confused	Silly	Excited	Surprised
Frightened	Wild	Irritable	Anxious
Frustrated	Happy	Shy	Brave
Relaxed	Relieved	Safe	Calm
Centered	Terrible	Lonely	Ignored
Disappointed	Nervous	Crazy	Capable
Important	Curious	Apologetic	Bashful
Aggressive	Glad	Enraged	Crabby
Determined	Awful	Balanced	Amazed

Sample Feelings Planets List

Planet of Confusion

Planet of Worry

Planet of Proud

Planet of Embarrassment

The Scared Planet

Planet of Boredom

Planet of Sadness

The Confident Planet

Planet of Joy

Planet of Peace

Planet of Anger

Planet of Hurt

Planet of Love

The Happy Planet

Planet of Guilt

Planet of Mad

The Lonely Planet

Planet of Wildness

My Feelings

Booklet

by _____

The HEALS Program

163

This is how I felt when _____
died:

This is Me...I am O.K. however
I am feeling!

This is how I look when I feel:

silly

happy

This is how I look when I feel:

afraid

confused

This is how I look when I feel:

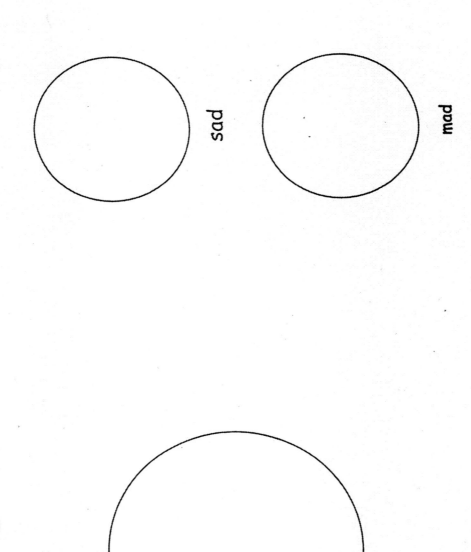

sad

mad

This is how I feel right now:

Session IV: Taming The Wild Things

Objectives & Learning Concepts

Objectives:

• To understand that anger and other intense emotions such as guilt, jealousy, and fear are natural responses when we lose someone or something special.

• To learn how to recognize early warning signs of uncomfortable emotions before they get out of control.

• To safely and creatively access and express anger and other uncomfortable feelings.

Learning Concepts:

1. To learn that anger or fear are natural responses when we feel our, or someone else's, mental, physical or spiritual well-being is threatened.

2. To understand that uncomfortable feelings serve as signals that can alert us when something does not feel right.

3. To realize that pent-up or unacknowledged anger, fear, or worry can turn into depression, illness, or rage.

4. To understand that there are specific signs and symptoms that help us recognize the different levels of anger or discomfort in other people, and about our own potential reactions to them.

5. To learn that anger has three main and immediate pathways out of the body: the mouth, the arms/hands, and the legs/feet. Like releasing the valve on a pressure cooker, it is important to find creative and safe ways to release anger and other intense emotions.

6. To acknowledge that when loss is experienced we may be unaware of how that loss affects our lives.

7. To understand that underneath our anger is often a deep sadness about something we feel should or should not have happened.

8. To realize that it is not okay to hurt yourself, someone else, or other people's property.

9. To learn that we can make choices to *respond* rather than *react* or to any situation.

167

10. To understand that anger, and other difficult feelings, are generally not the problem—it is how we handle those feelings.

11. To realize that we are all responsible for our behaviors.

12. To distinguish that there are different ranges of anger on a continuum and words to describe and express them.

Sample Session IV: Preschool/Kindergarten

~ Taming The Wild Things ~

Materials: centerpiece, flowers, bears, pillows, colored pencils, crayons or markers, paper, kooshball, HEALS Learning Agreement and Group Guidelines, *When Sophie Gets Angry—Really, Really Angry* book by Molly Bang, drum, art materials for angry art.

I. Introduction: Review the **HEALS Learning Agreement** and **Group Guidelines.** *Allow time for each participant to share a memento if they brought one. **Today's Topic**: Dealing with some of the more difficult feelings we sometimes have when we experience loss or change.

II. Inside Weather Scoop Attunement: If you could take how you are feeling right now and turn it into weather, what kind of weather would you be?

III. Session Activity:

> **A. Read *When Sophie Gets Angry—Really, Really Angry* book.**
> **Questions**: What did Sophie do when she got angry? What did Sophie do to help herself feel better? (ran, cried, climbed favorite tree, felt the breeze in her hair, watched the waves, let nature comfort her)

> **B. Talk about the Pathways of Anger.** Discussion questions: "What do you do when *you* get angry?" "What kinds of things do you do that help you to feel better?"

> "It is natural to feel angry when someone dies or we lose something important to us. But it is important that we learn **safe** ways to cope with those feelings, like Sophie did, or like some of the things group members have mentioned. Each of us needs to find the ways that work best for ourselves—because we are all different."

> **C. Practice Safe Anger Release:** angry drumming, angry dancing, angry art,
> *Mention that it is always best to find someone to *talk* with about your feelings.

IV. Sharing Time: Talk about how it felt to do the angry release activities. Explore what they can do at home when they get angry.

V. Flower Blossoms Centering Exercise: "Curl up on the floor and pretend you are a little flower seed planted just below the surface of the earth. Feel the soft earth on top of you being sprinkled by water and then warmed by sunlight. Keeping your chin near your chest begin to push up from the earth, green shoots (arms) growing towards the bright spring sunshine. As you stretch upwards begin to unfold your leaves and slowly show your beautiful, smiling blossom (face) to take in the world. Take a moment to enjoy this feeling of being rooted in the earth while shining your flower of light into the world. Seque into the **Closure Circle** by having the "flowers" hold one another's leaves and send their smile or a buzzing bee around the flower garden.

Sample Session IV: 1st-3rd Grade

∽ Taming The Wild Things ∽

Materials: centerpiece, flowers, bears, pillows, markers, paper, koosh ball, HEALS Learning Agreement and Group Guidelines, Barney's Anger Puppet Show script, puppets, legos, drum, drawing paper, large feathers, marshmallows in a basket.

I. Introduction: Review the last session. Review the **HEALS Learning Agreement** and **Group Guidelines.** Allow a few moments for sharing any mementos. Introduce **Today's Topic:** Dealing with some of the more difficult feelings we sometimes have when we experience loss or change.

II. Feelings Flavors Attunement: Share a flavor or taste that best describes what you are feeling in this moment.

III. HEALS Theatre Production "Barney's Anger:" (See *"Barney's Anger"* puppet show in this *Section IV* on *Puppetry*.) "It is natural to feel angry when someone dies or we lose something important to us. But it is important that we learn **safe** ways of coping with those feelings, like Barney did, or like some of the things group members have mentioned. Each of us needs to find the ways that work best for ourselves— because we are all different."

> **A.** Talk about the **Pathways of Anger.** Discussion question: "What do you do when *you* get angry?"
>
> **B. Safe Anger Release**—angry drumming and sounding & a *Marshmallow Fling Dance.* (See *Session IV: Additional Activities.*)

IV. Sharing Circle: Encourage the children to talk about how it feels to express their anger and what kinds of things they do to help them feel better?

V. The Velvet Goose Centering Exercise: (See *Centering Exercises, Velvet Goose,* in first part of *Section III: The Creative Mind.*)

VI. Pass The Squeeze Circle Closing: Pass the squeeze and give a little hop when you receive it.

*Reminders: In two weeks, at Session VI, we will be making Memory Boxes to commemorate our loved ones. If you have a special box you would like to use—please bring it in the next few sessions. We will also have boxes available.

Sample Session IV: 4th-6th Grade

∼ Taming The Wild Things ∼

Materials: centerpiece, flowers, bears, pillows, markers, paper, koosh ball, HEALS Learning Agreement and Group Guidelines, Pathways of Anger Poster (optional), paper plates and collage materials, glue

I. Introduction: Review the last session. Review the **HEALS Learning Agreement** and **Group Guidelines.** Allow a few moments for sharing any mementos brought. Introduce **Today's Topic**: Dealing with some of the more difficult feelings we sometimes have when we experience loss or change.

II. Body of Water Attunement: What body of water depicts what you are feeling in the present moment? It can be any form of water and can include sounds and movement and be mirrored by the group.

III. Session Activity: Invite the children to go around the circle and share where they feel anger in their bodies. (When they get angry, what is the first reaction their body wants to make?)

> A. Share **Pathways of Anger** (using poster, optional)
> B. **Masks of Anger:** Use paper plates and a variety of art materials to make angry or ugly masks.

IV. Sharing Circle: Share masks and brainstorm safe things to do when we get angry.

V. Centering Exercise: Hand Drum Circle—Have all group members get on their hands and knees facing the center of the circle. Each person places their hands on the either side of their neighbor's hands with palms on the ground. The leader then chooses which direction the Hand Drum will pass and taps the ground with one hand. The drum tap must continue round the circle of hands. This is very silly and confusing, requiring a lot of concentration to get it right. (It is also a great circle closure for kids who do not like to hold hands or touch others.)

VI. Closing: Silent Circle Squeeze pass with eyes closed. Silently leave the room…

*Reminders: In two weeks, at Session VI, we will be making Memory Boxes to commemorate our loved ones. If you have a special box you would like to use—please bring it in the next few sessions. We will also have boxes available.

Session IV: Additional Activities

～ Taming The Wild Things ～

A. Angry Art: Connect with any feelings of anger or frustration that have occurred since the death of the significant person. Express this in a three-dimensional clay sculpture with nails, wire, stones, twigs, etc.. **Option:** Invite the participants to allow the Angry Art to express itself through their writing.

B. Blowing Off Energy Balloons: Write or draw any uncomfortable or scary feelings you may be experiencing on a small piece of paper. Roll up the paper and insert into balloon. Blow all those feelings into the balloon and then release the air. (Environmentally friendly.)

C. Chaos Rhythms: Using the Chaos segment of Gabrielle Roth's *Initiation* tape allow the children to move their bodies to express the wildness of the music and to feel into and release their own feelings of chaos and frustration.

D. Feelings Bubbles: (Outdoors) Each child gets a bottle of bubbles and are instructed to think about anything that makes them mad, nervous, anxious etc. Have them say what it is they are releasing such as, "I am blowing out *the fear*" or "I am blowing out *the anger*" and blow it into a bubble, and watch it float away.

E. HEALS Puppet Theatre: Barney's Anger: (See *Section IV: Creative Mind, Puppetry*.)

F. Inside Me/Outside Me: Using lunch bags, glue feelings that you show to the world. On the inside glue the feelings you prefer to keep to yourself.

G. Jam Session: Allow the children to select a percussion instrument and to make "angry music" to express their own feelings of anger. After a while, encourage them to listen to each other and allow their anger to "dialogue" with the group or with one or two other group members.

H. I'm All Shook Up!: Make angry shakers from small containers filled with beads, seeds, rice, etc. Create a Shakin' Mad Band and dance together.

I. Make A "Wild Things" Box: Have each child make their own "Wild Things" Box using a shoe box, a paper towel cardboard tube and newspaper. (See directions for *Wild Things Box* at end of this segment).

J. Masks of Anger: Use paper plates and a variety of art materials to make angry or ugly masks.

K. Marshmallow Fling Dance: Allow the children to transform their anger by playfully dancing and throwing marshmallows at each other. In order for this to be safe, it is important that the children aim for only below the neck of other group members. **Note:** Only use soft, fresh marshmallows—not hard or sticky ones, and put some aside for the inevitable eating afterwards.

L. Nerf Balls Throw: Encourage them to throw Nerf balls at the wall or target saying the things that make them mad or frustrated.

M. Paper Towel Splat: Using wadded paper towels dipped in water, throw against a backboard or large wall. Messy Variation: dip the paper towels in paint and then throw.

N. Pathways of Anger: There are generally three main pathways in which the body releases anger. These pathways are: 1) The mouth 2) The hands and arms and 3) The legs and feet. Have group members identify which anger pathways they generally use by encouraging them to think about their knee-jerk reactions when they feel anger and frustration. Once the children have identified their dominant pathways, they can review a list of release activities that might be the most effective for their particular style. (See *Physically Releasing Anger Activities* in *Section I: The Backbone, Cautious Reflections on Anger.*)

O. Release through Recycling: There are several ways one can release anger that is actually helpful in preparing materials that are to be recycled: Stomp down old aluminum cans, old cardboard boxes, or plastic milk jugs. (Also drop or throw glass containers into the recycling bins and hear them "crash!") Shred and tear old paper or newspaper prior to recycling.

P. Ripped/Torn Art: Using torn paper from a physical release exercise, have the group members put together their pieces of paper using glue or tape to create a group collage or sculpture.

Q. Stress Balloons: Use heavy-duty, latex balloons for this activity. Attach a balloon to the mouth of a funnel and fill with any of the following fillers: salt, rice, flour, sand, beans, barley, peas, cornstarch or anything that is small enough. The texture of each filler gives the stress balloons their individual shape and feel. Inexpensive funnels can be made from a plastic water or soda bottle by cutting it off about two to three inches down from the neck. Once the balloon is full, slip it off the funnel and tie a knot in the end. Children of all ages love to make these and use to self-soothe when feeling nervous or tense. **Note:** Stress Balloons have a shelf life and may become quite fragile as the latex ages. Request children *not* to take them into classrooms in order to maintain good relations with the school, they can break and make quite a mess.

R. The Dance of Anger: Have the children move and dance out their anger to wild music or drumming.

S. The Explosive Machine: One person begins the human sculpture by repeating an angry sound and movement quietly. New sounds and movements are added by each participant who joins in. The angry machine escalates until it explodes. **Variation:** Use with musical instruments, pots and pans, etc. if you are in an environment where loud sound is not an issue.

T. Water Balloon Sploosh: Throw water balloons at an appropriate target or wall.

Suggested Books for Session V:

An Enchante Inner-Active Book: Exploring Anger by the Enchanted Family. CA: Enchante Publishing, 1994. Anger arises from a violation of what each of us think "should" and "should not" happen. This workbook encourages children to release anger and translate its energy into beauty and enthusiasm.

Painting The Fire: Exploring Anger by the Enchanted Family. CA: Enchante Books, 1994.

When Sophie Gets Angry—Really, Really Angry by Molly Bang. Questions: What did Sophie do when she got angry? What did Sophie do to help herself feel better? (ran, cried, climbed favorite tree, felt the breeze in her hair, watched the waves, let nature comfort her).

Sample Music for Session V:

Chaos on *Initiation* by Gabrielle Roth (or other discordant music),

1812 Overture by Tchaikovsky

Mars from *The Planets* by Gustav Holst

The Storm from *Canyon Suite* by Grofe

*Ask the children to bring in sample music that they feel expresses anger—check for appropriate language and content prior to using in group.

Session IV: Taming The Wild Things

Unraveling Anger Game

Goal: To have the group rank the following degrees of anger from the most mild to the most intense.

Directions: Cut out the word cards and distribute to group members. As a group have them lay them out beginning vertically with the most mild feeling on the bottom and the most intense feeling at the top.

Option: The group may also act out the words, demonstrating what a person might look and sound like if they were feeling that way, or share a time when they did feel that way!

MAD	ANNOYED	IRRITATED
MIFFED	TICKED OFF	RESENTFUL
BERSERK	ENRAGED	TESTY
GRUMPY	HOSTILE	TROUBLED
UPSET	CRANKY	FURIOUS
VICIOUS	IRATE	AGITATED
LIVID	GROUCHY	VIOLENT

IRRITATED	ANNOYED	MAD
RESENTFUL	TICKED OFF	MIFFED
TESTY	ENRAGED	BERSERK
TROUBLED	HOSTILE	GRUMPY
FURIOUS	CRANKY	UPSET
AGITATED	IRATE	VICIOUS
VIOLENT	GROUCHY	LIVID

Pathways of Anger Booklet

The HEALS Program

Safe ways to express anger with hands:

Draw a picture of the safe ways to express anger using your mouth that works *best* for you:

Safe ways to express anger with feet and legs:

Draw a picture of the safe ways to express anger with your feet that works *best* for you:

Draw a picture of safe ways to express anger with your hands that works *best* for you:

Safe ways to express anger through the mouth:

183

Pathways of Anger Booklet Sample

Safe ways to express anger with our hands.

throw snowballs   punch a pillow   tear paper

make an angry clay sculpture   hit a punching bag

write a letter   wad newspaper up and throw it

make an angry drawing   scribble   punch clay

Safe ways to express our anger with our feet and legs.

stomp feet outside   take a walk   kick a ball

jump rope   run   tap dance   ride your bike

skateboard   ride your scooter really fast   swing

dance   step on bubble wrap

Safe ways to express our anger with our mouth.

growl   scream into a pillow   cry

scrunch your mouth   make a "raspberry"

use a scream box   blow bubbles   sing loudly

speak gibberish   make sounds   yell

release slow, deep breaths out of our mouth

How to Make A

"Wild Things Box"

Children love Wild Thing Boxes for releasing loud and silly sounds when their energy is high or they are frustrated. The muffled sounds have the uncanny ability to make one laugh, transforming the energy in the child's emotional body into something lighter and more manageable. Be sure to encourage children to use the box to make sounds from their diaphragms rather than their throats so they do not strain their vocal chords. Demonstrate for them how to make sounds with the Wild Things Box that come from deeper within

Materials: shoe box, newspaper, cardboard tube (paper towel tubes), decorations such a contact paper, brightly colored scraps of paper or old wrapping paper, pictures or wild, ferocious beasts drawn or cut from magazines, or paint, tape, glue scissors.

.

1. Trace a circle the size of the tube on the end of the shoe box.

2. Cut out the circle and insert the tube halfway into the box.. You may secure it with tape.

3. Fill the box with wadded up newspaper.

4. Tape the lid to the box.

5. Wrap and decorate the box to express YOUR own Wild Things from within.

When I Get Really Mad Booklet

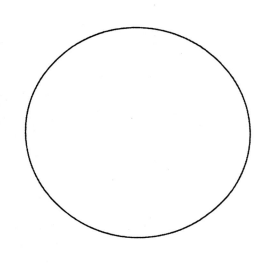

by _____

The HEALS Program

Just before I get mad, I first feel these things in my body:

I also feel these things in my mind:

Things I can say to others to
let them know I am feeling mad:

Things I can do for myself when I am
feeling mad:

Session V: Unfinished Business

Objectives & Learning Concepts

Objective:

• To provide the opportunity for each participant to express and complete any unfinished business they may have with the person who died.

Learning Concepts:

1. To understand the importance expressing feelings to loved ones, whenever possible, while they are alive.

2. To learn that as humans grow and change, the issues surrounding a particular loss may also change. The issues, regrets, and wishes of a 5-year-old child who has lost her mother, for example, will be different for her when she reaches the age of 12, 18, or 21 and on throughout the life cycle.

3. To explore that even though we may no longer see the deceased, it is still possible to communicate our thoughts and feelings to them.

4. To acknowledge that adults may overlook the bereavement needs of children due to their own intense feelings of grief.

5. To recognize that attending to unfinished business with a deceased person can deepen and enrich communication in other relationships.

6. To realize that holidays and birthdays may be difficult, and the re-emergence of intense grief is normal during these times.

Sample Session V: Preschool/Kindergarten

~ Farewell Rituals & Unfinished Business ~

Materials Needed: centerpiece, flowers, bears, pillows, HEALS Learning Agreement and Group Guidelines, cray-pas or markers, drawing paper, envelopes, koosh ball, Imaginary Journey, soft music, tape/CD player, dancing scarves, 10 acorns (optional).

I. Welcome & Introduction: Review the *Taming the Wild Things* Session—what do the children remember? Review **Learning Agreement** and **Group Guidelines.** Introduction to **Today's Topic:** Some of us have "unfinished business" or "wishes or regrets" after a person dies. Today is an opportunity to explore this incomplete work for ourselves.

II. Smell Attunement: Begin by talking about our sense of smell and how certain smells remind us of someone. Think of a smell that reminds you of the person who died and then invite each child to share their memory smell.

III. Session Activity: Imaginary Journey *Wishes & Regrets* (See *Imaginary Journeys—Wishes & Regrets, Pre-K, at the end this segment).* During the Imaginary Journey you will be inviting the participants to find a quiet place in the room to do some relaxation and explore some wishes or regrets they may have—to write or draw pictures of any wishes they may want to tell the special person who died. Let them know how much time they will have to draw. Gently help them prepare to transition to the next part of the activity by notifying them when there are only a few minutes left to finish their drawings. When they finish, they may return their art materials to the table and then go to the circle with their picture.

IV. Sharing Time: Each participant is invited to share their writing or drawings, if they choose.

V. Acorn Sprouts Centering Exercise: *"Curl up on the floor and pretend you are an acorn planted below the surface of the earth. You can feel the soft soil on top of you being watered by the rain and then warmed by the sun, causing your nutshell to soften so it can move as you to begin to expand, to unfold and grow towards the light. You slowly uncurl and move upwards, moving beyond your shell, stretching your branches toward the sky. Take a moment to see how good it feels to have your roots digging deeply into the earth while your branches are reaching toward the sun."* (If possible, give each child an acorn to keep as a memento).

VI. Hand Drum Circle Closure: Have all group members get on their hands and knees facing the center of the circle. Each person places their hands on the either side of their neighbor's hands with palms on the ground. The leader then chooses which direction the Hand Drum will pass and taps the ground with one hand. The drum tap must continue round the circle of hands. This is very silly and confusing, requiring a lot of concentration to get it right. (It is also a great circle closure for kids who do not like to hold hands or touch others.)

Sample Session V: 1st-3rd Grade

～ Farewell Rituals & Unfinished Business ～

Materials: centerpiece, flowers, bears, pillows, HEALS Learning Agreement and Group Guidelines, cray-pas or markers, paper, koosh ball, pencils and slips of paper, envelopes, Imaginary Journey: Changes in My Life, soft music, tape/CD player, dancing scarves, large feathers.

I. Welcome & Introduction: Review **HEALS Learning Agreement** and **Group Guidelines.** Introduction to **Today's Topic:** About changes and growth that they have experienced since their special person died, and things they wish their special person knew about them.

II. Memory Sound Attunement: Think of a sound that reminds you of the person who died.

III. Session Activity:

> **A. Imaginary Journey *Wishes & Regrets*** (See *Imaginary Journey Wishes & Regrets, Pre-3rd grade,* following this segment).
>
> **B. Writing:** Allow time to write about those wishes and or regrets on separate strips of paper. Now ask the children to select one of those pieces of unfinished business that has the most energy or power.
>
> **C. Art as Expression:** Ask each participant to gather together clay and clay tools. Invite the children to find a quiet place to sit and allow the clay to express what it wants to communicate to the significant person whom has died. Play soft, gentle music in the background. Allow 10-30 minutes depending on the age of the group and their attention span.
>
> About halfway into this claywork activity, quietly request that when the group members are finished with the clay they may get paper and pen and write whatever messages come from the clay. (Older students may be encouraged to use their non-dominant hand.) Provide envelopes for their writings, which may be sealed, if the participant does not intend to share their writing with the group. The participants may save their envelopes or released their wishes and regrets by one of the following methods with help from an adult: 1) Burning in a fireplace or campfire; 2) Releasing into a body of water such as a stream or ocean; or 3) Burying in the ground.

IV. Sharing Time: Allow time for sharing and witnessing the clay images. Some students may feel inclined to share their writing while others may choose to sacredly sit in silence. Either choice needs to be respected.

V. Soothing Rainstick Centering Exercise: To calm and quiet a group, pass a rainstick around allowing each person to turn it over once while everyone listens to the comforting sounds of rain.

Ask them to keep the quietness inside as long as they can. Request that they depart the group silently or use whisper voices.

VI. Roots of Love Closure: All group members are asked to stand very quietly, feeling their feet supported by the floor. Imagine their body sending a root down deeply into the earth. When the signal is given, they may touch their palms with the neighbors on either side of them and send this supportive and grounded energy around the circle and then out into the world (raise branches outwards and up).

Sample Session V: 4th-6th Grade

∼ Farewell Rituals & Unfinished Business ∼

Materials: centerpiece, flowers, bears, pillows, HEALS Learning Agreement and Group Guidelines, cray-pas or markers, paper, koosh ball, paper, envelopes, pens, Imaginary Journey Wishes & Regrets (4th-6th grade).

I. Introduction: Review last week and allow time for sharing special objects anyone may have brought. Review **HEALS Learning Agreement** and **Group Guidelines.** Introduction to **Today's Topic:** Some of us have "unfinished business" or "wishes or regrets" after a person dies. Today is an opportunity to explore any unfinished work or business for ourselves.

II. Smell Attunement: Think of a smell that reminds you of your special person that died.

III. Session Activity: Imaginary Journey of *Changes in My Life (See Imaginary Journeys Session of **Changes in My Life,** 4th-6th grades, at the end of this segment).* In this imaginary journey the children will be guided to think about the changes and growth that they have experienced since their special person died. They will be provided an opportunity to write or draw about things they wish their special person knew about them.

IV. Sharing Circle: Participants may share the changes they have experienced or things they wish they could say to the deceased.

V. Drumming Rhythms Centering Exercise: The participants dance to a drum beat placing the soles of their bare feet solidly onto the surface of the floor. **Variations**: 1) The entire group drums together using different instruments. 2) The entire group creates a "Jam Session" using any object that produces sound.

VI. Sound Band Circle Closure: Holding hands in a circle, standing up or sitting down, have each person go around the circle and create a sound. (Be creative and let ideas just happen, such as the sound of machines, or instruments, food cooking, emotions, etc.). Then pass a squeeze around the circle with a sound.

Session V: Additional Activities

∼ Farewell Rituals & Unfinished Business ∼

*Note About Guilty Feelings:
Some kids feel as if they are somehow responsible for the death of someone they loved or someone who is important to them because of something they did, didn't do or may have even thought. When we get angry or frustrated we might say things we really don't mean. Many children, teens and sometimes even adults, resort to "magical thinking"—they worry that there was something they could have done, and the person wouldn't have died. They need to be reassured that they did the best they could at the time and that words or thoughts do not make someone die.

A. Advice to Other People: Have the participants talk or write about the "Stupid things that people have said to me about this loss…"

B. Bubble Wishes: (Outdoors) Each participant receives a small bottle of bubbles. Have each one in turn think about any wishes they might have concerning their loss and then blow the wish into a bubble and releasing it. "I wish my dad hadn't died." (blow bubble away). Also, taking deep breaths are very helpful during times of stress.

C. Imaginary Journey of *Changes in My Life* (See Imaginary Journeys, Session V): In this imaginary journey the children will be guided to think about the changes and growth that they have experienced since their special person died. They will be provided an opportunity to write or draw things they wish their special person knew about them.

D. Imaginary Journey Wishes and Regrets: (See *Imaginary Journey on Wishes and Regrets at the end of Session V*). **Today's Topic:** To help the children express any Wishes or Regrets they may have surrounding the person who died. After a brief guided relaxation, the children are encouraged to write letters, poems or draw their wishes or regrets on paper to the person who died. Perhaps there are some things that they didn't have the opportunity to say before the death occurred. (See Imaginary *Unfinished Business Letter*) **Variation**: **Back to Nature:** Have the children write on pieces of bark or other objects from nature. Afterwards, the group can go for a walk in nature and decide where they will release their Wishes/Regrets (letting go in a stream, burying, burn in a fire pit, etc.). Upon releasing, the children may share how they felt about doing this activity or what they released.

E. Memory Stick: Tie notes and ribbons around a large stick that can be planted/placed somewhere special.

F. Regrets: Like the wishes idea, the children may write out their regrets onto strips of paper. These would be things that they said to the deceased that they now feel sad having said or things they did that they regret having done.

G. Wishes Strips: On strips of paper invite the children to write something they wish they would have said to the person who died or what they wish they had done with or for them. These messages may be saved in envelopes or released by burying, burning, letting it go into the air tied to an environmentally friendly balloon, or launching it into a body of water.

H. Worry/Wish Dolls: Using the tiny Guatemalan dolls that come either in the cloth bags or small wooden boxes, invite the children at the beginning of a session (or later in the session) to tell a worry or wish to the doll and then return it to the centerpiece. A child's ability to name their worries is a valuable healing aid. If possible, give each child a set of Worry Dolls to keep and use at home. At night, before they go to sleep, they may give a doll/s a worry and place it under their pillow.

I. Wreath of Wishes: Tie or stick notes, ribbons, special or sacred objects for the deceased person into a wreath. Hang somewhere special.

∾∾∾∾ Special Letter ∾∾∾∾

You may write a letter on this page to the person who died. It can be helpful to express things you wanted to say but never had the chance. It is okay to say whatever you want here, speaking from your heart.

Dear_____,

Session VI: Commemoration

Objectives & Learning Concepts

Objective:

• To provide the child with an opportunity to affirm the value of the deceased's life.

Learning Concepts:

- To explore and celebrate the gifts or "inner treasures" and the good memories that the deceased leave for us.

- To remember that, for some children, the qualities they appreciate about their special person who died may give them a sense of balance and an important legacy.

- To understand that following the death of a significant person certain holidays and anniversaries may be difficult. Having strategies in place to deal with these times will be helpful.

- To honor the unique qualities and interests of the deceased that made him or her special.

❧ Important Note:

Sometimes people in our lives may die and leave us with rather painful memories, particularly if they were abusive or violent. In such cases, the HEALS curriculum may need to be adjusted to allow for a participant to release some of the pain the person represents in their life. For this particular session, we encourage participants dealing with this issue to make **Treasure Boxes** rather than **Memory Boxes.** Inside, children can put special and beautiful objects and affirmations to help them feel good when they open their box.

Sample Session VI: Preschool/Kindergarten

∼ Commemoration ∼

Materials: centerpiece, flowers, bears, koosh ball, Learning Agreement and Group Guidelines, paper and pens, boxes to decorate, collage materials such as: glitter, gems, glue, sequins, small stones, fabric, colored contact paper, feathers, shells, etc., Imaginary Journey "Memory Box" script, Name Poem cards and pens/pencils (optional).

I. Introduction: Review the **HEALS Learning Agreement** and **Group Guidelines.** *Allow time for each participant to share a memento if they brought one. Introduce **Today's Topic**: Honoring the qualities and interests of your special person that made them unique.

II. Magical Feeling Fairies Attunement: If you could be a Magic Feeling Fairy representing a particular feeling you have today which Feeling Fairy would you be? (i.e. The Mad Fairy, The Sad Fairy, The Confused Fairy, etc.).

III. Session Activity:

    A. In Round Robin style, have each participant answer:

        What is Your Favorite Color?
        What was your special person's favorite color?

    B. Imaginary Journey "Memory Box:" (See *Imaginary Journeys: Commemoration at the end of this segment*).

    C. Name Poem Cards—have them available, if time allows, or children can put them in their Memory Box and have their family help them to complete at home).

IV. Sharing Circle: Allow anyone who would like to share their memory box with the group to do so.

V. Pass the Squeeze Closing Attunement: Pass the squeeze around the circle using **Pinky** fingers only.

*Remind the group that there are two more HEALS sessions left!

Sample Session VI: 1st-3rd Grade

∿ Commemoration ∿

Materials: centerpiece, flowers, bears, koosh ball, Learning Agreement and Group Guidelines, boxes to decorate, collage materials such as: glitter, gems, glue, sequins, small stones, fabric, colored contact paper, feathers, shells, etc., Name Poem Cards and pens/pencils.

I. Introduction: Review the **HEALS Learning Agreement** and **Group Guidelines.** *Allow time for each participant to share a memento if they brought one. Introduce **Today's Topic**: Honoring the qualities and interests of the special person that made them unique to us.

II. Animal Sound and Movement Attunement: Think about how you are feeling right now— if you could turn that feeling into an animal, what animal would you be? Show the group what sound and movement that feeling animal might make.

III. Session Activity:

   A. Hobbies: Have each group member share a hobby or something their special person enjoyed doing.

   B. Imaginary Journey "Memory Box": (See *Imaginary Journeys: Commemoration at the end of this segment*).

   C. Name Poem Cards—have them available, if time allows, or children can put them in their Memory Box and complete at home).

IV. Sharing Circle: Provide time for anyone who would like to share their Memory Box with the group to do so, or allow time to witness the beauty of everyone's creations.

V. Pass the Squeeze and make a **Beep! Closing Circle:** Pass the squeeze around the circle, when it comes to you, make a beep and pass the squeeze to your neighbor.

*Remind the group that there are two more HEALS sessions left!

Sample Session VI: 4th-6th Grade

∼ Commemoration ∼

Materials: centerpiece, flowers, bears, koosh ball, Learning Agreement and Group Guidelines, large poster board and markers, boxes to decorate, jars or containers for candles, 8 candles, collage materials such as: glitter, gems, glue, Tacky Glue, sequins, small stones, colored contact paper, tissue paper, shells, etc., Name Poem Cards and pens, and basket of objects to make sounds. Alternative: have the children make rolled beeswax candles and decorate them with cut-outs of colored beeswax decorations.

I. Introduction: Review the **HEALS Learning Agreement** and **Group Guidelines.** *Allow time for each participant to share a memento if they brought one. Introduce **Today's Topic**: Honoring the qualities and interests of the special person that made them unique to us while making a Memory Candle.

II. Feelings Hieroglyphics Attunement: Draw a symbol/hieroglyphic showing what you are feeling at this very moment using a marker on a poster board. Share the feeling and tell where it is in your body.

III. Session Activity:

> **A. In Round Robin style,** have each participant answer:
> What is your favorite music?
> What was your special person's favorite music?

> **B. Memory Candle:** This is a bottle, jar, or some sort of container that will hold a regular-sized candle. The container is decorated however the child chooses; and the candle is lit to remember the special person during holidays and other significant occasions.

> **C. Name Poem Cards,** optional, if time allows.

IV. Sharing Circle: Allow time for group members to share their candle holders and Name Poem
Cards.

V. Jam Session Closing Circle: Have each all members of the group use various objects that create sound and make music together.
*Remind the group that there are two more HEALS sessions left!

Session VI: Additional Activities

～ Commemoration ～

Note on Memory Attunements: It is helpful to have the group members go around the circle and share something unique or memorable about the person who died. A special Attunement or Imaginary Journey prior to any of the Commemoration activities will help them focus more deeply upon the person who died. Here are a few *Commemoration Attunement* samples:

- What **smell** reminds you of your special person?
- What was your **person's favorite smell** (or favorite color, food, activity/hobby)
- What is something your special person **taught you**?
- What **sound** reminds you of your special person?
- Tell us a **Favorite Memory** of your special person.
- Tell us **Something Silly** your special person did.

A. A Collection of Melodies: Certain songs remind us of people, places, and specific moments in time. You may want to bring together songs that remind you of your special person who died. Perhaps they could be put together on one tape and dedicated to your loved one.

B. Memory Box: Put into a box memories of the person who died. The child can write some of these memories on pieces of paper, make things to symbolize the memory, draw pictures, or anything else that has special meaning to you. The box may be decorated. **Variation: Mini Memory Boxes:** Make small boxes from greeting cards. They can be filled with little mementos, memories, poems, love.

C. Memory Candle: This is a bottle, jar, or some sort of container that will hold a regular-sized candle. The container is decorated however the child chooses; and the candle is lit to remember the special person during holidays and other significant occasions. **Alternative**: have the children make rolled beeswax candles and decorate them with cut-outs of colored beeswax decorations.

D. Memory Collage (add to Memory box activity—(use photographs and/or find and cut out pictures from magazines things that remind you of the person who died (i.e. favorite foods, hobbies, things they like to do, etc.). **Creative 3-D Collage Variation:** Put together pictures, objects, environments and symbols that reflect the qualities and essence of the person who died.

E. Memory Ornament: paste a photo of the person who died onto a Mini Memory Box, or in a small frame, attach a colorful ribbon, and use as an ornament.

F. Memory Scrapbook: Invite the child to assemble a scrapbook of the life of the person who died.

G. Name Poems: First step: the child writes their own name vertically. Second step: the child writes the significant person's name who died also vertically. Third step: the child describes the special qualities of each in a poetic form horizontally (as shown in the example):

D aring   **M** usical

A dventurous   **E** nergetic

N ice   **G** reat cook

When sharing Name Poems in the group, suggest that the participants share a few memories they have of their special person that reveal the qualities mentioned.

H. Name That Tune: If you were to make up the title of a song about the person who died—what would be the name of the song?

I. Rainbows of Memories: Make colorful rainbows from paper or fabric and have the children write their memories of the person who died on the strips of rainbow colors.

J. Timeline/Lifeline: Using photographs, drawings or magazine photos, create a timeline of your special person's life.

Name Poem

Favorite Color ————————

Favorite Food ————————

Favorite Music ————————

Hobbies ————————

Name Poem

Favorite Color ————————

Favorite Food ————————

Favorite Music ————————

Hobbies ————————

Name Poem

Favorite Color ————————

Favorite Food ————————

Favorite Music ————————

Hobbies ————————

Name Poem

Favorite Color ————————

Favorite Food ————————

Favorite Music ————————

Hobbies ————————

Session VII: The Jewels Within—Treasuring Ourselves

Objectives & Learning Concepts

Objective:

• To remind the children that they are strong and powerful—each unique in their own way—with wise and creative resources which can be called forth when needed.

Learning Concepts:

1. To understand that each of us possesses vast inner resources which may be tapped into when in the appropriate state of mind.

2. To learn how we are all connected with each other—as each of us improve the quality of our own lives, we concurrently improve the quality of life for everyone else.

3. To acknowledge that life is a series of changes—not all of them pleasant.

4. To realize that change provides an opportunity to learn skills that can strengthen us.

5. To understand that despite the impact of a loss that temporarily can cause us to perceive ourselves as cracked, broken, or splintered, we can simultaneously perceive ourselves as whole.

6. To know that life is a teacher that allows us to discover new parts of ourselves. When we experience loss, we may gain a greater insight into life.

7. To recognize that loss often leads us into a spiritual quest in an attempt to understand the nature of our journey through life.

8. To realize that death is a transition, or change, rather than an ending.

9. To understand that we are all very special people with talents, gifts, and treasures inside that we share with others and they share with us, enriching all our lives.

Session VII: Preschool/Kindergarten

∼ The Jewels Within—Treasuring Ourselves ∼

Materials: centerpiece, flowers, bears, koosh ball, Learning Agreement and Group Guidelines, drum, dancing scarves, basket of 8-12 smooth rocks/pebbles, one rough rock, acrylic paints and brushes, and newspaper.

I. Introduction: Review the **HEALS Learning Agreement** and **Group Guidelines.** *Allow time for each participant to share a memento if they brought one. Introduce **Today's Topic**: We are all very special people with talents, gifts and treasures inside that we share with others and they share with us, enriching all our lives.

II. Flighty Feelings Attunement: Using Dancing Scarves, one of the facilitators takes a moment to see how s/he is feeling. Then the children imagine, one at a time, they can fly and move around the room with the scarf in a way that shows how they are feeling. Other group members follow mirroring the same movements (and sounds if appropriate) with their scarves.

III. Session Activity:

    A. The Rock Ceremony: (See complete *Rock Ceremony* at the end of this section) Each child chooses a smooth pebble or rock from the stone basket and the facilitator explains the metaphor of the "tumbling" process we experience in life comparing a rough rock to a smooth stone.

    B. Painted Friendship Stones: All members of the group have a paintbrush and a small pot of colored paint. Children take turns painting their friend's stones with a stroke of their color. Let dry and save for the *Blessing of The Stones* part of the *Harvest Ceremony*.

IV. Sharing Circle: Move around to witness the beauty of all the painted Friendship Stones.

V. Roots of Love Closing Circle: All group members are asked to stand very quietly, feeling their feet supported by the floor. Imagine their body sending a root down deeply into the earth. When the signal is given, they may touch their palms with the neighbors on either side of them and send this supportive and grounded energy around the circle and then out into the world (raise branches outwards and up).

*Remind the group that next week will be our last session and we will need to say goodbye.

217

Session VII: 1st-3rd Grade

∼ The Jewels Within—Treasuring Ourselves ∼

Materials: centerpiece, flowers, bears, koosh ball, Learning Agreement and Group Guidelines, drum, Book: *Badger's Parting Gifts* by Susan Varley, clay and paper plates, Queen and King crowns (optional).

I. Introduction: Review the **HEALS Learning Agreement** and **Group Guidelines.** *Allow time for each participant to share a memento. Introduce **Today's Topic**: We are all very special people with talents, gifts and treasures inside that we share with others and they share with us, enriching all our lives.

II. Natural Environment Attunement: Be still and imagine yourself in a natural environment that reflects how you are feeling right now. Name or describe that place in nature.

III. Session Activity:

    A. Read *Badger's Parting Gifts*.

    B. Group Discussion of *Badger's Parting Gifts*: Talk about all the gifts Badger gave to his friends over his lifetime. Think of all the things you love to do and your special talents and interests. What is something you will be able to teach or pass on to another person one day?

    C. Queens and Kings Imaginary Journey (*see Queen and Kings Imaginary Journey at the end of this section*): Guide the children to become the Queens and Kings of a special Queendom or Kingdom. What would they do for or give to their loyal subjects to help them heal during a time of loss. Allow the children to express this in clay.

    (Option—have queen and king crowns that they can wear when they are sharing.)

IV. Sharing Circle: Allow the Queens and Kings to share their art forms and what they chose to give their people during a time of loss.

V. We Are All Thumbody Special Closing Circle: Standing closely together in a circle, have each group member hold up their right thumbs in the center of the circle. Then have them turn their thumb horizontally to the left, slipping it inside the closed fingers of the neighbor to their left. Everyone says. "We are each Thumbody Special!" Afterwards, witness the beauty of the pattern their clasped thumbs make together in the center.

*Remind the group that next week will be our last session and we will need to say goodbye.

Session VII: 4th-6th Grade

∼ The Jewels Within—Treasuring Ourselves ∼

Materials: centerpiece, flowers, bears, koosh ball, Learning Agreement and Group Guidelines, scarves, Gabrielle Roth's *Body Jazz* from Initiation, *River of Life Imaginary Journey* script, mystery bag of stones, tape/CD of Babbling Brook or other water music and tape/CD player.

I. Introduction: Review the **HEALS Learning Agreement** and **Group Guidelines.** *Allow time for each participant to share a memento if they brought one. Introduce **Today's Topic**: We are all very special people with talents, gifts and treasures inside that we share with others and they share with us, enriching all our lives.

II. Precious Stones Attunement: Take a moment to be still. What precious stone best describes you in this very moment?

III. Session Activity:

1. **Movement With Scarves** to Gabrielle Roth's *Body Jazz (On Initiation* CD)
2. **Imaginary Journey: River of Life**—have children select stones from a basket or a mystery bag. (use *Babbling Brook* tape or other water music for background)

IV. Sharing Circle: Share a memory of your special person that you carry with you.

V. Dancing Scarf Painting Centering Exercise: Have each of the group members take their dancing scarves (or Magic Carpets) create a collective painting on the floor—using the scarves as their paint colors. When each person is finished adding their scarf to the "painting" invite them to take a few moments to admire it from different angles.

VI. Pass a Circle Squeeze Closing Attunement: With eyes closed, pass a squeeze and send a **Beep!**

*Remind the group that next week will be our last session and we will need to say goodbye.

Session VII: Additional Activities

∼ The Jewels Within—Treasuring Ourselves ∼

A. Animal Medicine Cards: These beautiful Native American cards bearing pictures of animals may be turned over and mixed together. Invite each child to select a card and then read some highlights about that animal and its' special qualities, keeping the readings appropriate to their levels of understanding. Pictures of the animals may be used at the center of shields or Mandalas.

B. Badge of Honor: Create medals or badges that honor the participant's bravery in being able to try new things—even though they may be scary at first. (See *Section IV: Imaginary Journey: Badge of Honor*.)

C. Box Within A Box: Make little boxes within boxes to represent how we can allow for growth.

D. Circle of Me Mandalas: A mandala (or a circle) represents the self or wholeness. It can be used to draw how one feels, remembering that, even though we lose someone we love we may feel broken but in reality we are still a whole person. This wholeness is represented by the unbroken circle line of the mandala. Using pre-cut or printed circles, or circle stencils which the children can trace themselves, have them draw a picture(s) within the circle. It is very interesting to observe how their unconscious will lead the way when working with the boundary of the circle. Discussion of the symbolic meaning of Mandalas is not necessary prior to making them, but could be valuable when, or if, the children share their Mandalas with the group.

E. Create A Collage: Build something beautiful out of what the loss has brought to your life.

F. Dreamcatchers: Using brass rings, cut-out paperplates, willow branches, etc., weave dream-catchers. Explain the use of Dreamcatchers as protection. Great for discussing dreams they might have had of the person who died.

G. Dream Gift: Provide an Imaginary Journey where the deceased person has a gift for the child. Design an expressive arts activity to bring this into manifestation. Have the deceased bring the child a box, most beautifully wrapped, their idea of a perfect present. Guide the child to imagine unwrapping and opening the box to see what gift is inside waiting for them. Before sharing, invite the child to use art materials and paint, draw, or sculpt from clay what gift they received.

H. Magical Royal Messages: Have a piece of regular-sized paper for each child and at the top calligraphy or print their name with a Lord, Lady, or Sir in front of it. Remember to include the facilitators, too. Then beginning at the bottom of the paper, decorate the bottom section with something regal or whatever strikes your fancy and then put two paper clips one on each side of the bottom section. Each person begins with the paper that has his or her name on the top and then passes it to the person on their right who writes something they like about the person whose name is at the top of the paper, beginning just above the drawing at the bottom of the paper. When the children are finished, they fold the design at the bottom of the paper over what they have written, paper clip it securely, and pass it to the person on their right. The next person writes their nice comment just above where the paper clips are and then folds it one more time and secures the clips. This is continued until the paper is returned to the person whose name appears at the top of the Magical Royal Message.

I. My Own Image: Invite children to make small images of themselves that can arise from the box.

J. Name Boxes: Decorate little boxes that depict some kind of meaning of the children's names.

K. Name Collage: Each child puts their name on a large paper, decorating it in whatever way they choose (picture cut-outs, paint, marking pens, etc.). Have the child dance to their name or create a movement around the picture so all participants can dance to their name. **Let me Speak! Variation:** Use instruments to let the name speak.

L. Name Poems: Using each letter of your name, think of an adjective to describe yourself.

M. Painted Friendship Stones:. All members of the group have a paintbrush and a small pot of colored paint. Children take turns painting each friend's stone with a stroke of their color. Let dry and save for the *Blessing of The Stones* part of the *Harvest Ceremony*.

N. Palm Painting: Have the children divide up into pairs and massage one another's hands. Using poster paints invite each child to paint a design on their palm that symbolizes who they are. Then have them print it onto paper. **Variation**: 1) Palm Prints—Have each child print their Palm Print onto a large piece of paper, or onto Circle Puzzle pieces to create a group picture. 2) Palm Printed **Fabrics**—Have children put their printed palm onto fabric to make a circle centerpiece, flag, wall hanging, poster, tee shirt or pillow case.

O. Pass It On: Think about all your special qualities and talents. What kinds of things can you pass on to teach to another person?

P. Power Stone: Place stones of various shapes and sizes into a bag and then invite each child to feel around in the bag, without looking until they find the stone that feels just right when they hold it in their hand. The facilitator then asks for a child to volunteer to have special blessings put into their stone. The stone is then passed around the circle and as each child holds the stone, they put a special blessing into the stone. (This may be audible or inaudible.) Each child who wants to have their stone blessed by the group may have a turn. The child may wish to keep the stone in their pocket and if they are ever feeling low or lonely or nervous they may put their hand into their pocket and hold onto the happy blessings.

Q. Queens and Kings Imaginary Journey: Guide the children to become Queens and Kings of a special Queendom or Kingdom. What would they do for or give to their loyal subjects to help them heal during a time of loss? Allow the children to express this in some form of art such as clay. (Option—have Queen and King crowns for them to wear during sharing.)

R. Read *Badger's Parting Gifts* followed with a group discussion. Talk about all the gifts Badger gave to his friends over his lifetime. Think of all the things you love to do and your special talents and interests. What is something you will be able to teach or pass on to another person one day?

S. Seedlings for Life: To learn about the cycles of life and to affirm life—a seedling gift is given to each participant.

T. Shields: Shields are believed to have magical powers and are usually painted or decorated in accordance with the totem or vision dream of the owner. Native Americans believe shields provide protective powers or medicine to an individual, a tribe, or a family. The idea of shield-making could also be extended to the protection of our deceased, wherever they are now. Shields could be made out of natural materials found in the woods, collage materials, painted or drawn onto circular paper, board, or paper plates.

U. Tell Me What You Like About Yourself: In dyads, have the designated "questioner" ask their partner, "Tell me something you like about yourself." After the partner answers, the questioner repeats the question. Continue for at least 1 minute, and then have the partners reverse roles.

V. Ten Good Things About Me Booklet: This activity can be done following the reading of *The Tenth Good Thing About Barney* by Judith Viorst. After reading the story, have the children write or draw 10 good things about themselves in a small journal or booklet and share.

W. The Rock Ceremony: (See *Rock Ceremony* at the end of this section) Each child chooses a smooth pebble or rock from the stone basket and the facilitator explains the metaphor of the "tumbling" process we experience in life comparing a rough rock to a smooth stone.

X. Treasure Boxes: Using collage materials, magazine pictures, children's own photographs, things that represent them or are important to them to decorate the inside and outside of the box. This is a special place for the children to keep the treasures of their lives that come to them.

Y. Treasures in The Woods: Prior to taking the children on a walk into the woods, talk about a gift that their important person has symbolically left there for them, something that could be with them for the rest of their life. While walking, have the children be aware of going in and out of the dark parts of the woods. The moral of this experience is that the Dark Woods have treasures. Share with them the fact that they will receive many other gifts, and give to others as well.

Z. Unique Flowers: Have a different kind of flower that represents each member of the group. As you present the flower to each individual, share what special qualities that flower reminds you of that person.

Movement Activities

A. Animal Dance: Invite each child to pick an animal they would like to be in that moment. Have them pretend that their animal is wounded, and invite them to dance their way out of their wounds.

B. Dancing Our Qualities: Pick a topic from the following list and invite the children to explore a special quality they have or would like to have in their repertoire, and identify that quality with something from the chosen group, and name those qualities if possible (example: a tool in the garden; a fruit; a plant; a flower; a vegetable: an animal; a planet; a shape; a container; a body of water; a cloud; a precious stone; a fairy tale character or animal; a hero or heroine; a tree; a structure). Invite the children to draw, paint, or sculpt the image and colors of their quality. Follow this by having the children dance or move in whatever way this quality in them would move. If possible, allow some time for writing or journaling what has come. Another option would be to allow the group to mirror the qualities each participant chose.

C. Dancing Scarves Circle Sculpture: Divide the group into an inner circle and an outer circle. Persons in the inner circle face out towards the outer circle. Have each person in the outer circle hold one corner of a scarf and connect the opposite corner with a person in the inner circle using the corner of a scarf. Have the group untangle itself until it forms a circle without letting go of the scarves.

D. Dependent—Independent—Interdependent Parts: Create a large body sculpture with all participants. Each person takes a turn to pull away from the group and become an independent self, observing the whole, perhaps moving to their own beat, or creating an individual sculpture. When the individual person is ready, they reintegrate back into the larger sculpture.

E. Machine Sculpture: Create a machine sculpture by adding people one at a time who will perform a certain movement and sound for the machine. **Machine Reparation Variation:** Have the machine break and recreate itself into a new machine with new movements and sounds.

F. Rope Sculpture: Have all members hold onto a rope in a line or circle. Create a sculpture keeping everyone connected together.

The Rock Ceremony

Materials: a special bag containing polished rocks and one rough rock

Intent: To empower students and to open their awareness to some of the blessings and gifts that can accompany painful life experiences.

Activity: Taking the rough rock from the bag explain to the children (see following) how we all come onto this planet very similar to this rock. (Pass the rock around the group so each member has a chance to feel its roughness.)

> *"We are similar to rocks, because they begin as little chips of larger rocks, having lots of rough spots and edges that will later be smoothed out and polished by other rocks, the weather, water, course grit, and fine sand. This is called the "tumbling process."* (Show the polished stones and pass them around so each may have/hold one).

> *"Humans experience this same process as we are tumbled through life by one another, the knocks, the pain, the losses, the disappointments, and the hardships. Some of us will crack. But most of us will find that all the cracks, sharp edges, and rough spots are polished and we become creations of beauty. As humans we can bounce through our pain and losses to become all that we can be and fulfill our potential. And it is hard, and sometimes it hurts like crazy. But—oh, to be a beautiful, smooth stone!"*

> —Elisabeth Kübler-Ross

Have each child hold a polished stone in their hand and quietly think about the tumbling they have already experienced in their lives. The children may also be encouraged to think about the positive things they have learned through their tumbling experiences.

If time permits, allow the children to explore these ideas further by using some of the expressive arts: make a personal timeline of these tumbling experiences; draw or paint them; portray them in clay; enact them in a psychodrama; make sounds or music to them; write about them; share them with the group.

Dr. Elisabeth Kübler-Ross says very concisely, "Should you shield canyons from windstorms, you would never see the beauty of their carvings."

The Blessing of the Stones Ceremony

Materials: a Mystery Bag to hold enough smoothly tumbled stones for each person in the group to receive one. *May use Apache Tears (black obsidian formed into the shapes of tears by volcanic action) —very symbolic for the process of grief.

Intent: The following empowerment activity is designed to allow the participants in the group to give and receive positive affirmations and blessings by putting them into an individual's stone. The power of being blessed through this stone, by peers, provides a very special testimony and witness of each participant's value and worth as a human being. (Option: Can also be referred to as Good Luck Stones or Power Stones).

Blessing of the Stones Ceremony

Pass around the Mystery Bag of polished stones. One at a time, have each participant put their hand into the bag to feel the stones. Instruct the children to allow their hand to be guided to the stone in the bag that is meant just for them. When each child has connected to the right stone, he or she may take it out and keep it.

The following explanation is one example of how to introduce the Blessing of the Stones to their new owners:

> *"Now each of you has your very own special stone. Close your eyes and feel your stone. Feel the shape, the curves, the bumps, or any indentations. How does it make you feel? What is noticeable about your stone? Think about it's special qualities quietly to yourself for a moment.*
>
> *I invite you to open your eyes and look around at your friends in the circle and think about how special each person is. We are now going to pass each person's stone, one at a time, around our circle—allowing each person to bless that stone and empower it with a wish or positive comment about something you like about that person, or a wish for them."*

A facilitator models the blessing (ex. 'I bless this stone for you, Travis, with the wish that should you ever feel down, you will be able to hold this special stone, and remember how important your sense of humor is to me. Though you are a good friend and listen well, you have the ability to make people laugh. When I think of you—I smile.'"

Pass each individual stone around the circle until it returns to its rightful owner. It is okay to "pass" on this activity or put a silent blessing into the stone(s). Continue in this way until all the stones in the group have been blessed by everyone.

Session VIII: The Harvest Ceremony

Objectives & Learning Concepts

Objectives:

• To honor and witness all we have done during the HEALS sessions, individually and as a group.

• To remind the children that the techniques they learned in The HEALS Program may be used at any time in the future when their feelings need to be safely expressed.

• To receive permission to go on.

Learning Concepts:

1. To realize that though the pain following a death may be intense, there will come a time when it will lessen. Grief often comes to us in "waves" that wash over us and then recede.

2. To understand that the feelings that accompany the loss are universal. Everyone will experience loss as a natural part of the cycle of life.

3. To gain an understanding that it is okay to feel confused and not know the answers to everything.

4. To realize that to love someone new does not take away any of the love that we feel for the deceased person. Love is inexhaustible and limitless.

5. To learn about the process of grief.

6. To understand that griefwork does not have to be done alone.

7. To acknowledge there is great value in the experience of a closure ritual that helps each of the children feel they are special and important.

8. To learn many safe and creative ways to express feelings

Sample Session VIII: Preschool/Kindergarten

～ Harvest Ceremony ～

Materials: centerpiece, flowers, sword, crowns, bears, pillows, markers, camera, treasure box, memory boxes, folders, food (a special food, sparkling cider or juice in plastic, reusable champagne glasses), napkins, scrolled certificates, evaluations, pencils, and shopping bags for each child to take their artwork home.

I. Attunement: Share with the group what your favorite experience was in The HEALS Program. Have each participant think about a color that represents that experience, and share that with the group.

II. Session Activity: Honoring The Harvest: Allow time to review and honor where the children have been, the friends they have made and what they have done on their journey in The HEALS Program. (Have all the artwork, journals, and Memory Boxes displayed.)

> **A. Blessing of The Stones:** This activity is designed to allow the participants in the group to give and receive positive affirmations and blessings by putting them into an individual's stone. The power of being blessed through this stone, by peers, provides a very special testimony and witness of each participant's value and worth as a human being. (See *Blessing of The Stones* following in this segment under *Ceremonies*.)

> **B. The Crowning Ceremony:** The facilitators invite participants to come up, one at a time, to receive their scrolled certificate that officially gives them permission to continue to express themselves in safe and creative ways. Upon bended knee the children receive their scroll and are knighted and/or crowned Sir _____ or Lady _____ . Repeat this process until all the children are "knighted" or "crowned."

> **C. Feast** of juice and snacks

III. Evaluations (to be filled out by the children)

IV. Closure: * Remind the children that they can continue this work on their own. Encourage the children to find other adults and friends to talk with in the future.

> End with a ***Thumbody Special*** Squeeze Circle and a group hug.

Sample Session VIII: 1st-3rd Grade

～ Harvest Ceremony ～

Materials: centerpiece, flowers, matches, plastic sword, crowns, bears, pillows, markers, camera, treasure box, memory boxes, folders, candle and matches, food (a special food, sparkling cider or juice, cups, napkins, scrolled certificates, evaluations, pencils, and shopping bags for each child to take their artwork home.

I. Color Attunement: Take a quiet moment to see how you feel inside. If you could put that feeling into a color, what color would it be?

II. Honoring The Harvest: Allow time to review and honor where they have been and what they have done. (Have all the artwork, journals, and Memory Boxes displayed).

III. The Love-Light Ceremony: (see *Lovelight Ceremony*: *Individual Losses* at end of this segment).

IV. The Crowning Ceremony: The facilitators invite each participant to come up, one at a time, to receive their scrolled certificate that officially gives them permission to continue to express themselves in safe and creative ways. Upon bended knee the children receive their scroll and are knighted and/or crowned Sir _____ or Lady _____ . Repeat this process until all the children are "knighted" or "crowned."

V. Feast of juice and special snack of **Question Cookies**

VI. Evaluations (to be filled out by the children)

VII. Closure: *Remind the children that they can continue this work on their own, and that they can find other adults and friends to talk with in the future.

End with a **Hand Drum Circle** and a group hug.

Sample Session VIII: 4th-6th grade

∽ Harvest Ceremony ∽

Materials: centerpiece, flowers, matches, sword, crowns, bears, pillows, markers, camera, treasure box, memory boxes, folders, snack and sparkling cider, napkins, certificates, evaluations, pencils, magic sphere, and shopping bags for each child to take their artwork home.

*Have all the art projects the children have made placed on to the centerpiece of the circle.

I. Introduction: Review last session. Introduce **Today's Topic**—To honor and celebrate what we have done together and individually, to recognize the unending quality of life and love.

II. Color Attunement Take a quiet moment to see how you feel inside. If you could put that feeling into a color, what color would it be?

III. Session Activity: Honoring The Harvest: Allow time to review and honor where they have been and what they have done. (Have all the artwork, journals, and Memory Boxes displayed).

IV. Circle Puzzle: Following an Imaginary Journey, invite the participants to draw on the pieces of paper symbols and colors that represent themselves—but **do not reveal** that they all fit together to form a puzzle!

When all the pictures are drawn, lay them all out on the floor and have the participants witness them. Appeal to the curiosity of the group and ask them why they think the paper pieces are in such unusual shapes. Allow them to assemble the puzzle and enjoy their creation! (Tape puzzle pieces together on the back and display in the school, or allow each member to take their piece with them.)

V. The Crowning Ceremony: The facilitators invite each participant to come up, one at a time, to receive a wire star crown and to receive their scrolled **certificate** that officially gives them permission to continue to express themselves in safe and creative ways (handshake or hug, optional). Celebrate with **cookies and juice!**

VI. Evaluations (to be filled out by the children)

VII. Closure: * Remind the children that they can continue this work on their own, encourage them to find other adults and friends to talk with in the future.

End with Circle Closing of their choice and a group hug.

Session VIII: Additional Activities

∿ Harvest Ceremony ∿

A. Circle Puzzle: On a large piece of paper (3-5 ft. in diameter) make a circle and then draw enough free-form "puzzle pieces" to correspond to the number of group members. Cut out the individual pieces and mix them up so that they just look like unusual pieces of paper. Following a imaginary journey, invite the participants to draw on the pieces of paper, but don't let them know that they all fit together to form a puzzle. Important Note: Before the facilitator cuts apart the puzzle pieces—put an "x" on each piece. The children are instructed to decorate the side without the "x." If this is not done, the pieces will get turned and most likely will not fit together.

    1) **Individual Losses:** If each participant is grieving the loss of a different person, then there would be one puzzle piece for each participant. When all the pictures are drawn, lay them all out on the floor and have the participants witness them. Appeal to the curiosity of the group and ask them why they think the paper pieces are in such unusual shapes. Allow them to assemble the puzzle and enjoy their creation! (Tape together on the back and display or allow each member to take their piece with them.)

    2) **Group Loss:** If all of the participants are grieving the death of the same person, a puzzle piece representing the deceased could be in the center and each person then draws a symbol on their puzzle piece that represents a treasure they will always remember about this special person. Have the children assemble the puzzle when their drawings are complete and decide on a place of honor to hang the Circle Puzzle.

B. Crowns/Crowning: Make crowns and use these during a crowning ceremony to take the place of traditional graduation caps.

C. Dance of Life / Dance of Death: If expressive dance is something you enjoy or might like to explore, you may consider choreographing a dance that progresses through the cycles of life, culminating in death.

D. Knighting of Lords and Ladies: During the final session, the children can be knighted with a sword (plastic or metal replica) much like during the Medieval Ages. Boys especially seem to enjoy this ritual. Sometimes we invite the children to go into the best part of themselves and from that place write one very positive statement about each of the other members in the group. It is for this list of attributes that the child is then knighted.

E. My Dream Mural: Draw the outline of your body. Draw in the images of your dreams with colors and shapes.

F. Wands: A wand could be used to gently tap the children on their heads and then send them on their way into a life without their special person as they carry the knowledge that they are empowered to be their own person.

G. The Web: Using a "Web" (a long rope) invite all the participants to hold onto it with both hands, allowing for 5-10 inches between their right and left hand. Have the person with the end tie a knot in his/her piece and then cut it from the rest of the Web. Continue in this way until all members have a piece of "The Web".

H. Wise Owl's Advice: Use an owl puppet (or any other puppet) to ask the children what advice they would give to other grieving children who have experienced the death of a friend or family member.

Small Gift Ideas

A. Band-Aid for Your Heart: As a gift idea, give one of these to a person who is in grief with a small ribbon bow. "Even though we can't see it, we know that your heart is hurting."

B. Felt Heart Pins: Small felt hearts cut with pinking shears to symbolize the grieving heart.

C. Purple Hearts: (cut out from fleece) Given to the warriors of grief who are survivors of some of life's most painful moments.

D. Quality Cards: Give each child a set of Quality Cards printed on colored cardstock, or let them choose from a deck of cards and keep the quality card they have chosen. See sample at end of this segment.

E. Seedlings for Life: To learn about the cycles of life and to affirm life—a seedling gift is given to each participant.

F. Soft Feely Hearts: Small stuffed velvet or fleece hearts can be used like a worry stone in a pocket.

CREATIVE

Courage

A loving heart

Hope

Laughter

Strength

PATIENT

LOVEABLE

Sense of Humor

CAPABLE

CONFIDENT

PEACEFUL

239

Last Session Review Questions
Session VIII: The Harvest Ceremony

Our facilitators have been experimenting with a variety of fun ways to review and reflect upon the past seven sessions with the children. This is important both from the standpoint of helping the children remember the points along their journeys as well as helping facilitators evaluate what seems important from the children's perspectives. Remembering back eight weeks can seem like a very long time for children, especially if vacations, field trips and snow-days have stretched the sessions out, as they often do. Group members often find it valuable to have the facilitator briefly review what happened during each of the preceding 7 sessions. This helps the children remember where they have been—and for those who may have been absent to close the gap a little bit.

This review also helps prior to the children doing their post-group evaluations, reflecting on what they found helpful in their grieving process while participating in the HEALS group.

Harvest Questions can be integrated during the snacking part of the Harvest celebration. Depending upon time, each child may answer a question, or the group may discuss the question together or they may be baked inside a special *Harvest Cookie* (see below).

Harvest Questions

1. What has been your favorite experience in this group?
2. What did you like least about the group?
3. What one activity do you remember most from this group?
4. Tell something you learned about someone else's loved one.
5. What did you learn about feelings and grief?
6. What kinds of things might you keep in your memory box?
7. Where will you keep your Memory Box?
8. Is there anything you would like to add or change to this group?
9. How did this group help you with your loss?
10. Has this group helped make a difference in your understanding of grief? How?
11. Which feelings are not okay to have?
12. Would you ever want to be in a group like this again?
13. What are the Three Pathways of Anger?
14. Why did the group use a kooshball or talking stick?
15. Before you came to this HEALS group, was it difficult to talk about death? What about now?
16. Would you recommend this group to another child in grief? What would you tell them about the group?

Special Harvest Cookies

Print out questions appropriate for your group and the curriculum used. Cut into little strips of one question each. Fold each strip of paper very small and then wrap with aluminum foil, making sure to fold the seal well. Place wrapped question between two rounds of cookie dough and seal edges. Bake cookies. When serving, make sure to remind kids that these are special cookies and should be eaten Very Carefully!

One or more of the following ceremonies may be incorporated into the final HEALS session. As previously stated, these ideas are extended to you as suggestions to serve as a starting place from which to allow your own ideas to percolate.

The Love-Light Ceremony
(Single Memory Candle)

As a closure to the final HEALS support groups, we have found this ceremony to be a beautiful way to commemorate the passing of important people in our lives, while at the same time honoring ourselves. Rituals and ceremonies are wonderful ways to honor the past and then receive permission to journey into the future—being open to new possibilities. Taking the time to provide this enriching and nurturing experience also builds children's self-esteem as they are exposed to the idea that each of us is a unique and special human being worthy of loving and being loved.

Note: Most schools, for fire insurance reasons, do not allow the use of candles. Always seek permission to use candles in any public facility.

Materials: one large Memory Candle, a jug of water, and matches.

Love-Light Ceremony
The facilitator explains that the group will be participating in a special Love-Light Ceremony to honor those who have died. Discuss the important safety measures that need to be respected for this special candle ceremony.

The facilitator might begin the ceremony in this way:

"This special candle represents all the people in our lives who have died. While I light the candle, each person may quietly call out the names of the people who have died...(wait until all names have been called, then proceed...).

...When each of you were born you came with a very special gift—the gift to give love and receive love. This gift is like a light; it makes you feel warm and happy. We call it our Love-Light.

First you got used to your Mom, being inside of her and then outside. She probably cuddled you and fed you. You felt close to her. You lighted a Love-Light with one another. Each person who came into your life after your mother were people with whom you lighted more Love-Lights... can you name all those people with whom you have lighted Love-Lights for... (include fathers, grandparents, guardians, aunts, uncles, cousins, friends, and other significant, special people).

As you grew, you lighted more lights with new friends and people in your life. Each time you do this your inner Love-Light grows brighter and brighter. Take a moment to think about all the Love-Lights in your lives. The special people may be close by or far away, but they make your world brighter.

Yet, sometimes, as we have all found out, important people in our lives may get sick and die, or they grow old, or they may take their own life, or they may just go away and we don't see them anymore. This same thing may happen with our pets that we have grown to love. The warm and cuddly part is gone. You keep loving these persons or pets even though you no longer see them. Your Love-Light for them continues to burn. (Move the candle out of sight.)

And even though we can't see these special ones, their Love-Light is still burning.

When new people come into your life, you will most likely light new Love-Lights with them. Then there will be more people for you to love and who will love you. Think how bright your lights can be!

The important thing for you to remember is that the Love-Light you feel for the person who died will not go out. Loving is not like ice cream, where you scoop it out until it is all gone. Where love comes from there is an unlimited supply that never runs out. You can love as many people as you would like.

Remember, no one can make you blow out your Love-Light. You do not have to take away the love you feel for one person to love someone new.

*I think that you all understand about Loving. Your Love-Light is inside of you. This candle is only symbolic. When you blow **this** candle out, your inner Love-Lights are still burning. Would you all like to help blow out the candle? One, two, three blow!*

Now let us hold hands and have a moment of silence to feel our inner Love-Light."
(If there are any favorite songs, this is a good time to sing a few of them together.)

Resource:

The Love-Light Ceremony is a HEALS adaptation of the "Candle Ritual" Claudia Jewett describes in her book: *Helping Children Cope with Separation and Loss*. Harvard, MA: The Harvard Common Press, 1982.

The Floating Love-Lights Ceremony
(Individual Memory Candles)

As a closure to the final HEALS support groups, we have found this ceremony to be a beautiful way to commemorate the passing of important people in our lives, while at the same time honoring ourselves. Rituals and ceremonies are wonderful ways to honor the past and then receive permission to journey into the future—being open to new possibilities. Taking the time to provide this enriching and nurturing experience also builds children's self-esteem as they are exposed to the idea that each of us is a unique and special human being worthy of loving and being loved.

*Note: **Most schools, for fire insurance reasons, do not allow the use of candles. Always seek permission to use candles in any public facility.***

Materials: a floating candle for each loss, a large bowl of water, and matches.

Love-Lights Ceremony

The facilitator explains that the group will be participating in special Love-Light Ceremony to honor those who have died. Discuss the important safety measures that need to be respected for this special candle ceremony. *"These special candles represent the people in our lives who have died. As each one of you place a floating candle into the water, you may quietly say the name of the person or persons who died while I light the candles."*

Holding a candle the facilitator might say:

"When each of you were born you came with a very special gift—the gift to give love and receive love. This gift is like a light; it makes you feel warm and happy. We call it our Love-Light.

First you got used to your Mom, being inside of her and then outside. She probably cuddled you and fed you. You felt close to her. You lighted a Love-Light with one another. Each person who came into your life after your mother were people with whom you lighted more Love-Lights…can you name all those people with whom you have lighted Love-Lights? (Include fathers, grandparents, guardians, aunts, uncles, cousins, friends, and other significant special people.)

As you grew, you lighted more lights with new friends and people in your life. Each time you did this your own inner Love-Light grew brighter and brighter. Take a moment to think about all the Love-Lights in your lives. They may be close by or far away, but they make your world brighter.

Yet, sometimes, as we have all found out, important people in our lives may get sick and die, or they grow old, or they may take their own life, or they may just go away and we don't see them anymore. This same thing may happen with our pets that we have grown to love. The warm and cuddly part is gone. You keep loving these persons or pets even though you no longer see them. Your Love-Lights for them continues to burn. (Move the candle out of sight.)

Even though we can't see these special ones, their Love-Light is still burning for you and within you.

When new people come into your life, you will most likely light new Love-Lights with them. Then there will be more people for you to love and who will love you. Think how bright your lights can be!

The important thing for you to remember is that the Love-Light you feel for the person who died will not go out. Loving is not like ice cream, where you scoop it out until it is all gone. Where love comes from there is an unlimited supply that never runs out. You can love as many people as you would like.

Remember, no one can make you blow out your Love-Light. You do not have to take away the love you feel for one person to love someone new.

I think that you all understand about Loving. Your Love-Light is inside of you. This candle is only symbolic. When you blow this candle out, your inner Love-Light are still burning. Would you all like to help blow out the candles? One, two, three blow!

Now let us hold hands and have a moment of silence to feel our inner Love-Light."
(If there are any favorite songs, this is a good time to sing a few of them together.)

Resource:
The Floating Love-Lights Ceremony is a HEALS adaptation of the Candle Ritual Claudia Jewett describes in her book: *Helping Children Cope with Separation and Loss*. Harvard, MA: The Harvard Common Press, 1982.

The Medicine Circle Ceremony

Materials: One large Memory Candle set in a large circle of sand (sand can be poured onto a circular plastic sheet to represent the significant people who died), matches, basket of sacred and natural objects, photos and mementos of the deceased, and sage (optional).

Creating the Medicine Wheel

"We are going to be participating in a special Medicine Wheel Circle ceremony in memory of the people in our lives who have died. Native Americans use Medicine Circles for healing the earth, the sick, the wounded, and those in grief.

Today, because of our losses, we will be creating our own Medicine Wheel to help us with our grief. We will be going around the circle to allow each member of our "tribe" to place their mementos or a sacred object into the Medicine Wheel Circle, name the person/s who died and carefully walk around the Medicine Wheel Circle three times (if time is short—circle only once). We will follow with a moment of silence after each "circling" is completed."

Ceremonial Memory Candle:

"This candle represents those persons we love who have died. We call it a Love-Light. When each of you were born you came with a very special gift—the gift to give love and receive love. This gift is like a light; it makes you feel warm and happy. First you got used to your Mom, being inside of her and then outside. She probably cuddled you and fed you. You felt close to her. You lighted a Love-Light with one another. Each person who came into your life, after your mother, were people with whom you have lighted Love-Lights...can you each take a turn and name all those people whom you have lighted Love-Light for? (Include father, grandparents, guardians, aunts, uncles, cousins, friends, and other significant, special people).

As you grew, you lighted more lights with new friends and people in your life. Each time you did this your inner Love-Light grew brighter and brighter.

Take a moment to think about all the Love-Lights in your lives. The special people may be close by or far away, but they make your world brighter.

Yet, sometimes, as we have all found out, important people in our lives may get sick and die, or they get old, or they may take their own life, or they may just go away and we don't see them anymore. This same thing may happen with our pets that we have grown to love. The warm and cuddly part is gone. You keep loving these persons or pets even though you no longer see them. Your Love-Lights for them continues to burn. (Move the Memory Candle out of sight.)

Even though we can't see these special ones, their Love-Light is still burning for you. When new people come into your life, you will most likely light new Love-Lights with them. Then there will be more people for you to love and who will love you. Think how bright your lights can be!

The important thing for you to remember is that the Love-Light you feel for the person who died will not go out. Loving is not like ice cream, where you scoop it out until it is all gone. Where love comes from there is an unlimited supply that never runs out. You can love as many people as you would like.

Remember, no one can make you blow out your Love-Light. You do not have to take away the love you feel for one person to love someone new.

I think that you all understand about loving. Your Love-Light is inside of you—this candle is just symbolic. When you blow this candle out, your inner Love-Lights are still burning.

(facilitator blows Memory Candle out).

Now let us hold hands and have a moment of silence to feel our inner Love-Light."
(If there are any favorite songs, this is a good time to sing a few of them together.)

Resource:

The Medicine Circle Ceremony is a HEALS adaptation of the Candle Ritual Claudia Jewett describes in her book: *Helping Children Cope with Separation and Loss*. Harvard, MA: The Harvard Common Press, 1982.

The Blessing of the Stones Ceremony

Materials: a Mystery Bag to hold enough smoothly tumbled stones for each person in the group to receive one. *May use Apache Tears (black obsidian formed into the shapes of tears by volcanic action)—very symbolic for the process of grief .

Intent: The following empowerment activity is designed to allow the participants in the group to give and receive positive affirmations and blessings by putting them into an individual's stone. The power of being blessed through this stone, by peers, provides a very special testimony and witness of each participant's value and worth as a human being. (Option: Can also be referred to as Good Luck Stones or Power Stones).

Blessing of the Stones Ceremony

Pass around the Mystery Bag of polished stones. One at a time, have each participant put their hand into the bag to feel the stones. Instruct them to allow their hand to be guided to the stone in the bag that is meant just for them. When the children have connected to the right stone they may take it out and it is theirs to keep.

The following explanation is one example of how to introduce the Blessing of the Stones their new owners:

"Now that each of you has your very own special stone. Close your eyes and feel your stone. Feel the shape, the curves, the bumps, or any indentations. How does it make you feel? What is noticeable about your stone? Think about it's special qualities quietly to yourself for a moment.

Now open your eyes and look around the circle at your friends. We are now going to pass each person's stone, one at a time, around our circle—allowing each person to bless that stone and empower it with a wish or positive comment about something you like about that person, or a wish for them."

A facilitator models the blessing (ex. 'I bless this stone for you, Travis, with the wish that should you ever feel down, you will be able to hold this special stone, and remember how important your sense of humor is to me. Though you are a good friend and listen well, you have the ability to make people laugh. When I think of you—I smile.'"

Pass each individual stone around the circle until it returns to its rightful owner. It is okay to "pass" on this activity or put a silent blessing into the stone(s). Continue in this way until all the stones in the group have been blessed by everyone.

The Crowning Ceremony

The Intent: To create a ceremony honoring the path each child has taken through the grief process, recognizing that there may still be other layers remaining. To acknowledge the participant's willingness to explore their own grief, share that grief with witnesses, and support others on their journey. To review where we have been together during the guided visualization.

Materials: wire star crowns, candle and matches, sparkling cider, plastic glasses, chiming musical sphere, rolled diplomas tied with ribbon, tape player, relaxing music, pillows, little foods or treats such as Hershey Hugs or Kisses, paper lace doilies or napkins.

The Crowning Ceremony: Invite the participants to relax and get comfortable sitting on a pillow with their eyes closed. While quiet music is played in the background, one of the facilitators slowly and meditatively begins to reflect upon many of the activities and experiences throughout the course of the group sessions. As this is transpiring, the other facilitator very quietly begins to set the stage for the "graduation" ceremony (attempting to do anything that may be noisy in an outer room) placing the glasses of cider, cookies or candies on a paper doily or napkin in front of each participant. When the place settings are complete, the two facilitators go round to each participant, still with their eyes closed, and individually asks permission to place something on their head. If permission is granted, one facilitator places the star crown on the child's head while the other facilitator gently encircles their head with the magical fairy-like sound from the musical-sphere, while the rest of the group sits with their eyes closed in silence. When everyone has been crowned, the group is invited to open their eyes, behold each other, offer a toast for the group, and partake of the fare.

Following the "feast" each participant is presented with a scrolled diploma as their name is called. After receiving the diploma, each participant may share with the group anything that has been particularly meaningful or of significance to them personally.

Note: Depending on the age and gender of the group, you may choose to perform a Knighting Ceremony instead of crowning. (See *Knighting Ceremony, Session III: Additional Activities*.)

The HEALS Expressive Arts Loss Support Program

The HEALS Facilitators acting in accordance with the authority vested awards a

CERTIFICATE OF EXPRESSION

to

granting him/her

PERMISSION TO EXPRESS THEIR FEELINGS
In Safe and Appropriate Ways

given this _____ day of _____

_____
HEALS Facilitator

_____
HEALS Facilitator

A parting poem…

Thank you for being part of my life.

It is time to move on.

I bow inwardly

to the memory of you

and,

turning away,

stand straight

to face the new day."

—Molly Fumia

Puppetry

*"It is often easier for a child to talk through a puppet
than it is to say directly what he finds difficult to express.
The puppet provides distance, and the child feels safer to
reveal some of his innermost thoughts this way."*
—Violet Oaklander

Puppetry is often used by HEALS facilitators to begin an exploration of the expressive arts in a group situation. By providing just enough of a buffer, puppets enable children to experience and play with life and death situations, ethics, morals, and fantasy material in a very non-threatening way, while at the same time allowing them to utilize their own expressions and body movement. Facing difficult topics through the use of puppets and animal stories can ease the integration of these events into a child's life.

The two HEALS Puppet Theatre Productions in this section demonstrate how uncomfortable topics, such as feelings surrounding death, can be presented using puppets. In these stories when the expressive arts are initially introduced, the puppet/s are hesitant to explore death. By inviting the audience to accompany the puppets on the journey through the expressive arts, their fears and hesitancy disappear as the whole group learns to support one another. Individually, the participants learn to connect the mind, emotions, and the body while at the same time develop group togetherness.

Usually the playful air that accompanies the expressive arts dispels any reluctance on behalf of the participants. However, it is important to ask the audience if they would like to participate, offering the option to observe from a safe place.

Though all ages seem to enjoy puppetry, other forms of drama and psychodrama may be more appropriate when dealing with pre-teens and adolescents. Reading and/or acting out stories and plays about death and grief issues may be more applicable for older adolescents. Encouraging teenagers to write and produce their own puppet show for a group of younger children is a simple and safe way for them to give themselves permission to explore and play with the expressive arts with less peer pressure and self-consciousness.

Spontaneous Puppet Shows by Children

If time allows, or a filler is needed, spontaneous puppet shows put on by the children can provide valuable outlets for their expression enabling them to act out and gain control of their fears and emotional dilemmas. Encouraging children to integrate rhythm instruments, a drum, and/or their own sounds with the puppets can provide a vehicle for the outer expression of what they may be experiencing in their inner worlds. In this way the children are given the opportunity to "act" out their feelings or those held in the unconscious through verbal and non-verbal means. This trial "acting out" is a precursor for being able to deal with conflicts, ideas, or emotions in real life.

Improvisational puppet shows can be performed anywhere. If a theatre is not available—use the back of a chair or a table turned on it's side for the stage. The HEALS facilitators should offer a general sense of structure knowing that the enactment of feelings can have a critical effect on the safety of the group.

Knowing when to intervene and when to pull back to allow the group to take it's own course requires practice and is a skill well worth cultivating. Keep in mind the attention span and comprehension level of your audience and encourage the puppeteers to stay within certain time boundaries, perhaps letting them know how much more time remains to complete their performance.

We recommend using hand puppets, rather than finger puppets, to maximize fuller body movements on the children's behalf while at the same time helping to keep their attention more focused on what they are doing. Some children who tend to store tension and emotional memories that are restricting or blocking their growth may become violent with their movements, exhibiting lots of hitting and aggressiveness with the puppets. Though the reasons for this need to release vary, it is more important to find safe ways for its expulsion rather than attempting to understand the cause. Further repression of the emotion may result if the child chooses not to share the exact reason for the stored anger. Re-playing a child's original story and adding constructive ways to deal with the conflicts that arise provide a positive and beneficial role-model for what may be missing in the child's life.

Thus, being able to create a safe container with general guidelines and tools for the safe release of emotions, provides children with valuable skills that will serve them for the rest of their lives. Here the adult has a marvelous opportunity to model positive conflict resolution and how to cope in situations of crisis through the use of puppetry.

Interactive and Expressive Use of Puppets

- Adult and child together create a story, or dialogue.
- Have a variety of puppets available and allow each child to select a puppet. Then invite the child to speak through their puppet…they are to be the puppet. The adult can then ask questions such as "Puppet, how old are you?" or "Why did Jason pick you?" Have them introduce and tell something about themselves. The adult can ask the children if they ever feel like the character they chose.

Selecting Puppets

A good selection of puppets to have might include:

- several animals
- a man
- a woman
- two boys
- two girls
- a baby
- a dog with long ears
- grandparent figures
- a wizard or wise person
- a doctor
- a fireman
- a snake

- an angel
- a witch
- a crocodile
- a tiger
- a king
- a queen
- a cat
- a fairy godmother/father type
- several small stuffed animals
- a policeman
- a wolf
- monsters

The children may want to bring some of their own puppets from home or make a puppet that more closely represents the issues or story(s) they need to reenact.

HEALS Puppet Theatre Production

"Barney's Feelings"

HEALS Puppet Theatre Production: Barney's Feelings: This puppet show was written as an introduction to the expressive arts to help children access what they are feeling in the present moment. The script tells about a bear whose grandfather has died and how this loss is impacting on his relationships as well as his physical and emotional well-being. (This is also appropriate for Session I.)

Materials: theatre stage, two scripts, three puppets—one adult and two smaller offspring, paper folded into quarters, paper and colors for the Barney puppet (one of the younger puppets), an easel or box for a firm surface to write upon, assorted crayons, markers, or colored pencils, (**optional**: tape player and song from "It's Alright to Cry" sung by Rosie Grier from "Free To Be You and Me" by Marlo Thomas.

Ages: 2 1/2-12 years old

Environment: Preferably on the floor, and a nice clear space that will allow movement.

THE PLAY:

The play begins with Barney sitting quietly by himself, looking rather sad. Otto happily enters and wants Barney to play with him like as they have in the past. Barney is apathetic and doesn't respond to any of Otto's encouragements.

Otto: Hi Barney! Let's play!

Barney: No, I don't feel like playing.

Otto: Oh come on, we always play together on Friday afternoons!

Barney: Naah, I just don't feel like playing right now.

Otto: What's the matter Barney, don't you feel well?

Barney: I don't know what the matter is. I feel sad. I..I..I feel worried. I feel angry. I just don't know. I feel confused.

Otto: (sadly) Ohhhh….. touches Barney's shoulder.

(Enter, Big Bear)

Big Bear: Hi you two! What are you up to today?

Otto: Well, Big Bear, Barney is not feeling well today, and he doesn't feel like playing.

Big Bear: Are you feeling sick Barney?

Barney: No, not sick. I am sort of sad and confused.

Big Bear: Is there something bothering you?

Barney: I don't know…Why did my Grandfather have to die?

Big Bear: (Long pause) Oh! I didn't know that your Grandfather died, Barney. I am really sorry to hear that. Now I understand why you are feeling so sad and confused. Do you want to talk about it?

Barney: I don't know what to say…I feel awful inside, my tummy hurts. I am confused about things. I don't understand. I, I, I think I might cry…(begins to cry). (Big Bear touches his shoulder)

Big Bear: There, there. It's all right to cry. When things happen like losing someone or something important, it can create many different feelings. Crying can help get the hurt out of you…..It is really okay. (**optional:** *"Listen:" play song sung by Rosie Grier called "It's Alright to Cry."*

Big Bear: Barney, death *is* a part of life but most of us don't want to talk about it because it makes us sad or even scared. When someone important dies, it creates all kinds of feelings in us. It is healthy to be able to talk about those feelings and to express them in safe ways—like through the expressive arts.

Barney: What's "'spressive arts"?

Big Bear: Expressive Arts means using your body, making sounds and music, drawing and painting, and writing to express the feelings that are inside. Hey! Would you like to try some?

Barney: Yes, but it is scary for me to do those things by myself.

Big Bear: If you feel scared right now, how about asking the children here in this room if they would join you in trying a few expressive arts?

Barney: Oh, I am scared to ask them. What if they say no?

Big Bear: You'll never know until you try.

Barney: Okay… (Looking at the audience.) Would you like to try some 'spressive arts with me? (The kids all say Sure! Those who do not want to participate can be asked by the Big Bear to please move off to the edge of the circle or room and quietly observe.)

Big Bear: Okay children, please stand up (move anything like pillows or chairs out of the area). Let's begin by loosening up with some body stretching: Does everyone know what **inhale and exhale** mean? Let's try it together. (Do an inhale and hold it; and then a slow, loud exhale saying **"Ahhh."** Now, everyone reach for the sky taking a deep breath. Get up on your toes! Hold it. Now exhale "Ahhhh" as you slowly come down, bending as you go lower until you are grasping your knees in a ball position. That's it! You've got it! (Do a total of three times.)

• Does everyone know how to **freeze**? Let's practice that a few times. (A third person uses a drum or tape recorder. The children are instructed to move about quite wildly. When the drum or music stops they are to freeze. Practice a few times.)

• Okay. Now we are going to "feel" and try to move to that feeling. Let's begin with ANGRY. Think about how you feel when you are ANGRY. Let's have a temper tantrum, without touching any other people, to the ANGRY drum (pound drum fast and loudly.) You should freeze when drums stops. Well done!

- Now let's think of what it feels like to be SCARED and let's move in a scared way… Oh you did that so well!
- This time let's think of something SAD and feel it and move that way. Oh your bodies looked so sad, good job!

- This last time let us express what it feels like to be HAPPY. (Walk, wave arms, skip, dance, etc.) Great! (Freeze.)

- Now let's express confusion…(followed by any or all of the following):

Happy	Proud	Silly
Scared	Wild	Loving

Now very quietly you may go (or first row or section may go) and fetch a piece of paper and box of crayons/craypas, and return to the circle putting these things on the floor in front of you and your hands in your lap.

1. (Have them number their squares if not already prepared.) Think about ANGRY again. Look at your crayons and take out a color that feels it could represent anger. Draw your angry feelings in square one.

2. Do the same with Scared, Sad and Happy. When you are finished, put your crayons down and hands back in your laps please.

How was that for you Barney? How do you feel now?

Barney: I feel a little better, but not totally.

Big Bear: Well, these important feelings take time to heal. Do you know people that you can talk with about your feelings? Can you think of any people who might listen to you? (Your parents, friends, school counselors, teachers, minister, priest, rabbi, or HEALS facilitators.)

Barney: Thanks for being here for me, Big Bear (hug). And you too, Otto. (hug). And thank all of you children for helping me. It wasn't scary at all when you did it with me! Thanks Big Bear for showing me different ways to express myself.

Big Bear: Anytime....what are friends for? Well, I think it is time to go. Shall we say good-bye to the children?

Barney: Oh yes, good-bye! Good-bye!

Say Good-bye, put the puppets down and gather into a circle. Have an open discussion of the experience, responding to any questions the children want to ask. Remember to thank them for their great participation and cooperation.

HEALS Puppet Theatre Production

"Barney's Anger"

Materials: three bear puppets, two scripts, sticks, drum, pillows, newspapers, a few blocks or legos, and a screambox (optional).

THE PLAY:

The play begins with Barney and Otto, two young bears, who are having an argument. Barney is being very unreasonable. He is name-calling and breaks Otto's lego tower. Otto begins to cry and hits Barney. Big Bear is nearby and hears the conflict.

Big Bear: (enters) Whoa! Can we talk about what just happened?

Otto: (tearfully) Barney called me names, and then knocked down the beautiful tower I was building!

Big Bear: How did that make you feel Otto?

Otto: It makes me feel sad…and…and…angry. I guess I also feel sort of confused because I don't know why Barney would do that to me.

Barney: Well, I don't know why I hurt his house…I just felt angry. I wanted to break something…I am angry that my Grandfather died and I won't see him anymore.

Big Bear: Oh, I see, Barney. When someone important to us dies, it is natural to be angry. We are angry because now we can't be with them anymore. We remember all the memories and the things we did together. We realize that we won't have them in our life anymore. Learning to release our anger is a healthy thing to do. But do you think it is good if someone else gets hurt or something dear to someone gets broken in the process?

Barney: No, I suppose that is not very good. I am sorry, Otto.

Big Bear: Perhaps I can help you by giving you some ideas that are *safe* ways for expressing your anger.

Otto: What do you mean by *safe*?

Big Bear: I mean that there are many ways to release or let your feelings of anger and frustration come out without hurting anyone.

Barney: How?

Big Bear: Well, Barney, you mentioned that when you get angry you feel like breaking something. I will show you several ways to get your anger out safely and you can choose the one that feels right for you. Each person may have their own particular way that works well for them.

(Big Bear asks the children in the audience if they will stay with Barney while he gets out some of his anger.) Great! This group of children will be here for you so that you don't feel alone, Barney. We need each other when we are going through hard times. Okay, here are your choices:

1. pound this drum
2. stomp or dance
3. break sticks
4. yell or scream into a pillow
5. hit pillows with your fist
6. rip newspapers
7. scream into the screambox

Barney: Give me those sticks! (Barney puts a lot of energy into breaking the sticks making sound effects as he does, until he is tired.)

Big Bear: Now how do you feel?

Barney: I feel tired, but a good kind of tired. And it seems all the angry feelings are gone for now. Do you want to do it Otto?

Otto: Yes, please! I would like to pound on the drum!

Big Bear: (to audience) Each of you will now have a turn to express your feelings, too. We will be with you just as we were with Barney.

Allow time for participants to explore anger release materials.

(*How the participants are involved is up to the facilitators: it can be done individually; in small groups each with an adult to supervise the releasework and ground rules—perhaps two go at a time while others witness. **Be mindful of keeping this *very* controlled.**)

Big Bear: Grief comes to us sometimes in waves. As time goes on, the "down" times will be less and less and there will be more good feelings. Each time a wave comes it is important to express it safely in whatever way works for you. This will allow the healing to take place. If you ever get to the point where the feelings get too strong and scary like they did for Barney, make sure to go talk to someone you trust. Can any of you here think of someone whom you trust and feel comfortable talking to about your feelings? (a parent, teacher, counselor, HEALS facilitator, pastor, priest, rabbi, etc.) Good. Remember that feelings aren't bad as long as you get them out safely; that means not hurting yourself or others.

Barney: Thanks for being here, Big Bear.

Big Bear: It's my pleasure, Barney.

Otto: Yes, thank you for showing us safe ways for our feelings to come out. Hey Barney, wanna help me build my tower again?

Barney: Yeah! Let's go!

THE END!

The HEALS Program

Facilitator Tips for Imaginary Journeys

The goal of leading children through guided imagery is to slow down their brain wave patterns in order for them to relax into an alpha state. Helping them to create this calm state allows them to be able to focus on the activity they are being guided to explore. The following tips should help facilitators maximize guided imagery experiences for children. Imaginary Journeys can be done lying down or sitting in a chair. If children will be in chairs, it is best if they are sitting up straight with both feet on the floor.

- **Breath:** Take a set of three deep breaths to help you focus, center and relax first.

- **Tone:** Strive to keep your voice soft, smooth, calm, and relaxing, but not monotone.

- **Pace & Rhythm:** Speak your words to match your heartbeat—and your phrases to match the length of your breath.

- **Length:** For children, be mindful about the length of the Imaginary Journey, the developmental ages of the participants, and their attention spans.

- **Hearing Problems:** Be aware of any hearing problems of children in the group. Have children with hearing challenges sit/lie near you. Be aware of the effects of the music for these particular children if it is used for background. Some children with attention difficulties may find background music, in addition to your voice, and the mental images being stirred, overstimulating. To adjust: delete the background music, and allow them to keep their eyes open if need be.

- **Monitoring the Group:** Continually monitor the environment and the group to assure there are no unnecessary disruptions and that the children are present in the activity.

- **Alleviate Distractions:** To alleviate any potential distractions make sure children are far enough apart so that no one is touching. Sometimes visual contact should also be inhibited so that one or two children do not disrupt the silence for others. Set the tone so that distractions are not permitted and they understand this, then any needed reminders or discipline should be more easily handled. Arrange to have your co-facilitator become a "floater" if necessary and quietly deal with any children who are distracting.

- **Learning Styles:** Children usually learn through all their senses. Most tend to have one sense that is more dominant than others such as hearing (auditory), seeing (visual), or kinesthetic (touching). Kinesthetic learners may have more difficulties with guided imagery and seeing pictures in their minds. You can help them by incorporating all five senses into the design of an Imaginary Journey. For example, when imagining a scene, asking them what they are seeing, hearing, feeling, tasting or smelling is sure to touch upon at least one style or combination of their learning styles.

Imaginary Journey: Session II Tell The Story

"Floating Clouds"

Materials: dancing scarves, art materials, and soft music.

*Have the children select a colored scarf before you begin.

"I would like to invite you to wander around the room quietly until you find a spot that feels good...and then spread your scarf and lie down upon it...let your body gently move around until it finds a comfortable place...imagine it is a Floating Cloud...allow your body to rest and settle down on that cloud...very comfortably supported...I'd like to invite you to take some slow and deep breaths...allowing your body and mind to feel relaxed...comfortable...and safe...

Now, close your eyes and imagine that your cloud is gently beginning to move... slowly being pushed by a soft, warm breeze...you feel very comfortable...floating past other soft, billowy clouds...you just relax and watch them float by...and you know even though your cloud is cozy and soft, it is also very strong and will not let you fall...as you gently float, you are taken back to the time and place when you first learned about the significant person or loved one who died...think back to that time...remembering all the things that happened...where you were...who you were with...how you were told...what you experienced...remember the colors...the sounds...the smells...what do you remember about that time?

Hold that memory for a moment...I would like to invite you, when you are ready...to gather some art materials that are laid out, and find a quiet place in the room to draw or make images of the things you can remember about this time...we will be allowing about 10-15 minutes for this activity before we return to the circle...if you finish early, there is some paper and you may take a few moments to write about your memory. When you are ready...you may get up and gather your art supplies..."

The HEALS Program
Imaginary Journey: Session II Tell The Story

"Magic Carpet Ride"

Materials: dancing scarves, art materials, pillows, teddy bears, and gentle music

"I would like to invite you to quietly wander around the room until you find a spot that feels just right for you...now, spread your Magic Carpet like a picnic blanket and lie down or sit upon it...and let your body gently move around until it finds a comfortable place...then let it settle down on that spot, comfortably supported by the floor and your Magic Carpet...now I'd like to invite you to take some slow and deep breaths...allowing your body and mind to feel relaxed...comfortable... and safe...

Now, close your eyes and imagine that you are still on your carpet, but you are outside...the temperature is warm and comfortable...feel your Magic Carpet slowly lift up...and float...you know that it is strong and will not let you fall...and you enjoy the feeling of gently floating...you float up into the blue sky together...as you look around you see some lovely, white, billowy clouds floating past...you just relax and watch them float by...a light breeze begins to blow you gently... and you and your Magic Carpet float downwards...ever so gently...you are taken back to the time and place when you first learned about the significant person or loved one that died...

Think back to that time...remembering all the things that happened...where you were...who you were with...how you were told...what you experienced...remember the colors...the sounds...the smells...what do you remember about that time?... hold that memory in your imagination for a little while...

I would like to invite you, when you are ready...to gather [name the art materials] and find a quiet place in the room to draw or make images of the things you can remember about this time...we will be allowing about 10-15 minutes for this activity before we return to the circle...if you finish early, you may take a few moments to write about your memory...

When you are ready...you may get up, collect your art supplies, and find your quiet place in the room..."

The HEALS Program
Imaginary Journey: Session III Feeling The Feelings

"Journey to Planets of Emotions"

Materials: dancing scarves, enough large blank sheets of paper to represent each emotional planet they will be visiting (could be cut into large circles to represent planets), marking pens, refer to Planet of Emotions List for planet names).

"I would like to invite each of you to quietly choose a scarf or Magic Carpet...once you have chosen your scarf...begin to wander around the room until you find a special place to spread it out and lie upon it...feel yourself becoming very comfortable and safe on your Magic Carpet...in a moment you begin to feel the carpet move a little and lift off the ground...gently moving upwards until you are floating through the clouds, all pink and blue...as you are enjoying the colors and the warm, soft breeze, you notice several planets not far away...you think to yourself, "I'd like to explore these planets"...At that thought, you find that your Magic Carpet magically lands on one of those planets! I would like to invite you to get up and let's begin to explore this amazing world...

(All gather to one spot in the room around one of the blank circles titled, "Planet of Sadness").

Here we are on the Planet of Sadness...let's experience this planet fully by moving around in a sad way, making sad sounds as we walk around this planet...now choose a color that represents or looks like what you think sadness might look like, and draw sad images and symbols on the planet paper...there are so many sad feelings here...are you ready to leave your sadness here and explore another planet?...shake off the sadness and lets fly over to the Planet of Anger...

*Option: You may want to allow the children to share a time when they experienced the feeling while visiting each planet after the movement and drawing segments.

(Continue in the same way until all emotional planets you have chosen for the group have been explored such as the Planet of Wildness, the Scared Planet, the Quiet Planet, the Proud Planet, the Planet of Worry, the Planet of Joy and Happiness, etc.)

Let's all lay back down on our Magic Carpets so we can return to planet Earth...feel your carpet gently taking off...floating gently past the billowy clouds...being moved by a gentle breeze towards planet Earth...your carpet floats lower and lower until you feel it sinking softly onto the earth...

allow the earth to cuddle you as you lie quietly on your Magic Carpet and think about the journey you have just taken...

The feelings you have experienced are rich and varied and there are many, many more, some that do not even have names...none of the feelings are considered good or bad...you may enjoy some more than others, but they all play their part in the rhythm of life. Through experimenting with lots of feelings, you can learn to travel in and out of them, almost like dancing with them...you did that today with your Magic Carpets—you flew in and out of a variety of emotions...

When you lose someone or something you love you may feel many emotions...some briefly—others for longer periods...each of you may experience these emotions in your own way and in your own time because you are each unique and different and that is okay, even desirable...

We now must say good-bye to the Planets of Emotion, knowing you can visit them anytime you like...let's find our magic carpets and return to the circle so we can talk about our adventures on all the Planets of Emotion!"

Variation:

For older children: Take the children through a couple of planet explorations. Then, using blank paper planets, allow the children to decide and name various planets they would like to visit and allow them to facilitate the exploration, using the expressive arts as above.

The HEALS Program
Imaginary Journey: Session V Unfinished Business

"Changes In My Life"

Ages: 1st-3rd Grade

Materials: scarf, soft music, CD-tape player

"Select a scarf and wander quietly around the room until you find a place that feels just right... spread out your scarf and lie down upon it as if it were a magic carpet...

Give yourself permission to feel the floor beneath you...supporting you...notice your feet...let them relax...then your legs...allow them to feel very heavy but supported by the floor...now notice your belly...let go any tightness there...breathing softness into your belly...until it feels relaxed and soft... Now focus your attention on your arms... letting them completely relax...feeling all tension float out of them so they are limp...like a rag doll...now notice your elbows, your shoulder, your neck and feel them relaxing...being gently supported by your magic carpet... relax your face...feel all the muscles in your face and around your mouth gently let go...you might open your mouth a little and let your jaw drop to fully relax the muscles in your face...take a moment to enjoy your whole body feeling very relaxed....

In this relaxed state...think about your own life...particularly since your special person died... what changes have you experienced?...have you learned how to do new things that you want them to know about?...do you have any dreams or wishes that you would like to tell them?...what would you like them to know about you?....

When you are ready you will be able to gather some art materials and draw or write about the changes or dreams in your life that you would like to share with this person...

I do have one special request...that you find yourself a space, after choosing your materials, and that you go there and work alone...respect your neighbor's private space and your neighbors will respect your private space. You will have about _____ minutes to work.

When you are ready, I invite you to open your eyes...gather your materials and find a quiet place in the room to do this activity."

The HEALS Program
Imaginary Journey: Session V Unfinished Business

"Wishes & Regrets"

Ages: Preschool-3rd grade

Materials: drum, scarves, strips of paper, colored pencils or pens, and envelopes.

Note: You may begin this visualization by guiding the children to move about the room with their scarves to a beating drum, slowly softening the sound until it is barely audible. When they have almost stopped moving begin the guided visualization:

"I would like to invite you to quietly wander around the room until you find a spot that feels just right to you...lay your scarf down as if it were a magic carpet, and then quietly lie upon it...let your body move around until it finds a comfortable place...and then settle down quietly on that spot, comfortably supported by the floor.

Put your hands on your belly and take a long, deep breath, feeling your belly expand...and then gently release the air out of your mouth...take another long, deep breath, feel your belly expand again...and then release your breath gently out of your mouth...take one more deep breath, release it slowly...and feel your body, your belly and your mind relax...

And now I would like to ask you to think about your special person who died... imagine you can see them in your mind...is there anything you would like to say to them now? Maybe you didn't get a chance to say good-bye to them before they died...or perhaps there's something you said to them before they died that you wish you wouldn't have said? Are there things you wish you could tell that person about yourself?...and your life today?...things you can do now...ways you have changed or grown?

In a moment...you will be asked to gather some art materials and write about or draw pictures about any wishes you have that you would like this person to know ...envelopes will be provided if you would like to fold it up and keep your art or writings private...we will be allowing about 10 minutes for this activity...you may open your eyes and gather your materials...if you have any questions or need help quietly ask a facilitator for assistance..."

The HEALS Program
Imaginary Journey: Session V: Unfinished Business

"Wishes & Regrets"

Ages: 4th-6th Grade

Materials: drum, scarves, strips of paper, colored pencils, and envelopes.

Note: You may begin this visualization by guiding the children to move about the room with their scarves to a beating drum, slowly softening the sound until it is barely audible. When they have almost stopped moving, begin the guided visualization:

"I would like to invite you to quietly wander around the room until you find a spot that feels just right to you…lay your scarf down as if it were a magic carpet, and then quietly lie upon it…..let your body move around until it finds a comfortable place…and then let it settle down on that spot…comfortably supported by the floor…

Give yourself permission to feel the support of the floor beneath you…as you begin to settle into your body…being present in the moment…invite relaxation into your feet…your legs…your belly…feel your arms relaxing and falling heavy upon the floor…allow any tension to go into the floor…relax your shoulders…your neck…and your face…breathe peacefulness into your whole body…feeling relaxed and calm.

And now I would like to ask you to think about the person who died…is there anything you did not have the opportunity to say to that person before they died?… anything you wish you could say to them now? Perhaps there was something you said to them, or thought about them before their death…that you regret having said? See if you have any of these thoughts in your mind….and are there things your wanted to do with this person…places you wanted to go…that didn't happen? Is there something you wish they knew about you? Perhaps there are things that you did that you feel crummy about…give yourself permission to search your mind to locate any of these thoughts… feelings…regrets…or wishes that may be present in your mind or heart.

In a moment…as a way of releasing these wishes and regrets…I will be inviting you to write or draw any of these thoughts on little strips of paper…and as you do…allow yourself to let go of them…when you are finished…you may put them into an envelope…now you may open your eyes and gather some materials, returning to your special place to sit and write your wishes and regrets…"

The HEALS Program
Imaginary Journey: Session VI Commemoration

"Name Poems"

Materials: scarves (or small carpets), Name Poem cards, pens or pencils

"Find a scarf you like and slowly walk around the room until you find a spot that feels just right... gently lay your scarf out in this area and lie down upon it...wiggle around until your body feels comfortable...as you begin to relax...feel the support of the magic carpet beneath you...and...as you begin to settle into your space...bring your awareness...to your breath....and notice the way you breath in...and breath out...inhale...and exhale...as you observe your breathing...invite your body to relax with each breath you exhale...then slowly inhale...and gently exhale—letting go of any tension...inhale...exhale—releasing any concerns...any worries your might have...simply being with yourself...right here...right now...just being aware of your breath... (longer pause here—transition)

And now...I'd like to invite you to allow your mind to travel back in time to remember the important person in your life who died...the person you have been focusing on in our HEALS group...and as you do...give yourself permission to remember this person...and the relationship you shared with them...I'd like to invite you to recall some of the memories that remain with you...remembering the qualities that made this individual unique...as you reflect upon this person remember what they might have taught you...activities you might have done together...little things they might have done for you or others...foods or clothes they loved...their favorite music...jokes...movies... hobbies...allow those memories to bubble up into your awareness...as you focus on this person... what made this human being unique and special?...what did he or she represent?...what beliefs were important to him or her? Take a little time here to think about this person. (long pause)

In a moment...I would like to invite you to express these special qualities and thoughts...about your important person...in the creation of a Name Poem in honor of them...

You may begin waking up your hands and feet by gently moving them...and when you are ready, open your eyes...

When you rise you will notice that there are little cards and pens set up on the table for use in decorating your name poems...to commemorate and remember the unique qualities of your special

person...I would like to suggest you honor the silence while working on these cards so you do not disturb others around you who might be thinking about their significant person...if there is something particular you need or want please feel free to quietly ask an adult...when you are ready you may get up and gather your materials and find a quiet place somewhere in the room...we will be allowing about _____ minutes for this activity."

Imaginary Journey: Session VI Commemoration

"Memory Box"

Materials: boxes with lids, art and collage materials, glue, scissors, marking pens, paint, etc.

"I would like to invite you as you begin to relax...to feel the support of the floor beneath you...and as you begin to settle into your space bring your awareness to your breath...notice the way you breathe in...and breathe out...and as you observe your breathing—invite your body to relax with each breath you exhale...letting go of any tension...releasing any concerns....any worries....simply being with yourself...right here...right now...just being aware of your breath...(long pause here—transition)

And now I'd like to invite you to allow your mind to travel back in time to remember the special person in your life upon whom you have been focusing in the HEALS group...and as you do, give yourself permission to remember this person and the relationship you shared with him or her...was it warm and fuzzy?...or was it a prickly relationship?...and as you reflect on this person...I'd like to invite you to recall the memories that remain...remembering the qualities...that made this individual unique... give yourself permission to allow some memories to come, even if they are not very pleasant...people have light sides...and shadowy sides...they are not always perfect...perhaps some colors...or images come to your mind...as you reflect upon this person...maybe smells...foods...activities...music... hobbies...allow any memories to bubble up into your awareness...as you focus on this person...what made this human being unique?...what did he or she represent...what beliefs were important to him or her? (long pause)

And now...I would like to invite you to express these memories, images, thoughts...and feelings in the creation of a memory box...a box that can allow you to be with the memories and perhaps treasures stored in your mind...a box that can be filled with anything that represents...or reminds you of the person who died...

You may begin moving your hands...and feet...gently waking them up...When you are ready to open your eyes...you will notice that there are many art and collage materials set up on the table for use in decorating your memory boxes to commemorate and remember your special person...I would like to suggest you honor the silence while decorating your boxes so you do not disturb others around you who might be thinking about their significant person...If there is something particular you need or want please feel free to ask an adult...When you are ready you may get up and gather your materials. We will be allowing about _____ minutes for this activity."

Imaginary Journey: Session VII The Jewels Within

"Badge of Honor"

Materials: art supplies, colored paper, foil papers, streamers and ribbons, marking pens, glitter or glitter pens, stickers, jewels, glue, fasteners: safety pin or flat-backed pin, mat board or plastic conference badge, and a sample badge.

"Close your eyes and take a moment to focus on three long, slow deep breaths...1) feel yourself relaxing with each breath...2) your body and mind are growing very calm...3) and very quiet.... we are going to take a journey back in time...I invite you to think back to a time when you were afraid to do something—something you might have tried for the very first time and were not quite sure about it—such as going to school the first day...maybe speaking up for yourself the first time...or trying a new food...maybe trying to ride a bicycle or scooter for the first time...or taking a test...something you tried for the first time and had to work through feelings of being afraid or worried...I will be quiet while you think...while you remember...when you have thought of something, you may quietly raise your finger so I know that you are finished thinking...

Okay, now think about the feeling you had just before you tried the new experience...how did your mind and body feel?... then think about how you felt afterwards...did you allow yourself to feel Proud...Brave...Relieved...more Confident in yourself?...take time now to feel Proud or Brave or Successful... It takes Courage to try new things...in a few minutes, we are going to create a Medal or Badge that honors your bravery in being able to try new things—even though they may be scary at first...When you are ready...you may quietly get up, go to the art table and gather materials to make yourself a Badge of Honor...we will spend about _____ minutes to create this special project and then we will return to the circle..."

Imaginary Journey: Session VII The Jewels Within

"Kings and Queens"

Materials: plenty of colorful dancing scarves

*Set the stage so that all the participants know they are Kings and Queens about to take a journey. Invite the children to each choose a Royal Magic Carpet (dancing scarf).

"I invite all the Kings and Queens in this room to wander around until you find a comfortable spot…and spread your Royal Magic Carpet out and lie down upon it…you may close your eyes if that is your wish…

I humbly ask your Royal Highnesses to begin to breathe deeply and evenly…feeling your body relax as it is being gently supported by your Royal Magic Carpet…feel your Royal Carpet begin to gently move…and then lift off the ground floating higher and higher…until you are able to observe the great lands below you…a soft gentle breeze begins to blow and you float on your Royal Magic Carpet……… behold the mountains…the valleys…and streams…you carry on in this way until you see a familiar walled castle in the distance…it is your own home…your castle…of which you are the King or Queen… all the people…your Royal Subjects…have been waiting for your return…you see they have suffered the loss a beloved Knight and a beloved Knightess…and they know not what to do to help themselves feel better…they are awaiting your arrival and your leadership to help them in their grief…as you float nearer and nearer to the castle you are thinking about what you can do to help your Royal Subjects…

…You float right over the castle walls…past the tall spires and into the courtyard where everyone is waiting for you…so happy to see you after your travels…your Royal Magic Carpet gently floats down and lands on the soft grass in the courtyard….the people cheer to see you're safely home again amongst them…then one small child bends down on one knee and asks what the people of the Kingdom or Queendom should do for their grief…you share with them that you have given this much thought and that you have a plan…

Take a moment now to think more about your plan to assist your grieving people…remember…you are the King or Queen and you have the power to create whatever you want to help your grieving people…what is it you wish to do for them?…after you have thought about it…when you are ready you may rise and step off your Royal Magic Carpet…gather some art materials (to draw, write or create in clay) what your plan is for your Royal Subjects in your Kingdom or Queendom…when you are ready you may rise and gather your materials…"

(Option—have Queen and King crowns that thee children can wear when they are in sharing circle.)

Imaginary Journey: Session VII The Jewels Within

"Finding Your Power Animal"

Materials: soft music, scarves, drawing materials

Note: You may begin this visualization by inviting the children to move about the room with their scarves to a beating drum, slowly softening the sound until it is barely audible. When the children have almost stopped moving begin the Imaginary Journey.

"Wander around the room quietly until you find a spot that feels good to you...and then lie down upon your scarf. Let your body gently move around a little until it finds a pleasing position...and then let your body settle down into that position...comfortably supported by the floor and your magic carpet...I'd like to invite you to take three slow and deep breaths, inhale (breathing in)... exhale (breathing out)...inhale...exhale...and one more time...inhale...and exhale...allow your body and mind to feel deeply relaxed, and very safe...

Now, close your eyes and imagine that you are still on your carpet, but you are outside...the temperature is warm and comfortable...feel your magic carpet slowly lift up...and float...you know that it is strong and will not let you fall...you float up into the blue sky together...as you look around you see some lovely, white, billowy clouds floating past...just relax and watch them float by...some of these clouds are making silly shapes and that make you smile...you enjoy just floating about...and feeling good...

A light breeze begins to blow you gently over a lovely grassy area in a land that is familiar to you...the magic carpet floats downwards...downwards...ever so gently...and you land in a soft, grassy area...you look around...and notice something coming towards you...it is a special animal friend who wants you to take him or her for a ride on your magic carpet...you invite this special animal to join you...it doesn't matter how big this animal is because your carpet is magic and can accommodate any size, no matter how large or how small...together you and your special animal friend begin to float upwards on your magic carpet...into the sky...and over the land...passing the clouds again, until you are magically back in _____.

Your carpet slips quietly into this room and lands softly on the floor...as you adjust to being back here, take a few deep breaths and begin to wiggle your toes and your fingers...when you are ready...you may open your eyes and get a piece of paper and some markers and draw a picture of you and your special animal friend who has returned with you…if your animal has a message or a word or words of protection or power words to give you… you may want to write them down, too…

We will be allowing about _____minutes for this activity…when you are finished, you may put away your markers, get your scarf and picture, and return quietly to the circle."

Imaginary Journey: Session VII The Jewels Within

"River of Life Gifts"

Materials: a Mystery Bag of shiny stones and plenty of colorful dancing scarves, tape/CD player, and brook or river music/sounds.

*Prior to this imaginary journey, have each child reach into the Mystery Bag and feel for a special stone…they may take it with them on their imaginary journey.

"Take your large scarf and wander around the room until you find a comfortable spot…your scarf out and lie down upon it…you may close your eyes if you wish…

Begin to breathe deeply and evenly…and feel your body relaxing as it is being gently supported by the floor…now imagine that you are lying next to a brook…a cool stream…smell the cool, dampness of it…this stream is the life of your special person…their life that ran next to yours…for a time… notice all the smooth and shiny pebbles…hear the water bubbling over these stones…smoothing them…these beautiful, shiny stones are the things that were special to your person…things they loved…or did…or were good at…or taught you how to do…their gifts to the world…

Reach into the stream and pick a stone…and now feel the smoothness of the stone in your hand…it is a gift from the stream of the person's life—something they gave to you…which one have you chosen?…perhaps a special ability or knowledge they gave you…or a way you are like them that you will take with you throughout your whole life…feel how special it is…bring it into your heart and know that that part of them will always be with you…it will live on in you…treasure it…..

When you are ready…bring your shiny stone gift with you and sit quietly in the circle…"

• Created by HEALS Facilitator Sue Aldridge, Westminster, Vermont 2002

Section IV: Death Crisis Intervention

HEALS Death Crisis Intervention Support for Schools

The Chinese characters for crisis are "danger" and "opportunity." Such is the potential for either of these responses within a school where the death of a student or faculty member has occurred. Danger may result if the school community is denied time and space to grieve. Or the crisis can be growth promoting and allow the students and faculty to come together to support one another and accomplish individual grieving tasks. The HEALS goal is the latter.

The effects of a loss can permeate an entire school and parent community, leaving everyone in an immobilized state of shock. Some administrators and teachers may be in the throes of their own grief and need to be able to make conscious decisions as to how they, and the school, can best support each other and the students. Fear of emotions getting out of control tend to make some administrators and teachers want to carry on as usual. When this is allowed to prevail, those students and staff who are in need of talking, crying, sharing stories, receiving hugs, or being with their parents and support system are often left in a void where there is little or no safety net.

It is important to note here that each person's reaction to death can vary. For some individuals being alone is necessary; others may benefit from maintaining a routine; and others may need time to be with peers to grieve in their own way. These different reactions place the school in a very challenging position, because the staff cannot always provide for such a diverse variety of individual needs.

In addition to the intense emotional responses by those who knew or were close to the person who died, there can also be a tremendous impact on those who did not know the deceased. These students or faculty can re-experience deep emotional grief responses from previous losses that are often difficult for those around them to understand or perceive. This "triggering" effect of old losses is just as devastating emotionally for them as the immediate death the school community is facing.

For teenagers, experiencing the death of someone their own age can be especially traumatic because it shatters their sense of immortality. As they grow more and more independent of their parents, a feeling of vulnerability pervades their lives where they cannot imagine anything penetrating their powerful, magical shields. This is a healthy and necessary part of life's process which allows an adolescent to venture forth and to take risks—but soft spots can be found in their shields when confronted with a peer's death. For these reasons The HEALS Program developed special Death Crisis Intervention Teams, that are available upon request, to go into schools to provide the extra emotional support needed for students and faculty during times of death crisis.

What HEALS Death Crisis Intervention Teams Provide

The support given by a HEALS Death Crisis Intervention Team can be broad or minimal depending upon the needs of the students, faculty, and parents involved in the death crisis and how severe the trauma is. The HEALS DCI Team is usually assigned to a designated room to create a safe, comfortable environment within the school where the students and faculty can come during the day to share and process their feelings using the expressive arts. Materials included in the HEALS environment might be pillows, a centerpiece, a lighted candle (if the school permits), lots of stuffed teddy bears for cuddling, a few tables with art supplies, blank paper, envelopes, a graffiti table (covered with paper), a memory box(es), and perhaps some fresh flowers to create an inviting space that feels comfortable.

Soft, huggable teddy bears have proven to be very valuable assets in times of crises for all ages. If the cuddly "working bears" are allowed to leave the HEALS room, facilitators need to be prepared for the possibility that some of them may never return, unless some sort of check-out system is put in place.

Most of the support provided on the first day is on a drop-in basis, with permission from teachers. Facilitators, if there are a number of them, are scattered about the room. As the children first enter they may feel shy and a little hesitant as they begin to explore the HEALS environment. A facilitator might briefly explain what HEALS is, perhaps inviting the child or children into the circle to sit on pillows, maybe hold a bear, and chat together. After listening to a student(s), the facilitator may encourage the student or faculty member to put their feelings, memories, and/or pain into one of the available expressive arts materials. They may be invited to draw a picture, write a poem, or take care of some unfinished business with the deceased which can be placed into a memory box that the students may decorate. Worry dolls are useful in helping children get in touch with some of their fears. Naming the fear and giving it to the doll(s) "to help" may provide a release and lightening effect.

There will be students who come to the HEALS room just to be with others in the safe, unconditional environment. Choosing not to participate or chat is okay—some need space to be with their feelings in quiet ways.

A HEALS DCI Team is designed only to assist during the initial crisis (for the first day or two), and may be called upon in the future for consultation to recommend ritual and commemorative ideas appropriate for school settings. HEALS facilitators need to bear in mind that the primary goals are to enable the school to become independent in dealing with grief issues. The HEALS facilitators are available for consultation, suggestions, and recommendations for any future processing, commemoration, or closure rituals. Note: The most valuable gift care-givers can offer is to listen and be a witness to the pain.

Note: Organizations like the Red Cross and the International Critical Incident Stress Foundation provide excellent training in defusing and debriefing techniques and are highly recommended for any crisis response team. Their respective websites can be found on the Internet.

Calling The HEALS DCI Team Into Action

The counselor, nurse, or administrator at the school in crisis must make a request to HEALS in order for a Death Crisis Intervention Team to come and provide help. Once the school makes the request for HEALS support, a facilitator on the DCI team will be designated to act as the liaison with a school official. This liaison provides an assessment of the school's needs and determines with them how the HEALS DCI Team may best assist.

The responsibilities of the HEALS liaison are to:

 A. Assess if the school has a death protocol in place. If not, they can offer them a sample HEALS Death Protocol (see Death Protocol).

 B. Find out what information the school will be providing to the students and parents in regards to the details and circumstances of the death so all information is correct, pertinent, and consistent.

 C. Secure a quiet, safe room within the school where the HEALS environment can be set up—hopefully with a carpet and some tables and chairs (often in a library or empty classroom).

 D. Establish the time when HEALS DCI Team will arrive at school and request for any materials that will be needed.

 E. Provide all information, expectations, times, location, and the name/s of school liaison(s) to other HEALS DCI Team members.

The HEALS DCI Team will be responsible for gathering the materials needed such as the centerpiece and candle or flowers, kooshball, bears, pillows, worry dolls and stones, anger release materials such as a drum or punching bag, a memory box for the deceased, and a memory box for the family (in case of a divorced family, two family boxes should be provided), and art materials such as cray-pas, colored pencils, or crayons, plain and lined paper, and envelopes. Most schools will provide all the art materials, papers, and envelopes upon request. **Important Note:** If a Memory Box full of children's letters, cards and art are being sent to a bereft family, preview all materials being sent for appropriateness and withhold when necessary.

It is very beneficial for the DCI Team to attend any faculty meetings either at the beginning of the day or at the end to help support the faculty and brief them on how HEALS can help. Participation of this kind is not always possible or desired by the school officials. Sensitivity to their needs is of the utmost importance. Be aware of what attitude you bring with you into this situation—are you there to provide unconditional support or do you have an agenda? Maintain a sense of flexibility throughout the day.

Troubleshooting for Teachers and Students

Deep feelings may take time before they surface, therefore some children and teachers may have more difficulty concentrating at unpredictable moments throughout the first few days or weeks as the waves of grief pass over them. There may be moments when a student or teacher need to leave the classroom. HEALS facilitators and/or selected faculty are requested to walk through the halls of the school periodically as troubleshooters to locate any children or faculty who may be in need of some support. The faculty may issue special passes to help keep tabs on students who need to leave the classrooms or have appointments with the HEALS DCI Team.

Keeping the students safe while emotions are high is essential, especially for teenagers. Any student or faculty who is experiencing deep emotions should be encouraged not to drive or leave the school until they are feeling grounded and safe enough to leave and/or operate a motor vehicle.

Remember that being part of a DCI Team is emotionally challenging. The day(s) can be long and unpredictable. It is normal for periods of time to pass where no students or faculty are in need of support—and then suddenly there may be a flurry of people needing support. Note: Group appointments may need to be utilized.

Each death crisis is a unique experience. Once the initial awkward moments pass, before strangers become friends, connections are made with others touching the most precious gift of all human endeavors—sharing and receiving unconditional care.

The HEALS Program

Guidelines When Dealing With Children In Grief

• Gently encourage the truth to be told. If anyone is in denial, or over-protective, children will find out. A lack of information, or misinformation, can lead to wild imaginings or self-blame.

• If at all possible, it is best to tell children about a death that has occurred in familiar surroundings by someone who is close to them.

• Trust your intuition, instincts, and gut feelings.

• Encourage children to express their feelings and thoughts in safe ways.

• Help the children to understand that grief is a process and that s/he can make it through.

• Allow children to participate in conversations and rituals about death, before and after. Be prepared for morbid or unusual questions concerning the details of death.

• Any unusual behaviors or children concerning you should be brought to the attention of the appropriate persons (i.e. counselors, parents, etc.).

• Use appropriate death terminology such as dead, death, died.

• Allow yourself not to have the answers to everything—leave room for their doubts, questioning, and differences of opinion.

• Allow yourself to express your own emotions of grief.

• Share the knowledge that it is okay to laugh, play, and have a good time; it does not mean you do not love or care about the person.

• Help them realize that not talking about the loss will not make it go away.

• Be aware that children who did not know the person may still experience deep feelings of grief—they may be reacting to earlier losses or fearing of their own mortality.

• Keep a neutral stance—do not judge, blame, criticize, or give advice.

• Be aware that not only the child who may be "acting out" needs help, but that quiet or withdrawn behavior may be masking the pain.

• Maintain gentle structure and balance.

• Be aware that the child who is always moving about when you are talking together does not mean s/he is disrespectful; the child may simply need to move!

• **<u>ABOVE ALL ELSE:</u> Being an empathic listener and witnessing a child's story and pain is the best support you can possibly give to a child in grief.**

From *The Art of Healing Childhood Grief*, Black & Simpson, 2004

The HEALS Death Crisis Intervention Program:
Debriefing Groups of Children

Classroom and small group *debriefings* are generally done approximately 24 hours after a critical incident as opposed to *defusings* which are done immediately following a tragedy. These processes are slightly more structured and allow much more time. Do not attempt to force children to participate in the group process or include children who are psychological distressed. Additionally, these groups will not be supportive if there are students who are hurtful or divisive in any way. Establish a safe environment, both physically and psychologically, before proceeding.

Meeting with small groups of children following a crisis provides an opportunity to:

Objectives:
- To provide an opportunity for children to talk about the event that occurred
- To provide education and skills for coping with loss and trauma
- To assess children who may need extra support and make referrals

Protocol:
- State purpose
- Set rules for discussion: Everyone has a right to pass or not participate.
- Describe process (maintain appropriateness for developmental level of children)

I. Introduction of Facilitators (if necessary)

II. Safety: As in all critical incident situations, children need to feel safe. Discuss safety relative to to the critical incident and what children can do to feel empowered.

III. Exploration or Disclosure of Events: Using the talking stick/kooshball give each person an opportunity to speak using the following framework:

    A. Acknowledge the Crisis: Can you tell us what you know or understand about the event?

    B. Clarify any Misconceptions: Work for consistency of group experience—creating a shared narrative on a factual basis, provide correct information.

IV. Exploration of Reactions: Provide a color attunement exercise or invite the children to draw images or pictures using colors to express how they are feeling. For older children, provide an opportunity for them to make images in response to the following questions:

"What is happening within you (your body, your mind) at this very moment?"
"What happened?"
"What is the worst part of this event for you?"

Notes of Caution: 1) *If the drawing activity requests that the children create a drawing focusing on the tragic nature of a crisis event, be sure to also allow for a drawing that includes the positive aspects of the event, such as what they have learned. 2) For later debriefings, a few months down the line, it might be helpful to focus on how the children may have become stronger because of the incident.*

V. Sharing Circle: Allow the children to share their art and their reactions with the group.

    A. Normalize their Experiences and Reactions: Decrease the sense of isolation the children might be feeling after such an experience, and provide helpful handouts, if possible.

    B. Explore and Identify Coping Skills: Empower the children by discussing ways they can be safe, explore self-soothing techniques with them, and help the children identify who they can turn to if more support is needed.

VI. Closure: Allow each person to say something in closing or use the color feeling again to assess if there have been any emotional changes.

Death Crisis Intervention: Death of A Teacher

Teachers usually play very important roles in the lives of children. They spend large portions of time providing role modeling, nurturance, knowledge, skills, and friendship. Children often experience grief at the end of the school year when they must say good-bye to their teacher and prepare themselves for the next teacher. To go further and lose a teacher by death can be as profound as the loss of a family member.

In the event of the death of a teacher, the children will have many fears and questions. It can be very helpful if their concerns are shared within the group context of the classroom. In preparing the children for a future without their teacher, the following considerations may be helpful to alleviate further trauma for the students:

• Who will fill in for their teacher?

The children will need reassurance that a <u>familiar</u> person will be in the classroom with them until a permanent teacher is found. This person should know the children <u>and</u> the teacher who died so that as a group they can process their feelings and stories together about the beloved teacher. Providing an atmosphere of care, safety, and control will help them while they try to readjust.

• Provide a safe place for children and staff to be able to go to grieve or talk.

Have compassionate people available for children and staff such as counselors, nurses, parents, HEALS facilitators, clergy, etc.

• Introducing the new teacher:

The children need to be reminded when the new teacher begins, that s/he will not be attempting to replace their deceased teacher. No one can ever do that. Things may not be done exactly the same way the former teacher did them because they are not the same person. The professional who takes on the teaching position needs to be especially sensitive to the children's feelings. It will be a very difficult role; that person may need extra support from other members of the staff and the parents. The children may reject him/her trying to maintain their loyalty to the deceased teacher, or they may vent their anger and frustration towards him/her. The *Love-Light Ceremony* can be adapted to provide a nice opening to encourage the children to allow new people, like a new teacher, into their hearts.

• Changing the classroom

The new teacher should consider making slow changes to the classroom. By involving the children in creating the changes, they will be creating a team approach the transition. This is both respectful and helpful for the children in taking those first steps towards the stages of acceptance and integration of their loss.

The HEALS Program

Sample Letter to Parents

Regarding Death Crisis:

Dear Parents,

The students, staff, and community have recently lost a beloved friend and teacher, _____ . Miss/Mrs./Mr. _____ died on (date).

Please be aware that your son or daughter may have known Miss/Mrs./Mr. _____ quite well. Teachers and students who work together often develop close friendships.

You, as parents, may see unusual behavior patterns, but which are part of the normal grieving process, as your child attempts to come to terms with this tragedy.

On (Monday), when the students and faculty return to school, we will be holding a general assembly to talk about the loss of Miss/Mrs./Mr_____ .

We hope to be able to answer any questions or concerns the children may have, and to provide them with such resource people as counselors, teachers, community members, grief support counselors, and clergy for extra support during the day. Our guidance counselor and faculty will be monitoring all students and will call parents if any unusual reactions are observed.

All of us in our own way try to make sense of death. We encourage you to make yourselves available for your children to. Listen and accept what is said, even if it is irrational. Encourage them to express their feelings, but let them know we all have different ways of expressing our grief.

Miss/Mrs./Mr. _____ was a gifted and dedicated teacher who touched lives not only in our school but in many others as well. Her/his love of community, children, and teaching will be greatly missed and fondly remembered.

If you have any questions or need further information or support please do not hesitate to call.

Sincerely,

HEALS Death Crisis Intervention: Suicide

Suicide has an unusual aura about it that leaves many of the survivors feeling a deep sense of guilt and anger. Because the deceased <u>deliberately</u> took their own life, loved ones tend to think there was something they should or could have done. Children may wonder what they did that may have caused the suicide, or question if that person truly loved them, and if so, why would they leave? We often get phone calls from people who worry that commemorating someone's life who committed suicide may seem to make a hero of the deceased and is bad role modeling for children. However, if handled appropriately, the loss of life to suicide is an extremely important teaching moment for children. They may learn that all people are precious, and ways to seek help and support when life feels terribly hopeless.

The stigma a family feels after experiencing a suicide of one of its' members often isolates them from others. They feel as if something is wrong with them in that they didn't or couldn't prevent the suicide. A feeling of shame spreads over them. In these instances friends, professional help, and/or group support may be needed to help dissolve the stigma attached to grievers of a suicide.

Over-identification with the deceased is a danger children can experience as they try to cope with the tragedy. If a child focuses frequently on the similarities and how alike the deceased and he/she is, suicidal tendencies could develop. Help the child to understand that they may have certain similarities as the deceased but, in truth, they are different. Each person is an individual and has their own way of handling problems. The person who committed suicide was unable or didn't know any alternatives besides death to solve his/her troubles.

Responding to A School After a Suicide

When HEALS is invited into a school following a suicide crisis, it is generally either to provide support where students and faculty may drop-in and spend some time processing their feelings with a HEALS facilitator(s)—or to facilitate a support group session.

The suicide of a friend or classmate may bring up feelings of guilt and helplessness on the part of some students and staff members. This is a very common initial reaction as they feel the pain and hear the internal tape playing over and over inside their heads of "if only I had "or "I wish I hadn't." Invite the students to talk more about their regrets and share their relationship with the student who died and their feelings surrounding the suicide. It is valuable to give the students a copy of The HEALS Program *Suicide Warning Signs* in hopes that they may feel more competent and alert to notice suicidal messages expressed by other friends or classmates. Gently remind the students that they are not responsible for what anyone else ultimately chooses to do with their life.

Empower children by providing opportunities to learn skills for problem-solving. Discuss what kind of help the deceased could have sought so the child learns what resources are available for him/her if their life should ever become unbearable.

The following are useful guidelines in helping survivors of suicide developed by Dr. Robert G. Stevenson :

- Assist the bereaved to clarify their thoughts and feelings—<u>listening well</u>

- Put an end to unfounded rumors that cause unnecessary additional pain.

- Don't romanticize the suicide by saying that he or she is "better off."

- Commemorate the death by perhaps attending the funeral and allowing the survivors to sense your continuing friendship and support.

- Help the bereaved by recalling the complete person with human strengths as well as weaknesses.

Our HEALS DCI Teams are generally assigned to a designated room where the friends, classmates, and staff may come to get support and find a safe place to be with their pain, confusion, and grief. We arrange the room with pillows, a lighted candle, and stuffed bears that visually convey an atmosphere of relaxation and comfort as we attempt to aesthetically show respect for the deceased as well as a tranquil environment for the mourners.

If we are providing **support on a student drop-in basis**, we keep the mood very casual and are available to listen as the students wander in. After listening to a student(s), we might suggest that they may find it helpful to put their feelings, memories, and/or pain into one of the expressive arts. They may want to draw a picture, write a poem, or take care of some unfinished business with the deceased which can be placed into a memory box that the students may decorate. Sometimes the students just want a place to "hang out" and be with their feelings and this is to be respected.

Important Note: If a Memory Box or letters created by the children are to be sent to bereft family members, preview all materials being sent for appropriateness, withhold when necessary.

The HEALS Program

Suicide Warning Signs

If you suspect someone is thinking about suicide, watch the person, listen for messages, and look for any of these signs:

1. A previous suicide attempt

2. Increased sadness, tearfulness, moodiness, or irritability

3. Loss of appetite or excessive eating

4. Changes in sleeping patterns—sleeping too much or too little lasting at least several days

5. Withdrawal from favorite activities and relationships

6. Expressing feelings of helplessness and hopelessness

7. Evidence of alcohol or drug binges or other self-destructive behavior

8. Verbal comments that tell of plan to "end it all" or "I can't take it anymore."

9. Unusual neglect of personal appearance

10. Expressing suicidal thoughts or a preoccupation with death

11. Giving away or disposing of prized possessions such as pictures, tapes/CD's, toys, or clothing

12. Changes in school performances, suddenly getting poor grades

13. A profound depression in response to a recent loss or rejection

14. Personality changes of nervousness, agitation, or outbursts of anger

15. A change in behavior to lethargy and apathy

What To Do If You Suspect A Person Is Suicidal

- Take your feelings and the warning signs seriously
- Tell someone; a responsible adult
- Discuss it openly and frankly
- Show interest
- Be a good listener
- If at high risk, don't leave the person alone
- Get professional help

HEALS Death Crisis Intervention: Homicide

When someone in our community has been murdered, it is common to lose faith in our society and not feel safe in the world. We feel uncomfortable and scared.

The <u>initial psychological reactions</u> following a murder are intense and very different from the early stages of other grief experiences. The grievers tend to feel:

1. Overwhelming rage at the perpetrator

2. Violated (like a rape victim)

3. Compelled to seek revenge. (It is common for family members to purchase weapons after a homicide)

4. Terror, fear, helplessness, guilt, and phobias

The more justice is demonstrated—the better the coping of the survivors and the community. Since homicide goes through the criminal justice system, the immediate family does not receive the support from the health-care network. Unfortunately, the criminal justice system can tend to aggravate the family's grief. Families may have to deal with an autopsy in which they experience feeling victimized again. Then they may have to contend with police, prosecutors, and lawyers. To compound the situation, it is not unusual for inquiring reporters and media coverage to exacerbate the pain invading their privacy during this traumatic time. Hopefully this situation will change as sensitivity to the emotional needs of the family is heightened.

Suicide is a mental health issue, but homicide is not. When individuals say that they do not want to live any longer, we give them counseling and support in recognizing that they have choices. When someone says, "I could just kill him!", we, as a society, tend to dismiss such a statement, assuming that the person is just angry and making an idle threat. Unfortunately, in the wake of so many school shootings and rising terrorist's acts, it is imperative that we listen and take action when we hear these cries for help. Rage affects the body and the mind. Uncontrolled rage is what prompts homicides.

Children who witness the homicide of a parent are at great risk and need immediate <u>professional</u> intervention. Post Traumatic Stress Disorder results whenever a child witnesses the death of a parent. Long-term help is needed to process the horror of the murder.

Adults and children alike may experience a feeling of vulnerability and powerlessness. Other types of death can usually be explained, but when an act of violence is committed, there is often no explanation that will take away the feelings that arise. Earl Grollman maintains in his book *Talking With Children About Death* that "healing after a murder is a lifelong process."

Death Crisis Intervention and Homicide

Some of the most important things to keep in mind for HEALS facilitators working with children involved in a death crisis situation of a homicide are:

1. Provide accurate facts…be honest with the children
2. Listen to them…give hugs freely and often <u>if</u> the child wants them
3. Assure them that they are safe…often
4. Grieving takes time…allow for it.
5. Allow constructive ways to release feelings
6. Do not feel you must have all the answers
7. Grief issues may arise from past losses…be prepared to hear them
8. Children exhibit grief differently from adults (see Signs of Grief page 82)
9. Offer structure, but be lax in maintaining it for a few days
10. Do not remove the deceased's belongings immediately

Adults need to prepare themselves for the behaviors and questions that come from the children following a homicide. They often want to know *all* the morbid facts: How did _____ die?; Did _____ experience pain?; Did _____ know s/he was going to die?; etc.. The school needs to decide before the children arrive what they will be told. Each faculty member and HEALS facilitator should have the information in print. Remember: the children will obtain details from newspapers, friends, their families, etc. *Correct information is essential.*

Many educators may not realize the effects a violent death has upon children. Special attention should be paid to the changes in the behaviors of children who have lost someone important due to murder. (Information on organizations that can be contacted for support can be found in the resource section of this manual.)

Due to the intensity of this type of crisis, it is essential for the HEALS facilitators to take extra special care of themselves immediately following this crisis work. (See the section on *Facilitator Sustenance* in this manual.)

The HEALS Program
Supporting Children Through Disasters, Terrorist Attacks or Times of War

It is very difficult to know what to do first when a disaster strikes. Parents and caregivers have the more complicated task of having to balance their own reactions while supporting the children in their care. The following are suggestions adults might consider after a tragic event occurs to help them. It is followed by children's common behavioral responses to tragedies, disasters and war with tips on how to manage certain behaviors.

- **As adults or primary caretakers, it is important to be positive role models for children.** How you as an adult cope with your feelings and responses during and following a tragedy provides modeling for children in how to handle their own emotions and feel safe again following a crisis. Caregivers may admit their concerns to children, but need to assure them of their abilities to cope with the situation.

- **If at all possible, it is best to tell children about a tragedy that has occurred in familiar surroundings by someone who is close to them, preferably a family member.**

- **Use language that is simple and easy for them to understand.** Provide basic accurate facts that are appropriate for their age level. For very young children it would be more appropriate to use the words "naughty person" rather than "terrorist".

- **Safety is the primary concern of most children.** Reassure them of their own safety, and that adults in charge are doing their best to make sure we are safe.

- **Consider limiting children's exposure to television, radio and internet.** If children have seen traumatic events on the tv, process with them what they saw. Answer their questions simply and as honestly as possible. It is okay to *not* know all the answers to their questions. Be aware to also limit adult conversations about the tragedy within the hearing of children.

- **It's okay to share your own feelings such as shock, sadness, disbelief, anger.** Be sure to model constructive things you do to soothe yourself when strong emotions rise (i.e. talking with a friend, walking in nature, petting an animal, taking a bath, running, playing sports, playing music or doing art, seeking a counselor, etc.) Explore and encourage children to express their feelings and thoughts in safe ways, too. If you have fears or intense anger find another adult who can listen to you so you do not pass this along to your children. Children can usually tell when their parents are under stress—and they may internalize and blame themselves.

- **Allow children to ask questions about the tragedy or war.** Try to hear what is really being asked to understand their specific worries.

- **Return to normal daily routines as soon as possible.**

- **Children may overhear others say things that may be frightening, confusing or hateful.** It is important to encourage children to talk with a parent or teacher about what they heard.

- **Parents and caregivers should be alert to significant changes in a child's behaviors.** Appropriate support such as counseling or professional advice may be needed.

Children's Common Behavioral Responses to Tragedies & War

- Very young children may have difficulty expressing their fears and may benefit by drawing, painting, art activities, play through puppetry or toys. (Be aware that some children may act out the tragic events in their play, in this way they are trying to come to terms with what happened.)

- Children who are very young may ask repetitive questions as they try to understand or seek assurances about their safety. Provide them with reassurances as well as simple, repeated explanations that are developmentally appropriate.

- Younger children may express their worries by experiencing difficulty separating from parents, or refusing to attend school while adolescents may become more argumentative or show a decline in academic or school performance.

- Children may experience upsetting dreams or nightmares, and may regress to bedwetting. Provide them with comfort and understanding (not shaming!) and extra love and support.

- If children need more cuddling or want to sleep with a parent, indulge them for a little while, it should soon diminish. Leave extra lights on such as nightlights or hall lights.

- Many children experience physical complaints such as stomach aches, headaches, or dizziness with no apparent physical cause. They may visit the school nurse more than usual. This is usually a sign that they cannot concentrate in class and are in need of some "time out" and extra loving care.

- Children of all ages may experience loss of concentration and an inability to focus. Allow extra time for them to finish tasks, and provide written instructions for them regarding homework or tasks.

- Some children may withdraw from family and friends or not find pleasure in activities that they usually enjoyed.

- Children can feel more empowered if they can help those in need. Find ways they can support emergency workers, or gather donations for those in need. Being of service to the community or those affected by the tragedy or war can help children (and adults!) feel some power and control, and mitigate the effects of helplessness that often occurs when a tragedy strikes.

Post Traumatic Stress Disorder

The closer a child is to a disaster the more complicated their reactions might be. If they directly experienced, witnessed or participated in a tragic event, or had a friend or family member killed or seriously injured, they are more likely to experience difficulties or symptoms of PTSD (Post Traumatic Stress Disorder). Children with PTSD tend to have repeated episodes where they re-experience the trauma over and over in their sleep, dreams and play. This behavior does not diminish over time. What follows is a list of symptoms to be watchful for when working with these children. These symptoms may occur soon after the event or can surface months or even years later. To help prevent or minimize PTSD symptoms parents of children directly affected by a tragedy should seek professional advice. Pediatricians or family doctors can provide referrals to a children's therapist or psychiatrist.

PTSD symptoms:
- Persistent intrusive thoughts of the tragic event
- Refusal to return to school
- Clingy behavior towards parents such as "shadowing" them around
- Fears that are persistent and related to the tragedy
- Anxiety and fear of separation
- Sleep disturbances such as nightmares, night terrors, screaming during sleep that extend more than several days after the event
- Bedwetting
- Loss of concentration ability to focus
- Irritability
- Startle responses, jumpiness
- Changes in behaviors that are not typical for the child
- Physical complaints for which no cause can be found (stomach aches, headaches)
- Withdrawal from friends and family members
- Decreased activity or loss of interest in activities usually enjoyed
- Preoccupation with the tragic events

*Some of the above information was adapted from a commentary immediately following the September 11th Terrorist attacks in 2001 on Vermont Public Radio, September 12th, 2001. Permission to use this information was granted by the writer/commentator, Rebecca Coffey and Vermont Public Radio.

Helping Teachers and Parents Cope in the Aftermath of a Disaster, Terrorist Attack or Time of War

In the wake of a tragedy there are often emotional and physical responses that we as adults experience as we try to grapple with what has happened. These reactions may include the following:

Feelings of helplessness	Sadness/depression
Loss of appetite	Headaches
Inability to concentrate	Stomach problems
Increased use of alcohol or drugs	Memory loss
Nightmares	Anger/Revenge
Sleeping problems (too much or little)	Skin disorders or rashes
Shortness of breath	Increased heart rate

As teachers and parents it is essential to take time to meet your own needs so that you may be able to help and support those in your care. Here are some suggestions for self-care in the aftermath of a disaster or terrorist attack or during a time of war.

• Keep to your daily schedule and routines as much as possible.

• Take care of your own needs so you can be helpful to others.

• Talk with another adult to process your painful feelings. It is okay to let children know your feelings about the tragedy, but be mindful of their ages and how much they can integrate.

• Allow yourself to feel your feelings and find appropriate and healthy ways to self-soothe (i.e. hugging and talking with friends and family, walking in nature, petting an animal, taking a bath, running, playing sports, cooking, playing music or doing art, seeking a counselor, etc.)

• Slow down and do not have high expectations of yourself or others in the aftermath of a disaster. It is normal to regress or have difficulty focusing, or making decisions while coming to terms with what has happened. Do what is necessary and put the rest on a waiting list.

• Connect with your support systems and communities—friends, family, and religious groups or spiritual paths. Be willing to ask for and accept help from others.

• Transform feelings of anger or revenge to constructive actions to empower yourself. Make donations of blood, money, food, clothing, toys or health kits to help others in need.

• Increase physical activity to release stress.

• Be mindful of eating well-balanced meals and drinking more fluids. Decrease or avoid caffeine and alcohol consumption.

The HEALS Program

Children's Reactions to Trauma/Stress

Signs most often seen at school:

Crying/Sadness/Depression
Vulnerability/helplessness
Difficulty concentrating
Drop in school performance
Increased heart rate

Ambivalence
Worry/anxiety
Irritability/fighting
Social withdrawal
Shortness of breath

Anger/Revenge
Memory Loss
Distrust
Loss of appetite
Headaches, stomachaches

Signs most often seen at home:

Separation issues/not wanting to attend school
Regressive behaviors (thumbsucking, bedwetting)
Clinging, Fear of being left alone
Nightmares/terrors

Changes in eating/sleeping habits
Excessive fear of darkness
Isolation from rest of family/friends
Use or increased use of drugs or alcohol
(in adolescents)

Section V: Facilitator Sustenance
Helpful Gardening Tools

Our lives can be likened to gardens in which we plant the seeds of the fruits we want to germinate, grow, and bloom. As we continue on our path of self-fulfillment and actualization, we become more and more conscious of the stimuli we allow to enter our internal garden. We are the creators of our gardens, and as gardeners, we take full responsibility for the lack of bounty or abundance we create. Thus the first part of this section focuses on ways to care for our physical, mental, emotional, and spiritual well-being. The remainder of this section is divided into three gardening categories: Planting Seeds with Quotes and Poetry, Warming our Souls with Inspiring Literature, and Resources that Yield Growth. Our hope is that this section of the HEALS manual will enhance your inner garden with beauty, peace, creativity, and love

Taking Care of Yourself

Within you there is a stillness and a sanctuary
to which you can retreat at any time and be yourself.
—Hermann Hesse

When working with those who are grieving, it is important to know our limitations and spend time nourishing ourself. To be fully present for others is one thing, but to be fully present for ourself and attending to our own needs throughout the day is often more challenging and an incredible gift to give. When we provide for our own needs, we are more able to meet the needs of others without feeling drained or resentful.

In the beginning of this section of the manual, we will be addressing how to nourish and develop ourselves in four separate and yet interrelated areas: the *physical* (caring for our bodies), the *mental* (examining the way our mind perceives life), the *emotional* (gaining an awareness of what we feel in our body), and the *spiritual* (connecting with a reverence for a deeper quality of life). The remainder of this section will provide quotes, poetry, food for thought, inspiration, and resources to allow us to connect with that inner wisdom and knowing that we already possess. These suggestions are given with the belief that if you "indulge" in at least one of them daily, you will be giving and receiving love from the most important person in your life: YOU! As you love yourself you are more able to love others and receive love. We create a ripple effect that is limitless…………………………………………………………

When we are providing support for grieving individuals, it is important to not allow ourselves to become over-extended. When this occurs we are unable to be effective in a HEALS session. The signs of over-extension while providing grief support could include any of the following:

• inability to concentrate	• feeling signs of grief
• dread of going to the group	• feeling rushed all the time
• triggering of own issues	• unable to separate own issues
• inner resentment	• overreacting to another's grief
• failure to honor inner child	• non-completion of activities

The following suggestions may be helpful in gaining greater ease and control of your life:

• **Give yourself permission to say "No"** before or when you begin to feel over-extended. Remember that "No." is a complete sentence.

• **Strive to avoid giving anyone an answer until you have had time to think about it.**

• **Ask others for help.** Many of us do not realize that most of what we do can also be done by someone else. Most people enjoy helping. Let them!

Physical Well-Being

Revere the body and care for it, for it is a temple.
—Muktananda

You may live in a body which is a gracious, comfortable palace, an unknown residence, or a machine that can be pushed to extreme limits riding the edge of self-abuse. The body is often given little thought or attention until physical discomfort or dis-ease manifests. When this happens, the body is signaling you to pay attention to an imbalance existing between it and the mind.

Stress and trauma can have a powerful impact upon the body creating tension within the muscles and organs that can last for years. Mental, emotional, and physical tension can cause tightness in the body. This tension often blocks or draws an immense amount of energy from the body—energy that could be used in more creative and productive ways.

There are a variety of ways to release tension and blocked energy. We highly recommend that you explore some of the activities listed below and find the ones that make you feel revitalized both mentally and physically.

• yoga	• bodywork	• movement	• walking/hiking
• Tai Chi	• dancing	• running	• working out
• singing	• playing music	• bike riding	• horseback riding
• painting	• gardening	• bird-watching	• clayworking
• skiing	• sports	• breathwork	• bubble baths
• massage	• napping	• reading	• movie-going

Remember that these activities need not be strenuous to have a positive impact upon your mind and body. Be gentle, patient, and give yourself permission to change old patterns slowly without pain. The adage: No pain, no gain is not necessarily true.

When memories, daily stresses, and conflicts weigh upon the body there may be a temptation to repress them by indulging in substances to help numb the feelings and distract the mind. We encourage you to become aware of why you use certain substances or foods, and explore those food choices which are of the greatest value for your mind and body.

Another important element of physical well-being is to breathe deeply and fully. An old Yogic proverb states that "Life is in the breath: therefore s/he who only half breathes, half lives." Breathing deeply affects the quality of our physical and mental states. While the body can exist for many days and weeks without food, it will perish after a few minutes without air. Yogis believe this life-force or prana, when experienced deeply and properly, relieves tension and will improve the quality of our blood, complexion, and general health.

The ideal is to make every moment of our life a moment of wonder in which we are choosing the best and creating the most fulfilling life we can imagine.

Mental Well-Being

*Learn to forgive yourself, again and again
and again and again.*
—Sheldon Kopp

Many of us are aware of the fact that we have a nearly continuous inner dialogue going on in our minds. The mind is busy "talking" to itself, keeping up an endless commentary about life, the world, our feelings, our problems, other people, etc.

The effect of the words and ideas running through our minds is very important. Most of the time we aren't consciously aware of this stream of thoughts, and yet what we are "telling ourselves" in our minds is the basis on which we form our experience of reality. Our mental commentary influences and colors our feelings and perceptions about what is going on in our lives, and it is these thoughts that ultimately attract and create everything that happens to us.

Our attitudes (the way we view things) and activities (the things we do on a daily basis) are sometimes unconscious, habitual, limited, and are a result of the programming we absorbed early in life from the world around us. In order to move beyond programming, beyond knee-jerk reflexes, and operate from a deeper awareness, it is helpful to consciously listen to and become aware of what our mind is telling us. Allow yourself to pause and reflect on the content of these messages and ask yourself if that is truly what you believe or want to believe or are the notions rattling around in your mind what you have been taught through your socialization process. Weeding out the unproductive ideas and beliefs can be tedious and yet exciting. To take responsibility for the creation of our thoughts is an empowering and creative experience.

The following suggestions may be helpful in assisting the mind to become more fruitful and creative:

- **Choose how you want to see the world.** Are you coming from love or fear? Is your cup half empty or half full? Are you enmeshed in black and white thinking or is there room for gray?
- **Expect miracles.**
- **Carefully use your thoughts to create what you want in life.** You are capable of growth, change, and magic unless you choose to remain static.
- **Maintain a lightness and a sense of humor.**
- **And finally try to utilize this two-step formula for handling stress:**

    Step 1: **Don't sweat the small stuff.**
    Step 2: **Remember, it's all small stuff.**

Emotional Well-Being

But before I look out…let me first of all gaze within myself.
—Rainer Maria Rilke

As infants and toddlers we expressed all of our feelings, needs, and wants in pre-verbal and non-verbal forms. Those of us who grew up in western cultures were probably not encouraged to express our feelings. We were taught the inappropriateness of expressing ourselves, sometimes in harsh forms.

We want to encourage you to explore your emotional landscape and find safe, creative ways to discharge your feelings and supportive people who will accompany you in the process. In recalling your childhood and uncovering patterns you developed for survival or conflict-resolution, you may be able to understand their negative impacts on your life and relationships today. Quick knee-jerk *reactions* to situations as opposed to healthy *responses* from your deeper self are examples of learned behaviors.

Although revisiting the past can often be painful, the rewards have the potential for making the journey a most valuable one. Your past is your unique story and it contributes to who you are today. You have the power to transform the residual effects and release repressed feelings from the past in order to free up new resources of personal power and energy to create better relationships.

You are hopefully learning that the expressive arts are readily accessible tools with which to explore your inner world of thoughts and feelings. Give yourself lots of freedom to go into your private world of emotions, fantasies, memories, wishes, deepest thoughts and regrets. Know that feelings change and that we are rarely stuck in an emotion—unless we choose to be. It takes practice and attention to become conscious of our emotional states.

The following are suggestions you may find helpful in learning to stay in touch with your emotions:

• journal-keeping	• dream big	• drawing
• writing	• painting	• guided visualization
• bodywork	• singing	• creating rituals
• playing	• laughing	• stay in bed one full day
• meditation	• therapy	• centering exercises
• support groups	• releasework	• walking in nature
• yoga	• claywork	• rest when tired
• dreamwork	• poetry	• assertiveness training
• LOVE yourself	• reaching out	• breathe, then respond

Deep inside you there is a child who is the keeper of your emotions. Strive to nurture this child and allow his/her creative forces to bloom for you; and when you are truly nurtured you will be able to be your best. So take time to tune into your feelings, trust your intuition, and make decisions that are for the highest good of all—including yourself.

Spiritual Well-Being

The most beautiful experience we can have is the mysterious.
—Albert Einstein

spir-it: n 1. a life-giving force: soul the animating principle. 2. the active presence of God in human life.

spir-i-tu-al-i-ty: adj 1. of, relating to, or consisting of spirit or sacred matters.

If you are not already on a path seeking spiritual fulfillment—the meaning of life and why you are here—facing death may trigger the onset of a spiritual quest. It has been a common thread throughout history to ponder the meaning of life—to sense that everything happens as part of a plan or purpose even though the pattern is hidden from us.

While some may prefer to deny the existence of death, there are those who are able to contemplate their own death, which in turn enables them to participate more fully in living. This awakening beyond that of normal consciousness opens us up to the beauty of life, miracles, wonderment, awe in what is around us, and reflection on our soul's purpose.

Being open and respectful to another's viewpoints and spiritual beliefs is essential in doing griefwork. It is not necessary to understand or believe in someone else's path to be open to and accepting of their beliefs as they share them with you. Each individual's belief system is important to them and provides them with structure and meaning. It is vitally important to respect another's beliefs and not attempt to convert them to your belief system. When accompanying someone into their dark night of the soul, humility is a valuable quality to cultivate. Regardless of a person's beliefs or life situation, it is helpful to remember that you will never meet anyone who you are better than!

The following are ways to take care of yourself spiritually while doing bereavement work:

- meditation
- prayer
- cultivating wonder/awe
- writing & poetry
- opening the heart
- immersing self in nature
- expressing yourself
- chanting
- creating affirming rituals
- attending your church, temple, mosque, meeting house, spiritual center, or places sacred to you.

The following quote by Martha Graham from <u>Dance to the Piper</u> by Agnes de Mille underlines the importance we each have to be fully who we are in order to give our special talents and gifts to ourselves and others:

There is a vitality, a life-force, an energy, a quickening that is translated through you into action and because there is only one of you in all of time, this expression is unique. And if you block it, it will never exist through any other medium and be lost. The world will not have it. It is not your business to determine how good it is nor how valuable nor how it compares with other expressions. It is your business to keep it yours clearly and directly, to keep the channel open. You do not even have to believe in yourself or your work. You have to keep open and aware directly to the urges that motivate you. Keep the channel open.

My Vow and Intent as a HEALS Facilitator

When working with an individual or group the following principles are to be kept in mind in order that The HEALS Program will remain uniform and the facilitators clear as to their role in the process:

1. I am a trusted facilitator of The HEALS Program.

2. I will set aside my personal "stuff" when I am working with children in bereavement. If something arises during one of the sessions, I will take care of it following the session with my co-facilitator or one of the program coordinators, a trusted friend, a therapist, or by myself.

3. I will strive to trust my intuition and be flexible. It is more important to connect with a child than to accomplish what is spelled out on my session objectives.

4. I am not expected to "fix" each and every situation. Being a good listener and asking carefully chosen questions are always more valuable than preaching.

5. I will look for opportunities to empower children, to help them find their own solutions and answers.

6. I will follow The HEALS Framework when planning each session. I will ask for feedback from the program coordinator if I wish to pursue a different course.

7. I will offer a gentle approach to the children in my group.

8. I will attempt to continue my own spiritual growth in whatever way best works for me.

Seeds of Inspiration

Art by Dale Schwarz

The Road Not Taken

Two roads diverged in a yellow wood,
And sorry I could not travel both
And be one traveler, long I stood
And looked down one as far as I could
To where it bent in the undergrowth;

Then took the the other, just as fair,
And having perhaps the better claim,
Because it was grassy and wanted wear;
Though as for that the passing there
Had worn them really about the same,

And both that morning equally lay
In leaves no step had trodden black,
Yet knowing how leads on to way,
I doubted if I should ever come back.

I shall be telling this with a sigh
Somewhere ages and ages hence:
Two road diverged in a wood, and I--
I took the one less traveled by,
And that has made all the difference.
                                    -Robert Frost

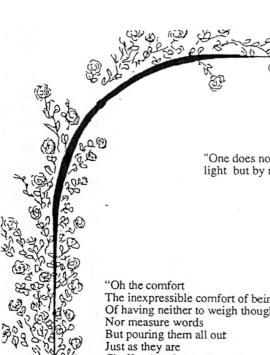

"One does not become enlightened by imaging figures of light but by making the darkness conscious."
-Carl Jung

"Oh the comfort
The inexpressible comfort of being safe with a person
Of having neither to weigh thoughts
Nor measure words
But pouring them all out
Just as they are
Chaff and grain together
Sure that a faithful hand
Will receive them
Keep what is worth keeping
And with a breath of kindness
Blow the rest away."
-Shoshone Saying

"Whatever you can do, or dream you can, begin it.
Boldness has genius, power, and magic in it."
-Goethe

Do not follow
where the
path may lead,
Go, instead, where
there is no path
and leave a trail.
-anonymous

"The creative individual not only respects the irrational in himself, but courts the most promising source of novelty in his own thought... The creative person is both more primitive and more cultured, more destructive and more constructive, crazier and saner, than the average person."
-Frank Barron

348

"After a while, you learn the subtle difference between
holding a hand and chaining a soul,
And you learn that love doesn't mean leaning,
and company doesn't always mean security.
You begin to learn that kisses aren't contracts
and presents aren't promises.
You begin to accept your defeats
with your head up and your eyes ahead
with the grace of a woman or gentleman,
not the grief of a child.
You learn to build all your roads on today
because tomorrow's ground is too uncertain for plans,
and futures have a way of falling down in mid-flight.
After a while you learn that
even sunshine burns if you get too much.
So you plant your own garden
and decorate your own soul instead of waiting
for someone else to bring you flowers.
You learn that you really can endure...
that you are strong...that you do have worth...
that you are beautiful..."

"Every act of creation is first
of all an act of destruction."
-Picasso

"It is not true that life is one damn thing after another--
it is one damn thing over and over."
-Edna St. Vincent Millay

"For a successful journey all you need is a good pair of
shoes and an open mind."
-Advice given by woman in airport

"I was so cold I almost got married."
-Shelley Winters

"Until one is committed
there is hesitancy, the chance to draw back,
always ineffectiveness.
Concerning all acts of initiative (and creation),
there is one elementary truth,
the ignorance of which kills countless ideas
and splendid plans:
that the moment one definitely commits oneself,
then Providence moves too.
All sorts of things occur to help one
that would never otherwise have occurred.
A whole stream of events issues from the decision,
raising in one's favour all manner
of unforeseen incidents and meetings
and material assistance,
which no man could have dreamt
would have come his way."

349

Universals

Virginia Satir called them universals-- "an old truth I made up the other day," she would say. Here is a selection from the wealth of her one-liners:

Art by Dale Schwarz

All children need touch; touching is a universal language.

Humans are geared toward growth, so you can always go in that direction. All living systems go toward balance.

The event is never what you have to deal with. Rather, it is the feeling engendered by the event.

Other people's behavior is about where they are at that moment--it does not define you.

Learn to look for the self-esteem issue behind every manifestation. Self-worth is behind every defensive stance, waiting to be born.

The twin ways to restore self-esteem: take a deep breath and give yourself a message of appreciation.

Family of origin issues need to be settled so you can get along in the present family.

There is the pain of recognition and the pain of blame. We cannot avoid the former, and we can learn from that. It is when we blame ourselves or others that we get stuck in pain.

In every new encounter, practice appreciations, not judgment. When your body feels tight, you're into judging. What you judge in another is something in yourself (a projection).

Unless we matter, have a dream, we die.

Freedom is not from the oppressor, but to have choices.

You can't erase anything; you have to evolve it.

Change, growth, influence take place by attraction; not by threat. Punishment doesn't change anything, not a deterrent. Behaviors that don't fit harmony, love, or growth fall away.

Section VI: Bibliography

There are three bibliographical sections in the HEALS manual. The first is an annotated collection of children's books on grief and emotional literacy which we use often in The HEALS Program curriculum. The second section contains children's books found to be sensitive and helpful in dealing with children's bereavement issues. The third section provides a rich resource of adult reference books for adults discussing death, dying, and suicide followed by a selection helpful expressive arts books.

Children's Books Used
With The HEALS Program Curriculum

Bang, Molly. **When Sophie Gets Angry—Really, Really Angry**. NY: Blue Sky Press, 1999. Everybody gets angry sometimes. And for children anger can be very upsetting and frightening. In this book children will see what Sophie does when she gets angry. People do lots of different things when they get angry. What do you do?

Curtis, Jamie Lee. **Today I Feel Silly & Other Moods That Make My Day**. China: Harper Collins Publishers, 1998. We all have moods that change each day. This book helps kids explore, identify, and even have fun with their ever-changing moods. Includes a Fun Wheel at the end of the book that kids can use to describe how they feel today.

Kent, Jack. **There's No Such Thing As a Dragon**. NY: A Golden book, Western Publishing Company, Inc.1975. (currently out of print—find an old copy—it is great!!)

Mellonie, Bryan and Ingpen, Robert. **Lifetimes: The Beautiful Way to Explain Death to Children.** NY: Bantam Books, Inc., 1983. Describes the cycles of life, beginnings and endings in plants, insects, animals and people. A touching book with lovely illustrations.

Sendak, Maurice. **Where The Wild Things Are.** NY: Scholastic, Inc., 1983. A little boy named Max learns about his wildness by getting sent to his bedroom where he becomes King of The Wild Things. When he becomes lonely and hungry he decides to give up being King of The Wild Things and finds his dinner waiting for him.

Seuss, Dr.. **My Many Colored Days.** NY: Alfred Knopf, Inc., 1996. Helps young children realize that they have moods, too, and can express how they feel through color and words.

Varley, Susan. **Badger's Parting Gifts.** New York: Lothrop, Lee & Shephard Books, 1984.
A warm story of how a group of woodland animals experience the loss of their dear friend Badger. Each one remembers a treasured experience, the "gifts" that Badger shared with them.

Brown, Margaret Wise. **The Dead Bird.** New York: Harper Junior Books, 1958. Brown, Teaching concepts: Death is final; Everything eventually dies; People have feelings when death/change happens.

Enchanted Family. **An Enchante Inner-Active Book: Exploring Anger.** CA: Enchante Publishing, 1994. Anger arises from a violation of what each of us think "should" and "should not" happen. This workbook encourages children to release anger and translate its energy into beauty and enthusiasm.

Children's Bibliography On Death and Dying

Abercrombie, Barbara. Charlie Anderson. New York: Margaret K. McElderry Books, 1990.

Bartoli, Jennifer. Nonna. New York: Harvey House, 1975.

Beckhorn, Susan Williams. The Kingfisher's Gift. New York: Philomel Books, 2002.

Bernstein, Joanne E. & Gullo, Stephen V.. When People Die. New York: E.P. Dutton, 1977.

Blackburn, Lynn Bennett. Timothy Duck: The Story of the Death of A Friend. Omaha, NB: Centering Corporation,1987.

Burningham, John. Grampa. New York: Crown Publishers, 1984.

Buscaglia, Leo. The Fall of Freddie The Leaf. Thorofare, NJ: Charles B. Slack Co., 1982.

Carlstrom, Nancy White. Blow Me a Kiss, Miss Lilly. Harper Collins Publishing, 1990.

Cazet, Deny. A Fish in His Pocket. New York: Orchard Books, 1987.

Coerr, Eleanor. Sadako and The Thousand Paper Cranes. New York: G.P. Putnam's Sons, 1977.

Cohen, Miriam. Jim's Dog Muffin. New York: Greenwillow Books, 1984.

Creech, Sharon. Absolutely Normal Chaos. New York: Harper Collins, 1990.

Dabcovich, Lydia. Mrs. Huggins and Her Hen Hannah. New York: E.P. Dutton, 1985. de Paola, Tomie. Nana Upstairs, Nana Downstairs. New York: G.P. Putnam, 1973.

Di Camillo, Kate. The Tiger Rising. Cambridge, MA: Candlewick Press, 2001

Egger, Bettina. Marianne's Grandmother. New York: E.P. Dutton, 1986.

Fender, Kay and Philippe Dumas. Odette—A Springtime in Paris. Kane/Miller Publishing, 1991.

Goble, Paul. Beyond the Ridge. New York: Bradbury Press, 1989.

Gray, Diane. Together Apart. Boston, MA: Houghton Mifflin Co., 2002

Greene, Constance C. Beat The Turtle Drum. New York: Viking Press, 1976.

Jampolsky, Gerold. There's A Rainbow Behind Every Dark Cloud. Berkeley, CA: Celestial Arts, 1978.

Jampolsky, Gerold. <u>Straight From The Siblings: Another Look at the Rainbow</u>. Berkeley, CA: Celestial Arts, 1978.

Haas, Jesse. <u>Unbroken</u>. New York: Greenwillow Books, 1999.

Harris, Audrey. <u>Why Did He Die?</u> Minneapolis, MN: Lerner Publications Co., 1965.

Hazen, Barbara Shook. <u>Why Did Grandpa Die?: A Book About Death.</u> New York: Golden Book, 1985.

Heide, Florence and Gilliland, Judith Heide. <u>Sami and The Time of The Troubles.</u> NY: Clarion books, 1992. (War)

Hodge, John. <u>Finding Grandpa Everywhere: A Young Child Discovers Memories of a Grandparent.</u> Omaha, NE, Centering Corporation Resource, 1999.

Johnson, Marv and Joy. <u>Where's Jess?</u> Omaha, NE: Centering Corporation, 1982.

Jordan, MaryKate. <u>Losing Uncle Tim.</u> Niles, Illinois: Albert Whitman & Company, 1989.

Keller, Holly. <u>Goodbye, Max.</u> New York: Greenwillow Books, 1987.

Kohlenberg, Sherry. <u>Sammy's Mommy Has Cancer</u>. New York: Imagination Press, 1993.

Kraus, Robert. <u>Owliver</u>. New York: Windmill Books, 1974.

Kübler-Ross, Elisabeth. <u>Dougy's Letter.</u> Head Waters, VA: Elisabeth Kübler-Ross Center, 1979.

Kurth, Judith. <u>Bebe and Bobo Bury a Squirrel.</u> Reedsburg, WI: Hammer Funeral Home, 1985.

Madenski, Melissa. <u>Some of the Pieces</u>. Boston, MA: Little, Brown and Company, 1991.

Marshall, Bridgett. <u>Animal Crackers: A Tender Book About Death and Funerals and Love.</u> Omaha, NB: Centering Corporation, 1998.

Miles, R.. <u>Annie and The Old One</u>. Boston, MA: Little, Brown and Company, 1971.

Munsch, Robert. <u>Love You Forever.</u> Willowdale, CA: A Firefly Book, 1983.

Pascoe, Judy. <u>Our Father Who Art in a Tree</u>. New York: Random House, 2002.

Paterson, Katherine. <u>Bridge To Terabithia.</u> Camelot, NY: Avon, 1977.

Pomerantz, Barbara. <u>Buddy, Me and Memories.</u> New York: Union of American Hebrew Congregation, 1983.

Sanfor, Dori. <u>It Must Hurt a Lot: A Child's Book About Death.</u> Multnomah Press, 1985.

Smith, D.B. <u>A Taste of Blackberries</u>. New York: Crowell, 1973.

Stevenson, James. <u>Don't You Know There is a War Going On?</u> New York: Greenwillow Books, 1992. (War)

Stiles, Norman. <u>I'll Miss You Mr. Hooper</u>. New York: Random House, Children's TV Workshop, 1984

Stull, Edith G.. <u>My Turtle Died Today.</u> New York: Holt, Rhinehart & Winston, 1964.

Tobias, Toby. <u>Petey</u>. New York: G.P. Putnam's Sons, 1978.

Thompson, Colin. <u>How to Live Forever.</u> New York: Knopf, 1976.

Tresselt, A. <u>The Dead Tree</u>. New York: Parent's Magazine Press.

Varley, Susan. <u>Badger's Parting Gifts</u>. New York: Lothrop, Lee & Shephard Books, 1984.

Warner, Sally. <u>This Isn't About The Money.</u> New York: Viking Press, 2002

Viorst, Judith. <u>The Tenth Good Thing About Barney</u>. New York: Macmillan Publishing Company, 1971.

Wahl, Mats. <u>Grandfather's Laika</u>. Minneapolis: Carolrhoda Books, Inc., 1990.

White, E.B. <u>Charlotte's Web</u>. New York: Harper Junior Books, 1952.

Whitman, Martha Hickman. <u>Last Week My Brother Anthony Died</u>. Nashville, TN: Abingdon Press, 1984.

Wild, Margaret. <u>The Very Best of Friends</u>. New York: Harcourt Brace Jovanovich Publishers, 1989.

Wiles,Deborah. <u>Love, Ruby Lavender</u>. New York: Random House, 2001.

Wilhelm, Hans. <u>I'll Always Love You</u>. New York: Crown Publishers, 1985.

Zemach, Margot. <u>Jake and Honeybunch Go To Heaven.</u> New York: Farrar, Straus & Giroux. 1982.

A Bibliography For Adults

Berlinsky, Ellen B. and Biller, Henry B. Parental Death and Psychological Development. Lexington, MA: D.C. Heath & Company, 1982.

Borden, A. and Kass, D. They Need To Know: How To Teach Children About Death. Englewood Cliffs, NJ: Prentiss Hall, 1979.

Chapman, Gary and Campbell, Ross. The Five Love Languages of Children. Chicago, IL: Northfield Publishers, 1997.

Dellasega, Cheryl Dr.. Surviving Ophelia. Cambridge, MA: Perseus Publishing, 2001.

Dillon, Illene L.. Exploring Grief with Your Child. Palo Alto, CA: Enchante Publishing, 1994.

Doka, Kenneth. Living With Grief After a Sudden Loss. Hospice Foundation of America, 1996.

Emswiler, Mary Ann. Guiding Your Child Through Grief. New York: Bantam Books, 2000.

Fassler, Joan. Helping Children Cope: Mastering Stress Through books and Stories. New York: The Free Press, 1978.

Feinstein, David and Peg Elliott Mayo. Rituals for Living and Dying. San Francisco: Harper Collins, 1990.

Fogarty, James A.. The Magical Thoughts of Grieving Children: Treating Children With Complicated Mourning and Advice for Parents. Amityville, N.Y: Baywood Publications, 2000.

Fox, Sandra Sutherland. Good Grief: Helping Groups of Children When a Friend Dies. Boston, MA: New England Association for the Education of Young Children, 1985.

Fry, Virginia. Part of Me Died, Too: Stories of Creative Survival Among Bereaved Children & Teenagers. New York, NY: Dutton Children's Books, Penguin, 1995.

Gaffney, Patricia. Circle of Three. New York: Harper Collins, 2000.

Goldman, Linda. Breaking the Silence: A Guide to Help Children With Complicated Grief— Suicide, Homicide, AIDS, Violence, and Abuse. Philadelphis, PA: Brunner-Routledge, 2001.

Good Grief Program, The. Books and Films On Death and Dying for Children and Adolescents: An Annotated Bibliography. Boston, MA: Junior League, 1985. (Plus yearly supplements).

Greenspan, Stanley Dr.. Building Healthy Minds: The Six Experiences That Create Intelligence and Emotional Growth in Babies and Young Children. Cambridge, MA: Perseus Publishers,1999.

Grollman, Earl. <u>Explaining Death To Children</u>. Boston, MA: Beacon Press, 1967.

Grollman, Earl. <u>Talking About Death: A Dialogue Between Parent and Child</u>. Boston, MA: Beacon Press, 1967.

Gurian, Michael. The Soul of The Child: Nurturing The Divine Identity of Our Children. New York: Atria Books, 2002.

Guest, Judith. <u>Errands.</u> New York: Ballantine Books, 1997.

Huntley, Theresa. <u>Helping Children Grieve: When Someone They Love Dies.</u> Minneapolis, MN: Augsburg Fortress, 2002.

Jampolsky, Gerald. <u>Love Is Letting go of Fear</u>. Berkeley, CA: Celestial Arts, 1979.

Jewett, Claudia L. <u>Helping Children Cope with Separation and Loss.</u> Harvard, MA: The Harvard Common Press, 1982.

Kanyer, Laurie A.. <u>25 Things to Do When Grandpa Passes Away, Mom and Dad Get Divorced, or The Dog Dies: Activities to Help Children Suffering Loss or Change.</u> Seattle, Washington: Parenting Press, 2003.

Kidd, Sue Monk. <u>The Secret Life of Bees.</u> New York: Viking, 2002.

Knott, Eugene J., Ribar, Mary, Dusen, Betty M., King, Marc. <u>Thanatopics: Activities and Exercises for Confronting Death.</u> Lexington, MA: Lexiton Books, 1989.

Krementz, Jill. <u>How It Feels When A Parent Dies</u>. New York: Knopf, 1981.

Kübler-Ross, Elisabeth. <u>On Children and Death.</u> New York: Macmillan Publishing Co., 1983.

LeShan, Eda J. <u>Learning To Say Good-Bye When A Parent Dies.</u> New York: Avon, 1976.

Lombardo, Victor S. and Lombardo, Edith Foran. <u>Kids Grieve Too!</u> Springfield, IL: Charles Thomas, 1986.

Lonetto, Richard. <u>Children's Conceptions of Death</u>. New York: Springer Publishing, 1980.

Marta, Suzy Yehl. <u>Healing the Hurt, Restoring the Hope: How to Guide Children and Teens Through Times of Divorce, Death, and Crisis With the Rainbows Approach.</u> Emmaus, PA: Rodale: Distributed by St. Martin's Press, 2003.

Meltzer, David, editor. <u>Death: An Anthology of Ancient Texts, Songs, Prayers, and Stories.</u> San Francisco, CA: North Point Press, 1984.

O'Toole, Donna. <u>Growing Through Grief: A K-12 Curriculum to Help Young People Through All Kinds of Loss</u>. Compassion Books, 1989 Raleigh, NC: Burnsville, North Carolina, 1987.

Rogers, Carl.R. <u>A Way of Being</u>. Boston: Houghton Mifflin, 1980/1995.

Rogers, Carl R. <u>On Becoming a Person.</u> Boston: Houghton Mifflin, 1961/1995.

Rogers, Carl.R. and J. Jerome, Freiberg. <u>Freedom to Learn</u>. Merill, 1994.

Rowling, Louise. <u>Grief in School Communities: Effective Support Strategies.</u> Philadelphis, PA: Open University, 2003.

Stein, Sara, Bonnet. <u>About Dying: An Open Family Book For Parents & Children Together.</u> New York: Walker & Co. (Center for Preventative Psychiatry, White Plains, NY)

Sternberg, Franki and Sternberg, Barbara. <u>If I Die and When I Do: Exploring Death With Young People</u>. Englewood Cliffs, NJ: Prentice-Hall, 1980.

Viorst, Judith. <u>Necessary Losses</u>. New York: Fawcett Gold Medal, 1986.

Wass, Hannelore, and Corr, Charles. <u>Helping Children Cope With Death: Guidelines and Resources</u>. Washington: Hemisphere, 1984.

Webb, Nancy Boyd. <u>Helping Bereaved Children: A Handbook for Practitioners</u>. New York: Guilford Press, 2002.

Worden, J. William. <u>PDA*Breaking Free of Fear to Live a Better Life Now</u>. Englewood Cliffs, NJ: Prentice-Hall Inc., 1976.

Suicide and Children

<u>Bibliography on Suicide and Suicide Prevention</u>. Chevy Chase, MD.: National Insititute of Health.

Cottle, Thomas J. <u>Golden Girl: The Story of An Adolescent Suicide</u>. New York: Putnam Publishing Group, 1983.

Giovacchini, Peter. <u>The Urge to Die: When Young People Commit Suicide</u>. New York: Macmillan, 1981.

Gordon, Sol. <u>When Living Hurts</u>. New York: Yad Tikvah Foundation, 1985.

Klagsbrun, Francine. <u>Too Young to Die: Youth and Suicide</u>. Boston: Beacon Press, 1971.

Expressive Arts Bibliography

Adair, Margo. Working Inside Out. Wingbow Press, 1984.

Adamson, Edward. Art as Healing. Boston, London: Coventure, LTD., 1984.

Benzwie, Teresa. A Moving Experience. Tucson: Zephyr Press, 1987.

Biffle, Christopher. The Castle in the Pearl. New York: Harper & Row, Publishers, 1990.

Brookes, Mona. Drawing with Children. New York: St. Martin's Press, 1986.

Capacchione, Lucia. The Creative Journal for Children. Boston & Shaftesbury: Shambhala, 1982.

Capacchione, Lucia. The Creative Journal For Children: A Guide for Parents, Teachers and Counselors. Boston, MA: Shambala Publications, Inc., 1982.

Capacchione, Lucia. The Creative Journal: A Handbook for Teens. Boston, MA: Shambala Publications, Inc., 1989.

Capacchione, Lucia. The Power of the Other Hand. Boston, MA: Shambala Publications Co., Inc., 1988.

Carr, R. Be A Frog, A Bird or A Tree. Garden City, NJ: Doubleday, 1973.

De Mille, Richard. Put Your Mother on the Ceiling. New York: Viking Penguin, Inc., 1976.

de Peyer, Katia. Dancing with Myself. Willow Springs, Missouri: Nucleus Publications, 1991.

Franck, Frederick. The Zen of Seeing. New York: Random House, 1973.

Furth, Gregg M. The Secret World of Drawings. Boston: Sigo Press, 1988.

Garfield, Laeh Maggie. Sound Medicine: Healing with Music, Voice, and Song. Berkeley, California: Celestial Arts, 1987.

Gawain, Shakti. Creative Visualization. Bantam Books, 1978.

Keyes, Laurel Elizabeth. Toning —The Creative Power of the Voice. Marina del Rey: DeVorss and Co. Publishing, 1990.

Murdock, Maureen. Spinning Inward. Boston & London: Shambhala, 1987.

Oaklander, Violet. <u>Windows to Our Children</u>. New York: The Center for Gestalt Development, 1988.

Oster, Gerald D. and Patricia Gould. <u>Using Drawings in Assessment and Therapy</u>. New York: Brunner/Mazel, 1987.

Rhyne, Janie. <u>The Gestalt Art Experience</u>. Chicago: Magnolia Street Publishers, 1984.

Roth, Gabrielle. <u>Maps to Ecstasy</u>. San Rafael, California: New World Publishing, 1989.

Rubin, Judith Aron. <u>Approaches to Art Therapy</u>. New York: Brunner/Mazel, Inc., 1987.

Rubin, Judith Aron. <u>Child Art Therapy</u>. New York: Van Nostrand Reinhold, 1978.

Steinman, Louise. <u>The Knowing Body</u>. Boston & London: Shambhala, 1986.

Wohl, Agnes and Bobbie Kaufman. <u>Silent Screams and Hidden Cries</u>. New York: Brunner/Mazel, 1985.

Appendix A

Miscellaneous Handouts &
Related Articles

Helping Children Handle Special Days

Holidays, birthdays and other special occasions can be very difficult times of the year for children in grief, especially at school when everyone is excitedly preparing and creating art for special occasions such as Mother's Day. But for a child in grief special occasions can magnify their pain of loss. The following is a sample list of holidays that are normally joyous occasions.

New Year's Day	Valentine's Day	Easter
Passover	Mother's Day	Memorial Day
Father's Day	The Sabbath	Rosh Hashanah
Birthdays	Grandparent's Day	Yom Kippur
Ramadan	Halloween	Thanksgiving
Hanukkah	Christmas	Independence Day

...And any other cultural, religious holidays, traditional family vactions, graduations, weddings, marriages, bnew birthds, changing from one grade to the next, a new teacher, a new home, etc.

Grieving children need their teachers to be aware of their losses and/or special circumstances and make adjustments to projects in the classroom that involve special days. For example, invite the child to think about how he/she might like to celebrate Mother's Day in their own way—making a card for the person who is now the primary caretaker in teh child's life. Or perhaps the child may want to draw a picture or write a letter or poem to their deceased parent—telling them a little about himself, or thoughts they have.

Alternatively, the other children in the classroom could be encourage to create a card for this child with drawings and writings that focus on the special qualities that they appreciate him or her. Caring adults and teachers may give a special card or perhaps some extra quality time to a child who has lost a family member. Simple, small acts of caring and acknowledgement from teachers, school personnel, and peers can go a long way to help a grieving child feel supported and less isolated in their community. Many successful adults who were traumatized by loss in childhood say they can remember at least one caring person who made a difference. School staff have a noble opportunity to affect a child for the rest of his or her life every single day at work! What an awesome job!

Creating New Family Traditions for Special Days

When someone we love dies, holidays and anniversaries can be particularly difficult. Maintaining family traditions is very important, but is not always possible. Adding some self-created rituals or new traditions that integrate our loss can deepen the meaning of holidays.

A family in grief can greatly help one another by preparing *in advance* for special days. When planning, include time for each family member to share any feelings they may have about the upcoming holiday. Encourage children to come up with ideas and suggestions of things they would like to do to help keep the memory of a loved one alive at family gatherings. New traditions can expand the meaning and depth of special days even more for each member of the family when they are included in the creative process. Here are some ideas of new traditions children and teens have come up with to help them remember a loved one through the holidays:

• Draw a picture of your loved one	• Light a candle next to their picture
• Visit their grave	• Do an activity together that s/he enjoyed
• Write memories down on slips of	• Make up a family verse for a holiday song paper, and read them out loud
• Give a gift in memory to a needy person	• Bring basket of cookies to senior citizen's center
• Decorate a bush or tree for birds or squirrels	• Volunteer at a soup kitchen
• Donate time or services to a charity	• Read a special prayer, story or poem
• Tie written wishes/memories on tree	• Create a scholarship to keep the memory of the loved one alive
• Decorate a wreath with pictures and were items loved by the person who died	• Share stories and memories, give each that other permission to talk about the deceased
• Tell stories about the ornaments on the tree, create a special ornament with the items the deceased loved	• Decorate a wreath with pictures and favorite
• Plant a memorial tree or garden	• Make or give a Memory Book
• Make a donation to a charity in the deceased person's honor	• Wrap a favorite memento of the loved one and give it to a grieving family member
• Make their favorite food for the holiday meal time	• Decorate a Memory Candle and light it at
• For Chanukah, recall a memory of your loved one each night as you light the Menorah	• Family sponsors a needy child, an elderly person, or an animal in memory of the deceased

☙ Remember: Be kind and gentle with one another on these days, and keep things simple!

The HEALS Program
Journal Activities

- Draw a happy time you remember with the person who died.

- Draw or write about the funeral or memorial service, if you went to one. If not, draw what you heard about or wish you could have done as a final good-bye.

- Draw or write about what you think happens after a person dies.

- Write or draw about the things that make you sad. It could be something you miss or will not miss about the person who died…or perhaps things you will miss doing with the person.

- Draw a timeline of the losses you have had.

- Draw a circle and color in it whatever symbols or colors come to you.

- Name 10 good things about yourself.

- Name 5 things about the person who died (positive or negative).

- Draw a picture of how you feel inside.

- Draw a picture of what you think death looks like or what you think happens after someone dies.

- Draw a name design and/or poem about the person who died.

- Draw or write what you have been mad about since your loved one or important person died.

- Draw a picture of your person who died.

MEMORY BOX REMINDER: We will be making Memory Boxes in our HEALS group very soon. Please bring a box to decorate, and any pictures or special things you would like to put on or in your Memory Box.

REMINDER: We will be making Memory Boxes in our HEALS group very soon. Please bring a box to decorate and any pictures or special things you would like to put on or in your Memory Box.

REMINDER: We will be making Memory Boxes in our HEALS group very soon. Please bring a box to decorate and any pictures or special things you would like to put on or in your Memory Box.

REMINDER: We will be making Memory Boxes in our HEALS group very soon. Please bring a box to decorate and any pictures or special things you would like to put on or in your Memory Box.

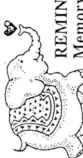

REMINDER: We will be making Memory Boxes in our HEALS group very soon. Please bring a box to decorate and any pictures or special things you would like to put on or in your Memory Box.

347

Appendix B

Resources & Referrals

The HEALS Program Materials Resources

Journals

Hardbound white journals can be used for artwork and spontaneous writing. These sturdy 8 x 10 inch books have a special binding, known as the Otabind method, that "opens flat" for easy drawing.

Lerner Publications Co.　　　　　Toll-free 1-800-328-4929
241 First Avenue North
Minneapolis, MN 55401

Dancing Scarves

The colorful Dancing Scarves we use for movement, release, imaginary journeys, and just for fun are available through:

Creative Moves by Sportime　　　Toll-free 1-800-283-5700
One Sportime Way
Atlanta, Georgia 30340

Music

Some of our favorite inspired and innovative composers of music we use during our Imaginary Journeys both in the training and in working/playing with the children are:

The Secret Garden (harp, bells, cello)　　　Mark Kelso, Muddy Angel Music
Songs from A Secret Garden　　　　　　　　www.muddyangel.com
Phillips, Polygram
Norway

Music by Marcey (harmonic sounds)　　　Therese Schroeder-Sheker
P.O. Box 831210 Celestial Harmonies　　　(*Rosa Mystica*-harp)
Richardson, TX 75083-1210　　　　　　　P.O. Box 3012
　　　　　　　　　　　　　　　　　　　Tucson, AZ 85751

Movement

We often use **Body Jazz** music, from the CD *Initiation* by the Gabrielle Roth & the Mirrors, to gradually loosen and awaken the children's bodies prior to HEALS activities. Body Jazz as a warm up exercise can be found on a CD titled *Initiation*.

The Moving Center   (201) 642-7942
P.O. Box 2034
Red Bank, NJ 07701-0902

Feather Maks
Beautiful and exotic feather masks for movement and creative expression can be ordered from:

Oriental Trading
Toll-free 1-800-228-0475

Children's Grief Video
The video "***Death of a Friend***" is available for rental through:
New Dimension Media
85803 Lorane Highway
Eugene, Oregon 97405-9408

National Resource Organizations

National Directory of Children's Grief Services

The Dougy Center for Grieving Children
3909 S.E. 52nd Avenue
P.O. Box 86852
Portland, OR 97286
(503)775-5683

Bereavement Resources Catalogues

Compassion Books
477 Hannah Branch Road
Burnsville, North Carolina 28714

(800)970-4220 (914)247-0116

www.compassionbooks.com

Mental Health Resources
346 Saugerties Road
Saugerties, NY 12477

Homicide

The following are organizations that can provide support, information, and workshops for parents and friends of those who have died by violence:

POMC (Parents of Murdered Children)
100 East Eighth Street, Room B-41
Cincinnati, OH 45202
Canada

Victims of Violence
P.O. Box 393
Boulton, Ont. L7E 1A0

Families and Friends of Murder Victims
P.O. Box 80181
Chattanooga, TN 80181
Washington, D.C. 20004

NOVA (National Organization
for Victim Assistance)
717 D. Street, N.W.

Families and Friends of Missing Persons
and Violent Crime Victims
P.O. Box 27529
Seattle, WA 98125

Suicide

American Association of Suicidology
2459 South Ash
Denver, CO 80222

Lifeline Institute (for youth suicide)
9108 Lakewood Drive, S.W.
Tacoma, WA 98499
New York, N,Y, 10169

National Save-A-Life League
4520 Fourth Avenue, Suite MH3
New York, N.Y. 11220
Aurora, IL 60506

Omega (for families of suicides)
271 Washington Street
Somerville, MA 02143

Samaritans
500 Commonwealth Avenue
Boston, MA 02215
   Rockville, MD 20857

Survivors of Suicide - National Office
Suicide Prevention Center, Inc.
184 Salem Avenue
Dayton, OH 45406

Friends for Survival, Inc.
5701 Lerner Way
Sacramento,CA 95823

National Committee on Youth
Suicide Prevention
230 Park Avenue, Suite 835

Survivors of Suicide
c/o Advent Christian Church
905 East Edgelawn

Survivor Support Programme
10 Trinity Square
Toronto, Ont. M4G 1B1 Canada

Suicide Research Unit
National Institute of Mental Health
5600 Fishers Lane, Room 10C26

Afterwards: A Letter For and About (a
quarterly newsletter)
c/o Adina Wrobleski, Editor
Minneapolis, MN. 55436

O'Toole, Donna. Growing Through Grief: A K-12 Curriculum to Help Young People Through All Kinds of Loss. Compassion Books, 1989 Raleigh, NC: Burnsville, North Carolina, 1987. *A very good source for suicide education can be found in this book.)*

Drunk Driver Victims

MADD (Mothers Against Drunk Driving)
Suite 310
Hurst, TX 76053

SADD (Students Against Driving Drunk)
P.O. Box 800
Marlborough, MA 01752

RID (Remove Intoxicated Drivers)
699 Airport Freeway,
Schenectady, N.Y. 12301 0669

PRIDE
19 Ovida Avenue
Islington, Ontario M9B 1E2
Canada

References

Barrett, Elizabeth. Brown, Karen. Zimmerman, Dr. Jill. (1996). Circle of prevention: an educational support group for children of chemical-abusing families. St. Paul, MN: Children Are People Support Groups.

Bowlby, John. (1973). Attachment and loss. volume II: separation. New York: Basic Books.

CASEL (Collaborative for the Advancement of Social and Emotional Learning). (1995, September). Status Report: Mission & Position Statement. New Haven, CT: CASEL Status Report.

Capacchione, Lucia. The power of the other hand. North Hollywood, CA.: Newcastle Publishing Co., Inc., 1988.

Dass, Ram & Gorman, Paul. (1985). How can I help?: stories and reflections on service. New York: Alfred A. Knopf, Inc..

Dellasega, Cheryl Dr..(2001) Surviving ophelia. Cambridge, MA: Perseus Publishing.

Demasio, Antonio. (1999). The feeling of what happens, New York, Harcourt Brace.

Dillon, Illene L.. (1994). Exploring grief with your child. Palo Alto, CA: Enchante Publishing.

Emswiler, Mary Ann. (2000). Guiding your child through grief. New York: Bantam Books.

Fogarty, James A., (2000). The magical thoughts of grieving children: Treating children with complicated mourning and advice for parents. Amityville, N.Y.: Baywood Publications.

Fox, Sandra Sutherland. (1985) Good grief: helping groups of children when a friend dies. Boston, MA: New England Association for the Education of Young Children.

Furth, Gregg M.. (1988). The secret world of drawings. Boston, MA: Sigo Press.

Gaffney, Donna. (1988). The seasons of grief: helping children grow through loss. New York: New American Library.

Gardner, Howard. (1993). Multiple intelligences: the theory in practice. New York: Basic Books.

Goldman, Linda. (2001). Breaking the silence: A guide to help children with complicated grief—suicide, homicide, AIDS, violence, and abuse. Philadelphis, PA: Brunner-Routledge.

Goleman. Daniel. (1995). <u>Emotional intelligence: why it can matter more than intelligence</u>. New York: Bantam Books.

Goleman. Daniel. (1995, November). *What's your EQ?* <u>The Utne Reader</u>.

Goleman. Daniel. (1995, December). *The educated heart.* <u>Common Boundary</u>.

Goleman. Daniel. (1993, February). *Raising peaceful kids in a violent world.* <u>Parents</u>, 68.

Goleman. Daniel. (1992, January). *Wounds that never heal.* <u>Psychology Today</u>.

Gordon, Audrey K. and Klass, Dennis. (1979). <u>They need to know: how to teach children about death</u>. Englewood Cliffs, NJ: Prentice Hall Inc..

Greenspan, Stanley Dr.. (1999). <u>Building healthy minds: the six experiences that create intelligence and emotional growth in babies and young children</u>. Cambridge, MA: . Perseus Publishers.

Grollman, Earl, edit.. (1967). <u>Explaining death to children</u>. Boston, MA: Beacon Press.

Grollman, Earl A.. (1990). <u>Talking about death: a dialogue between parent and child</u>. Boston, MA.: Beacon Press.

Gurian, Michael. (2002). <u>The Soul of The Child: Nurturing The Divine Identity of Our Children</u>. New York: Atria Books.

Heegard, Marge Eaton. (1992). <u>Drawing out feelings</u>. Minneapolis, MN.: Woodland Press.

Hendricks, Gay and Wills, Russel. <u>The centering book: Awareness activities for children, parents, and teachers</u>. Englewood Cliffs, NJ: Prentice Hall, Inc., 1975.

Huntley, Theresa. (2002). <u>Helping children grieve: When someone they love dies</u>. Minneapolis, MN: Augsburg Fortress.

Jacobi, Jolande. (1942). <u>The psychology of c.g. jung: an introduction with illustrations</u>. London, England: Routledge & Kegan Paul Ltd..

Kanyer, Laurie A., (2003). <u>25 things to do when grandpa passes away, mom and dad get divorced, or the dog dies: Activities to help children suffering loss or change</u>. Seattle, Washington: Parenting Press.

Kessler, S. (1994, Spring). *Emotional literacy.* <u>Great Ideas in Education, Number 2</u>, 4.

Kubler-Ross, Elizabeth. (1983). <u>On children and death</u>. New York: Macmillan Publishing Company.

Kübler-Ross, Elisabeth. (1969). <u>On death and dying</u>. New York: Macmillan.

Lichter, Paul. (1979) *Communicating With Parents of Handicapped Children.* <u>Teaching Exceptional Children</u>. Winter.

Marta, Suzy Yehl. (2003). <u>Healing the hurt, restoring the hope: How to guide children and teens through times of divorce, death, and crisis with the rainbows approach</u>. Emmaus, PA: Rodale: Distributed by St. Martin's Press.

Morgan, John D., edit..(1991). <u>Young people and death</u>. Philadelphia, PA: The Charles Press.

O'Toole, Donna. (1985). <u>Bridging the bereavement gap: a comprehensive manual for the preparation and programming of hospice bereavement services</u>. Burnsville, NC: Compassion Books.

O'Toole, Donna. (1989). <u>Growing through grief: a k-12 curriculum to help young people through all kinds of loss</u>. Burnsville, North Carolina: Mountain Rainbow Publications.

Rando, Terese. (1993). <u>Treatment of complicated mourning</u>. Champaign, Ill.: Research Press.

Rogers, Carl. (1980) <u>Empathic: an unappreciated way of being</u>. Houghton Mifflin Co..

Rogers, Natalie. (1993). <u>The creative connection: the expressive arts as healing</u>. Palo Alto, CA: Science and Behavior Books, Inc..

Roth, Gabrielle and The Mirrors. *Initiation* (CD). Redbank, NJ: Raven Recording, 1988.

Rowling, Louise. (2003). <u>Grief in school communities: effective support strategies</u>. Philadelphia, PA: Open University.

Webb, Nancy Boyd. (2002). <u>Helping bereaved children: A handbook for practitioners</u>. New York: Guilford Press.

Wolfelt, Alan. (1983). <u>Helping children cope with grief</u>. Muncie, IN: Accelerated Development Inc..

Zohar, Danah. (1982). <u>Through the time barrier</u>. London: Paladin Books.

~ Epilogue ~

The material presented in this manual has flowed through us—sometimes coming as a labored trickle and at other times as an inundating flood. The journey down this "river" has filled us with awe and humility. Our greatest gift has been to be granted windows into the souls of many dear children and adults, to witness their pain, and then watch them access their own healing energy to transform the feelings of grief into a source of spiritual strength and awareness.

Our vision has been clear, our obstacles few. Some little rivulets have branched from our initial mission and new curriculums like The HEALS Pet Loss Program and The Children in Changing Families Program have taken on their own flow. Other programs are developing, and we are grateful for the pure, clear and strong ways they are coming into form. Requests and new challenges come and our course is sometimes altered and adapted to meet the need, but the core approach is constant: When we create safe spaces for each of us to be open and vulnerable— healing occurs.

The development of The HEALS Program has been effortless and effortful. For the past fourteen years, as we have come together, the ideas and directions we were to take have been remarkably clear, as if we were each responding to the same compass. We have been simultaneously stirred from deep sleeps with ideas and thoughts calling us from our beds. In 1990, we both were awakened at 2:30 a.m.. Perched at our computers, we simultaneously worked on defining *What HEALS Is* for a half-hour and then returned to sleep. As such, this affirms and demonstrates to us that a synchronistic force is working in our midst.

This powerful force continues to affirm that "something greater than us" is helping us bring these healing creations into our needy world, a world where pain and suffering are part of our everyday existence. We do not want to deny the pain and suffering in this world. Instead, we are committed to shining a light on it so children can learn that everything happening in life can be discussed, explored, felt and expressed.

Everything that has come to us (and through us) has been given fully and completely to this body of work. We have held nothing back. The experiences and learnings are not ours to possess. Love does not possess—it gives freely of itself. There were times when we felt depleted and exhausted—and still as the challenges and inspiration continued to come—we responded.

We have honored each calling, believing that this creative healing approach for children (and the child in each of us) is to be in our world and in our schools. As we have journeyed into schools throughout this country, our eyes and hearts have been opened to the need for adults to do their own healing work and have the essential training and tools to help grieving children traverse the bumpy terrain of loss.

We are humble servants doing what we believe we have been called to do—doing it from the best of our human ability. There has been a strong sense of many visible and invisible hands supporting us along the way. We have not functioned in a vacuum. For all of you who have helped us on our way, we want to express our heartfelt gratitude.

And we thank each of you using this manual for giving from your full hearts to the children in your world, to those children who have lost a loved one, and for helping the hearts of grieving children to open and blossom, petal by petal.

Anne & Penelope
The Art of Healing Childhood Grief
4th Edition,
Vermont, 2004